LEGAL ETHICS

IN A NUTSHELL

Third Edition

By

RONALD D. ROTUNDA

University Professor and Professor of Law

George Mason University School of Law

THOMSON

WEST

Mat #40590881

© West, a Thomson business, 2003, 2006
© 2007 Thomson/West
      610 Opperman Drive
      P.O. Box 64526
      St. Paul, MN 55164–0526
      1–800–328–9352

Printed in the United States of America

ISBN: 978–0–314–18040–7

TEXT IS PRINTED ON 10% POST CONSUMER RECYCLED PAPER

to
Don

*

PREFACE

Most lawyers practicing today took a required course in Legal Ethics while in law school, followed by a specific bar examination on that same subject. It was not always so. When I started teaching, my law school did not even offer the course. In those days, it was easy for law students to learn the Golden Rule: Thou shalt not lie, cheat, steal, . . . or advertise.

Times have changed. The emphasis on legal ethics began in 1974 as part of what Spiro Agnew then referred to as our "post-Watergate morality." I started teaching legal ethics because the Dean knew I was the new boy on the block, and had been a lawyer for the Senate Watergate Committee.

Some people think that ethics can be taught only at mother's knee. It's a little more complicated than that. Those who think of ethics as intuition are often the same people whom courts routinely disqualify because they do not appreciate the complexities of the rules of conflicts of interest. Many lawyers today are, for instance, ignorant of recent developments regarding conflicts of interest and attorney disqualification. Several years ago, one of my former academic colleagues, who also practiced law, said she did not buy malpractice insurance because her contract with her clients required them to waive their malpractice claims. Her listeners nodded knowingly, oblivious to the fact that her standard waiver agreement violated state ethics rules, was not enforceable, and could cause her to lose her license.

One need not rely on anecdotal analysis. The few existing empirical studies show that many lawyers often are unaware of basic information about the law governing the practice of law. Consequently, many malpractice suits arise out of violations of professional ethics. In recent years, several major law firms have settled for substantial sums various malpractice claims based on ethical violations, and several criminal actions have brought into focus the role of lawyers. For example, on June 15, 2001, a federal jury convicted the 89-year-old accounting firm of Arthur Andersen of obstruction of justice for impeding an investigation by securities regulators into the financial debacle at Enron, the center of a massive securities fraud. Shortly after the verdict, Andersen informed the government that it would cease auditing public companies within weeks, effectively ending its professional life. "In interviews, jurors said that they reached their decision *because an Andersen lawyer had ordered critical deletions to an internal memorandum . . . .*" Kurt Eichenwald, *Andersen Guilty in Effort to Block Inquiry on Enron*, NEW YORK TIMES, June 16, 2002 at Section 1, pp. 1, 22 (emphasis added). The lawyer in question advised a partner to edit an internal memo about Enron's financial disclosures.

What we call "lawyer's ethics" is real "law" in the same way that the Rules of Civil Procedure are law. These ethics rules are not mere advice. Instead, they impose substantive requirements on lawyers and judges and are just as complex as the rules of civil practice or the rules of evidence. Many ethics rules cannot be known through some sort of innate awareness nor are they automatically infused into ordinary human beings once they are admitted to the bar.

This Nutshell is intended to offer an initiation to this complex topic. Because the American Bar Association has been the undisputed leader in developing ethics rules, this book is organized around the ABA Model Rules of Professional Conduct. Almost all jurisdictions base their ethics rules on this ABA product. Even when a jurisdiction, such as California, uses a different format, the substantive rules reflect the substantial ABA influence.

In addition to the ABA Model Rules, each jurisdiction has its own rules, which are derived from the ABA Rules but often with non-uniform amendments. There is also case law, the commentators, and influential advisory ethics opinions of various bar associations and the ABA Ethics Committee. In addition, the *American Law Institute's Restatement of the Law Governing Lawyers, Third*, has been an important and helpful tool. I will refer to all of these sources but, given the limited nature of a Nutshell, I am limited in discussing them in detail. For that, one should turn to other secondary sources such as (please forgive the shameless self-promotion): Rotunda & Dzienkowski, *Legal Ethics: The Lawyer's Deskbook on Professional Responsibility* (ABA & Thomson West, 4th ed. 2007) (a treatise on legal ethics, published jointly by the ABA & Thomson West Publishing), or, Rotunda & Dzienkowski, *Professional Responsibility: A Student's Guide* (ABA

& Thomson West, 4th ed. 2007) or Rotunda, *Professional Responsibility* (Thomson West, 7th ed. 2004) (Black Letter series). Finally, do not forget that ethical lawyering goes well beyond the four corners of the ABA rules: the kind of lawyer you are affects, and is affected by, the kind of person you are.

If I might miss something here or there, please bear in mind the words of Judge Henry de Bracton, who beseeched over 750 years ago: "I ask the reader, if he finds in this work anything superfluous or erroneous, to correct and amend it, or pass it over with eyes half closed, for to keep all in mind and err in nothing is divine rather than human."

RONALD D. ROTUNDA

March, 2007
Arlington, Virginia

OUTLINE

OUTLINE

*

TABLE OF CASES

References are to Pages

A

B

C

D

H

I

J

K

L

M

R

S

T

U

V

W

Z

*

LEGAL ETHICS

IN A NUTSHELL

Third Edition

*

INTRODUCTION: THE PREAMBLE, SCOPE, AND RULE 1.0

1. A Historical Perspective

A. The Hoffman Resolutions

The present ABA Model Rules of Professional Conduct have a long lineage that goes back over a century and a half. In 1836, in an era when the legal profession was subject to virtually no regulation, David Hoffman, an attorney who founded the School of Law at the University of Maryland, published for his students fifty "Resolutions In Regard to Professional Deportment."

Hoffman's exhortations may sound antiquated, or at least quaint, to the modern ear. E.g., "What is morally wrong cannot be professionally right, however it may be sanctioned by time or custom." Resolution 33. Some modern commentators have belittled his advice as Victorian moralizing. Yet, he marked the beginning.

B. Sharswood's Lectures

A generation later, in 1854, Professor (and Judge) George Sharswood published, *A Compend[ium] of Lectures on the Aims and Duties of the Profession of Law*. Sharswood agreed with many of Hoffman's specific recommendations, but there were important differences, probably more in degree than in kind. Sharswood was more interested than Hoffman in rules that lawyers could understand and the bar enforce.

Sharswood's lectures greatly influenced the Alabama Bar Association, which published its "Code of Ethics" in 1887. Alabama, in turn, paved the way for the American Bar Association to adopt its own ethics rules.

C. The ABA Canons of Professional Ethics

Various other states followed Alabama's lead, but there was no model code of lawyers' ethics until August 27, 1908, when a nationwide voluntary bar association, the American Bar Association, approved 32 Canons of Professional Ethics based on the Alabama model.

The ABA began with a very small, elite membership in 1878. From its inception through 1893, its annual meetings drew only about 75 to 100 people. In the twentieth century, ABA membership steadily grew and its goals expanded.

Initially, the ABA did not call its ethics rules a "model." In fact, the ABA had more ambitious goals. At first, it treated its Canons of Professional Ethics as private law governing those lawyers who chose to join that Association. In 1940 it announced: "The Canons of this Association govern all its members, irrespective of the nature of their practice, and the application of the Canons is not affected by statutes or regulations governing certain activities of lawyers which may prescribe less stringent standards." The ABA's remedies were limited. It could expel a member from its association for noncompliance with its rules, but one did not need to be admitted into the ABA in order to practice law, just like one does not have to join a choir in order to sing.

Nevertheless, the impact of the ABA Canons soon extended beyond membership in the ABA. Many states supreme courts adopted the ABA Canons as court rules, allowing for suspension or disbarment in case of violation. Courts also cited them as authority even when they were not court rules. In addition, the ABA established an Ethics Committee to interpret its Canons. These ABA Ethics Opinions proved to be influential when courts decided issues such as disqualification, legal malpractice, and discipline.

D. The ABA Model Code of Professional Responsibility

Over the years, the ABA amended these Canons of Ethics to take into account the changing nature of legal practice. But it was not until 1969 that the ABA adopted a completely revised set of rules, the Code of Professional Responsibility. In keeping with the view that the Code was "law" that governed ABA members regardless of state law, this Code (which the ABA House of Delegates approved on August 12, 1969) had an "effective date" of January 1, 1970. Until 1976, the ABA membership application included a promise to abide by the ABA Canons of Ethics and, later, by the ABA Code of Professional Responsibility.

Recall that the ABA purported to treat its Canons as private law (a contract among its members) governing those lawyers who chose to join that Association. The Antitrust Division of the Department of Justice, as well as other groups, noted serious antitrust problems when lawyers agree with each other to abide by certain purportedly "ethical" restrictions that restricted competition. For example, the ABA ethics rules had initially imposed serious restrictions on advertising of legal services and urged minimum fees. (Yes, there are those who argued it was "unethical" to charge too little!) A private agreement that restrains trade violates the antitrust laws.

In 1978, in response to this criticism, the ABA formally acknowledged that its Code was really only a "Model" or proposed Code. To emphasize this change, the ABA changed the title of its Code of Professional Responsibility to the *Model* Code of Professional Responsibility. There is no antitrust violation when the ABA, or any other organization or individual, lobbies to persuade the legislative, judicial, or executive branches of government to enact rules, because the First Amendment protects the right to petition the government. If the relevant government body promulgates rules, the private entity or individual who obeys a state law that limits competition is not conspiring in restraint of trade because one cannot "conspire" with the state.

The ABA was quite successful in persuading state and federal courts to adopt its Model Code as law. State courts cited the Model Code as evidence of the law even in states where it had not been officially adopted. Similarly, courts have often cited and relied on ABA Opinions interpreting the Model Code as influential, though not binding.

2. The ABA Model Rules of Professional Conduct

A. The Kutak Commission and the 1983 Model Rules

Less than a decade after the ABA Model Code of Professional Responsibility was promulgated in 1969, the ABA established a Commission to create another code of ethics for the legal profession. Between 1977 and 1983 the Kutak Commission, named after its chairman, the late Robert J. Kutak, created a new code of conduct for lawyers that completely revised the format, organization, and language of the Model Code. The Model Rules were, in part, a response to criticisms about the Model Code's focus on litigation, its relative neglect of lawyers' transactional work, and its three-tiered structure of canons, disciplinary rules, and ethical considerations. Now, there is a three-tiered system of eight titles (e.g., ''Client–Lawyer Relationship''), disciplinary rules (called ''rules'' or black letter rules) and comments.

The ABA House of Delegates approved the Kutak Commission's product in August 1983. This time, the ABA House of Delegates specifically defeated a motion to set an "effective" date. There is no "effective" date because the proposed law does not bind ABA members. Instead, it binds lawyers practicing in a jurisdiction only if the court has adopted some form of the ABA Rules as substantive law. In a sense, the ABA Model Rules are a lot like the uniform laws that are the products of the National Commission on Uniform States Laws. The Uniform Laws are not law until a state adopts them, and sometimes a state approves the law with non-uniform changes. When you practice law, you will follow the law of your jurisdiction, but in the meantime we study the ABA Model Rules just like the course in criminal law may study the Model Penal Code, even though each state has its own criminal code.

B. The Role of the Comments

The ABA says that its Model Rules follow an approach that the American Law Institute popularized by its various Restatements. The Model Rules place the Rule in text (often referred to as the black letter text), and then include, in official "Comments," additional material that elaborates and amplifies on the Rule. The Comments are sometimes like legislative history explaining the reasons behind a rule. At other times, the Comments refer to particular examples. However, unlike the American Law Institute's Restatements, the Model Rules provide no series of hypothetical illustrations. And, there are no official "Reporter's Notes."

C. "Ethics 2000"

In 1997 the ABA established a Commission called "Ethics 2000," to revise the Model Rules. Things often take longer than we expect, and it was not until 2002 that the Commission completed its work and the ABA House of Delegates adopted a series of major revisions to reflect the Ethics 2000 project. The ABA has kept the format of the 1983 Rules, but clarified some language and dealt with new issues that were only dimly foreseen in 1983. The ABA has lobbied various state jurisdictions, which have often adopted some or all of the 2002 Model Rules revisions.

D. Restatement (Third) of the Law Governing Lawyers

In 1986 the American Law Institute ("ALI"), a prestigious group of practicing lawyers, judges, and academics, began drafting a Restatement of the Law Governing Lawyers. Unlike the ABA's Model Rules, the Restatement is not meant as a code of regulations that the ALI expects state courts to adopt. Instead, it is a series of principles, also called "black letter rules," followed by commentary and illustrations. Because the Restatement analyzes and systematizes the law governing the practice of law, it goes beyond ethics rules to cover other areas that affect the practice of law, such as tort doctrines relating to malpractice and vicarious liability, evidentiary issues related to the work-product doctrine and attorney-client evidentiary privilege, agency rules and related areas.

The purpose of the Restatement is not only to restate what the law is but also to nudge the developing case law in a particular direction. This Restatement follows in the tradition of other Restatements that the ALI has drafted.

Although the ALI has never before drafted a restatement of the law of lawyering, it titled its project, "Restatement of the Law, Third." However, there is no "Restatement, Second," or "Restatement, First," resulting in confusion for all but the cognoscenti. The ALI chose to title its first Restatement on Lawyers the Restatement, Third, because it was a part of its third major series of Restatements covering various topics.

3. A Brief Note on the Terminology of Legal Ethics

The most fundamental legal skill consists of determining what kind of legal problems a situation may involve, a skill that necessarily transcends any particular specialized knowledge. However, a little specialized knowledge would not hurt. The ABA Model Rules represent an important source of this specialized knowledge. In examining any problem involving legal ethics, we should first apply our traditional legal skills to the fact situation and then evaluate how the Rules deal with the problem. Sometimes the Rules may be too vague; at other times they may be quite specific, but may appear to be bad policy. A conclusion that a Rule represents bad policy is important, because the law is not static: what the law ought to be is very relevant, because the "ought" influences the "is."

The Rules prescribe what *must* or *must not* be done. The Rules of Professional Conduct sometimes also advise what a lawyer *should aspire to do*. The predecessor to the Model Rules—the ABA Model Code of Professional Responsibility—expressed this sentiment in rules that were called "Ethical Considerations" or ECs. These provisions represent aspirational conduct for the lawyer.

Lawyers may only be disciplined for violating mandatory rules, even though they should strive to meet the aspirational goals. Although a violation of an EC was not designed to be disciplinable under the Code, in some cases courts disciplined an attorney for violating an EC. However, when we look at the situations more carefully, we will see that the conduct in question fell below the minimum level of acceptable conduct and the principle could be derived from a Disciplinary Rule (DR), even though the particular prohibition might be expressed more clearly in the EC. Courts do not always carefully and precisely explain what they are doing.

Some of the ECs and DRs were also cast in terms of what the lawyer *may* do in her sound discretion. The lawyer need not engage in the conduct, but was authorized to do so. The client might not like what the lawyer did and could always fire her, but the client could not charge the lawyer with violating ethics rules.

The ABA Model Rules of Professional Conduct continue these distinctions between what must be done, what should be done, and what may be done.

When the black letter Rules use imperatives such as "shall" or "shall not," violations are disciplinable. Rule 6.1 in contrast, is aspirational, because it says a lawyer "should aspire" to engage in pro bono work, for 50 hours a year.

If a Comment uses the term "should," or "may" it does not add to the mandatory obligations to the Rules but it does provide guidance for practicing in compliance with the Rules. Therefore, conduct that violates an explicit aspirational Comment does not subject the lawyer to discipline unless it also violates a more broadly drafted Rule.

4. The Relationship of Legal Ethics with Other Law

Legal Ethics is "law" in the same way that the Rules of Evidence are law, because they both are rules of the court and those rules apply to lawyers the same way any other law applies to lawyers.

The law of ethics relates to, and is often derived from, other law. The lawyer's ethical duty to keep the client's confidences incorporates the evidentiary attorney-client privilege, as well as the law of agency (the lawyer is a fiduciary) and the law governing work product. The lawyer's duty of competence is related to the law of tort and of malpractice. The lawyer's retainer agreement with the client involves the law of contract, and takes into account that the lawyer is a fiduciary of the client. The Model Rules must also be interpreted in light of constitutional principles, particularly those related to freedom of speech.

5. The Public Image of Lawyers

It is true that one of Shakespeare's characters, Dick the Butcher, says that the first thing he would do, if he assumed power, would be to "kill all the lawyers," but Dick was an unsavory character and, in context, he meant that the only way for his revolution to succeed was to kill those who represented the law.

Lawyers, like other professionals, help people. Granted, unlike engineers, we construct no bridges; unlike doctors, we mend no bones; unlike architects we design no buildings; unlike artists, we paint no portraits. There is little that we do that the human hand can touch. But—if we are doing our jobs professionally—we take on other people's burdens; we relieve stress; we pursue justice; we take the veneer of civilization and make it a little thicker.

6. The Introductory Sections of the Model Rules of Professional Conduct

The introductory section to the Model Rules is divided, like ancient Gaul, into three parts.

A. The Preamble

Part I is titled, *Preamble: A Lawyer's Responsibilities.*

The Preamble advises lawyers that they have a "special responsibility for the quality of justice." It then summarizes many of the obligations of lawyers, while emphasizing the importance of lawyers to the rule of law.

B. Scope

PART II of the introductory section to the Model Rules is entitled *Scope*.

First, the Scope section advises that the Model Rules are "rules of reason. They should be interpreted with reference to the purposes of legal representation and of the law itself." The Scope note emphasizes that some Rules are imperatives, some permissive, and others define the nature of the relationship between lawyers and others. The Rules are thus partly obligatory and disciplinary and partly descriptive in that they define a lawyer's professional role. Comments do not add obligations to the Rules but provide guidance for practicing in compliance with the Rules. Scope, ¶ 14. [Unless otherwise indicated, all citations and paragraph numbers are to the 2003 Model Rules.] Sometimes the Comments remind lawyers of their obligations under other laws. Scope, ¶ 15.

If a lawyer fails to comply with an obligation that the jurisdiction's rules of professional conduct impose, the lawyer is subject to discipline. If the lawyer is disciplined, he or she may be suspended from the practice of law, or disbarred, or subject to a reprimand. Whether there is a sanction and what the severity of the sanction should be are issues that are not discussed in the Model Rules of Professional Conduct, but are found in other law. The ABA has developed model rules governing the procedures and sanctions for legal discipline, as well as proposals to mediate client-lawyer disputes in general and fee disputes in particular.

The Scope section of the Model Rules advises (and many lawyers pray) that a lawyer's violation of a Rule should "not itself give rise to a cause of action against a lawyer nor should it create any presumption that a legal duty has been breached." Scope, ¶ 20. The Scope is insistent that the Rules "are not designed to be a basis for civil liability," and that "the purpose of the Rules can be subverted when they are invoked by opposing parties as procedural weapons." However, the plea that the ethics rules should not be used in malpractice cases or in disqualification motions may be likened to whistling past the graveyard. If one is frightened when crossing a graveyard at night, it does no harm to whistle, but the whistling provides no real protection either.

Courts routinely refer to the ethics rules in malpractice cases and have also raised them *sua sponte* and used them to disqualify lawyers. Courts have also relied on these same ethics rules to reject fee arrangements that violate them. Lawyers often object to this transposition of legal ethics into the realm of disqualification motions and malpractice, but it is a natural and virtually inevitable progression. The rules of ethics are judicially imposed court rules. It is more than a little inconsistent, for example, for a court to promulgate a rule that states that a lawyer cannot represent a particular client because to do so would violate Rules 1.6 and 1.9(b), (governing confidences and secrets of a former client), and then allow the lawyer to appear before the court in blatant violation of the Rule—particularly when the purpose of that Rule is to protect that former client. Similarly, it is not logical for a court to promulgate an ethics rule requiring that contingent fees be in writing and then enforce an oral contract to the detriment of a party whom the Rule was drafted to protect.

Some courts act inconsistently in this area, but it is important to remember that discipline is not the only way that the courts enforce the ethics rules governing lawyers. In spite of the protestations in the Scope section, courts often use the legal ethics rules to impose tort liability on lawyers. One court has categorized the various approaches in the case law into four different classifications:

"First, some courts hold that professional ethical standards conclusively establish the duty of care and any violation constitutes negligence per se. Second, a minority of courts finds that a professional ethical violation establishes a rebuttable presumption of legal malpractice. Third, a large majority of courts treat professional ethical standards as evidence of the common law duty of care. Finally, one court has found professional ethical standards inadmissible as evidence of an attorney's duty of care." *Allen v. Lefkoff, Duncan, Grimes & Dermer, P.C.* (Ga.1995).

The Restatement of the Law Governing Lawyers has adopted the third alternative, and the 2002 revisions to the Scope section now concede that tort liability may result from violations of the Model Rules. Scope, ¶ 20: "Nevertheless, since the Rules do establish standards of conduct by lawyers, a lawyer's violation of a Rule may be evidence of breach of the applicable standard of conduct."

Courts may impose other sanctions. Some courts may require the lawyer to forfeit some or all of the lawyer's fees because of ethical lapses. If the attorney's conduct is particularly egregious, the court may even impose the very harsh penalty of dismissing the pending litigation.

C.   Terminology: Rule 1.0

PART III is the Terminology section.

The Terminology section, called Rule 1.0 in the 2002 revisions of the Model Rules, defines the major terms that are used throughout these Rules. Most of these definitions are self-explanatory.

The Rules, as revised in 2002, acknowledge the changes in technology since the ABA House of Delegates originally approved the Model Rules in 1983. Thus, in defining "writing," Rule 1.0(n) makes clear that the term includes either a tangible or "electronic record," including e-mail. And a "signed writing" includes an electronic signature. These acknowledgements are nothing new for a generation that grew up thinking that everyone has a video recorder and it is perfectly natural for televisions to be 42″ wide and only 3″ thick. But remember that to the generation that developed the 1983 Rules, computers were new, telephones did not come with a complex instruction manual, and science fiction meant a Jules Verne novel, not the ''Attack of the Clones.''

RULE 1.1:   COMPETENCE

1.   Experience versus Competence

It is no accident that Model Rule 1.1 requires competence, for the drafters of the Model Rules believed that the first rule of legal ethics is competence. Not only the law of malpractice but the law of ethics requires lawyers to be competent.

The lawyer need not necessarily be experienced in a particular matter in order to be considered competent in that matter. There is a first time for everything. If a lawyer has to be experienced in a matter before undertaking that matter, he would never be able to acquire the initial experience. Moreover, even a novice lawyer has training in the common denominator of all legal problems: legal method, and the analysis of precedent and evidence.

The lawyer need not have the necessary degree of competence prior to accepting the employment. The lawyer may properly accept the matter and then acquire the necessary competence, through study and preparation in a novel area of law. The Model Code added a specific caveat that this preparation should not result in "unreasonable delay or expense to his client." This limitation is implicit in the requirement of the Model Rules that the preparation be "reasonable."

17

Sometimes, the best way to acquire the necessary competence is through working with more experienced lawyers. Training and close supervision are particularly important in developing certain skills (e.g., trial practice, negotiation). Consequently, trial lawyers typically do not start trial work by handling major, complex cases all by themselves. Instead, they work with other, more experienced, lawyers. The younger lawyers—those who are supervised— have the duty to become competent in an area before undertaking it, and the supervising lawyers, such as partners in law firms, have the responsibility to make reasonable efforts to ensure that all of the lawyers in their firm or under their supervision conform to the rules of professional conduct, including the rule requiring competence.

The lawyer's duty to become competent includes the duty to remain competent. A lawyer has an ethical duty to engage in continuing legal education and study in order to maintain his or her competence. The lawyer also may establish the necessary competence by associating in the matter with another attorney (outside of the law firm) who is already competent. Before the lawyer's association with someone in another law firm is proper, the client must consent to it. Rule 1.1, Comments 6, 2; Rule 1.5, Comment 7.

Because what is "competent" is a function of reasonableness, a different standard of competence applies in an emergency. Rule 1.1, Comment 3. A lawyer in such cases may give advice reasonably necessary in the circumstances "where referral to or consultation or association with another lawyer would be impractical.''

If workload prevents a lawyer, including a public defender, from providing competent and diligent representation to existing clients, she must not accept new clients. If the court assigns clients, the lawyer should request that the court not make new appointments. If the lawyer is representing a client, she must move to withdraw from representation if she cannot provide competent and diligent representation. ''If the court denies the lawyer's motion to withdraw, and any available means of appealing such ruling is unsuccessful, the lawyer must continue with the representation while taking whatever steps are feasible to ensure that she will be able to competently and diligently represent the defendant.'' The lawyer's legal supervisors ''must make reasonable efforts to ensure that the other lawyers in the office conform to the Rules of Professional Conduct.'' ABA Formal Opinion 06–441 (May 13, 2006).

2.   Malpractice and Competence

Clients can waive a lot of rights, but the ethics rules do not permit the client to waive, prospectively, the lawyer's duty of competence. If a client has suffered harm due to her lawyer's incompetence, we can expect that a suit for legal malpractice, as well as disciplinary action, may follow.

The inalienability of the client's right to a competent lawyer has one exception: sometimes a client may partially waive his or her right to competent

representation *if* another, independent lawyer separately represents and advises the client at the time
of the waiver decision to surrender or not assert
any malpractice liability. In general, a lawyer may
not ask the client to agree to incompetent representation; however, Rule 1.8(h)(1) provides that a lawyer may make an agreement "prospectively limiting
the lawyer's liability to a client for malpractice" if
the client "is independently represented in making
the agreement . . . ." This issue is discussed in connection with Rule 1.8(h).

RULE 1.2: SCOPE OF REPRESENTATION AND ALLOCATION OF AUTHORITY

1. The Creation of the Attorney–Client Relationship

The attorney-client relationship is a special type of contract—special because of the fiduciary relationship between the lawyer and her client. The lawyer becomes a particular kind of agent of the client with special responsibilities. There are three basic ways that the attorney-client relationship may commence.

- First, the prospective client manifests to the lawyer the intent to retain the lawyer, who agrees to the proposal.

- Second, the prospective client manifests to the lawyer the intent to retain the lawyer and the lawyer fails to manifest a lack of intent to be so retained under circumstances where it would be reasonable to do so. For example, assume a prospective client, fearing that his driver's license may be revoked, calls the lawyer's office and asks the lawyer to represent him in the revocation proceeding in 10 days. The prospective client knows that the lawyer often handles these types of cases; the lawyer's secretary tells the prospective client to mail the relevant papers, and he does so. The secretary does not mention that the lawyer will not decide to take the case until later. The lawyer does not communicate to the prospective client until the day before the hearing, when he says that he will not take the case. The prospective client detrimentally (and reasonably) relied on the lawyer by not seeking another lawyer when it would have been a lot easier to do so. In these circumstances, it would be reasonable for the trier of fact to conclude that there was an attorney-client relationship because the lawyer did not manifest a lack of intent to accept the client's retention. See the Restatement of the Law Governing Lawyers, Third, § 14(1)(b).

- Third, the attorney-client relationship may be formed when a tribunal, acting within its authority, appoints a lawyer to handle a matter. See Rule 6.2.

In order for an attorney-client relationship to be formed, it is not necessary that the client pay or agree to pay any money. Rule 6.1. Lawyers may work for free if they wish. Note also that paying a fee does not, by itself, create an attorney-client relationship with the payer if the circumstances indicate that the lawyer is to represent someone other than the payer. A typical example is when the insurance company pays a lawyer to represent another party, an insured.

For the attorney-client relationship to exist, it is not necessary that the client sign a written agreement. Other rules governing lawyers may require that there be a written fee agreement [e.g., Rule 1.5(c)], but those rules are for the protection of the client, not the lawyer. The purpose of the Rules of Professional Conduct is to impose regulations that govern lawyers, not clients. The obligations of the lawyer and client are not symmetrical because the lawyer is a professional with fiduciary duties to the client.

As a professional, the lawyer is *not* like a cab driver waiting at a taxi stand. While a cab driver must accept the next fare, the lawyer does not have to accept every client who walks through the door. However, it may be improper for a lawyer to refuse a case for the wrong reason. The Model Code made this point more clearly than do the Model Rules. To achieve the goal of making legal services fully available, the Code advised that a lawyer—

"should not lightly decline proffered employment. The fulfillment of this objective requires acceptance by a lawyer of his share of tendered employment which may be unattractive both to him and to the bar generally." EC 2–26.

The rules governing the practice of law make it clear that a lawyer may accept a case even though she believes her client will ultimately not prevail. Thus, a lawyer need not refuse a civil case merely the lawyer disagrees with the client's legal position, unless that position is a frivolous one, but a lawyer must refuse a case if she is unable to give it competent attention. Rule 1.1. A lawyer also must refuse a case if the client seeks to maintain a frivolous action. Rule 3.1. If the lawyer's personal beliefs about the issue at hand are so powerful that it impairs her effective representation, then she must not take the case. Rule 6.2(c) & Comment 2. Thus, a lawyer may accept criminal defense work (say, a criminal rape charge) even if she believes her client is guilty, but if she in fact believes her client must be punished, or has other personal feelings that are so strong that she could not perform the work competently, she must not take the case.

2. The Allocation of Authority Between Client and Lawyer

In the middle of a trial, the lawyer cannot consult with her client on matters such as whether to object to a question that the other lawyer has asked on the grounds that it may violate the hearsay rules. By the time the lawyer explained the hearsay rule, its various exceptions, and the benefits and risks of presenting an objection, the opposing lawyer would have moved on to other witnesses and the particular question will have become ancient history. On the other hand, we expect that the client and not the lawyer will make the decision as to whether to plead guilty or not guilty in a criminal prosecution.

The ethics rules therefore attempt to lay out basic guidelines to distinguish between those matters where the lawyer must let the client make the decision and those where prior client consent is unnecessary. As a general principle, the lawyer is entitled to make decisions in matters that do not affect the merits of the cause or substantially prejudice the client's rights, although, even in these cases, there may be situations where it would be prudent for the lawyer to confer with the client. In other situations, the client has the exclusive authority to make decisions. The lawyer is the professional fiduciary (not the guardian) of the client, who is the client (not the ward) of the lawyer.

The client decides whether to settle a civil suit, or to plead guilty. In criminal cases the client has the final say as to whether or not he will testify on his own behalf, or whether to waive a jury trial. Rule 1.2(a). The client decides the *objectives* of the representation but the lawyer must reasonably consult with the client with respect to "the *means* by which the client's objectives are to be pursued," Rule 1.2, Comment 1. Rule 1.4(a)(2).

Lawyers also have the right (*i.e.*, the power) to grant reasonable requests of opposing counsel that do not prejudice the client's rights. The ethics rules authorize lawyers to grant a "reasonable request for a postponement that will not prejudice the lawyer's client." Rule 1.3, Comment 3.

For example, assume that the defendant's attorney, while preparing an Answer to the Complaint, needs more time to complete some research, so he asks the plaintiff's attorney for a one-week extension in the time allowed to file the Answer. The extension will not prejudice the client's case. The ethics rules do not give the plaintiff a right to forbid his attorney from granting this specific request. The plaintiff may hate the defendant and try to order his lawyer to grant no extensions (no matter how reasonable the extension is), but the lawyer is acting ethically if he ignores this particular order. The plaintiff may always fire his lawyer for his refusal to obey instructions, but he may not successfully charge the lawyer with unethical behavior. By the way, if the lawyer had obeyed his client's order and refused to grant a reasonable postponement, the defense will move for a continuance. The judge will grant this motion, and will be perturbed at the plaintiff's lawyer for not agreeing to it in the first place.

The client usually has a great deal of power to modify the division of lawyer-client responsibility. For example, the client may hire the lawyer only for a specifically defined purpose. Similarly, the lawyer may ask the client's permission to forego action that the lawyer believes is unjust, even though such action is legal and is otherwise in the best interest of his client. And although the traditional rule is that the client alone can settle, a client may properly tell her lawyer, "Use your judgment as to whether or not to accept any settlement for at least $25,000."

Total freedom of contract is not the law here, however. Thus, the power to draft a specific contract (or retainer) between the lawyer and client may not be used to violate the ethical codes or other law. The lawyer may not ask the client to agree to representation so limited in scope as to violate the rule requiring competence. Nor may the client, by contract, surrender the right to terminate the lawyer's services or the right to settle litigation that the lawyer might wish to continue.

The lawyer or client may of course also affect the extent of client control by terminating the client-lawyer relationship. In other words, the client can always fire the lawyer, who then must withdraw, even if the client seeks to terminate the lawyer for a less than noble reason. Rule 1.16(a)(3) & Comment 4. For example, if a client decides to fire the lawyer because the lawyer has just hired an African–American associate, the lawyer has no right to prevent the client from terminating the representation. The client is obviously acting for a racist reason, but the ethics rules compel the lawyer to withdraw. Other law, such as civil rights laws, may impose sanctions on the client, but the rules of ethics require the lawyer to cease representing the client who has fired him.

The lawyer, in turn, may withdraw from further representation notwithstanding the client's protests if the client insists on pursuing an objective that is not illegal, but that "the lawyer considers repugnant." This is discussed below in the analysis of Rule 1.16. As a matter of constitutional law, the Supreme Court has held that an indigent criminal defendant can insist that his appointed counsel press every non-frivolous appeal. *Anders v. California* (S.Ct.1967). However, the indigent client has no constitutional right to compel his appointed counsel to present a *particular* non-frivolous *issue* on appeal, if the appointed lawyer's professional judgment is that this issue would weaken the appeal. *Jones v. Barnes* (S.Ct.1983). For example, the lawyer may decide that presenting one argument would undercut another argument that has a greater chance of success.

3. Counseling or Assisting the Client in Criminal or Fraudulent Conduct

A lawyer may not knowingly counsel or in any way assist a client to commit a crime or fraud. Unfortunately, . the Rules do not clearly define "counsel" and "assist." Obviously, the lawyer may not drive the getaway car in his client's bank robbery. But can a lawyer advise his client that the criminal penalties for robbing a state bank are less than the penalties for robbing a federal bank, or that there is no extradition for bank robbery from a particular Latin American country?

In general, if the actions of a non-lawyer in the same circumstances would make the non-lawyer civilly liable, or give the non-lawyer a defense to such liability, the same activities by a lawyer in the same circumstances generally make the lawyer liable or give that lawyer a defense. However, the lawyer is not liable for simply advising the client that a proposed action is unlawful and could have dire consequences.

There are three basic exceptions to the general rule that a lawyer will be civilly liable to a non-client for assisting the client if the client is liable. Let us turn to those three areas and then consider in more general terms the question of fraudulent conduct.

FIRST, the law does give the lawyer an absolute privilege under the law of defamation to publish defamatory material about a non-client in communications preliminary to a proceeding before a tribunal, or as a part of such a proceeding in which the lawyer participates as counsel. The principal rationale for this exception to the general rule of liability is that imposing the risks of liability on the lawyer in this circumstance would unduly impede a client's access to the courts.

SECOND, a lawyer assisting his client in a civil or criminal proceeding is not liable to a non-client for the tort of malicious prosecution *if* the lawyer acts primarily to aid the client in obtaining a proper adjudication of the client's claim. The rationale is the same as the rationale for the defamation privilege: imposing on the lawyer a risk of civil liability would unduly impede the client's access to the courts. If, however, the lawyer had no probable cause to believe in his adversary's culpability, and if the lawyer acted with malice (which itself may be inferred from the lack of probable cause), a malicious prosecution suit against the lawyer would lie.

THIRD, in the case of advising a client to breach a contract, the lawyer is not liable to a non-client for advising his client as to whether proposed client conduct is lawful, or for counseling his client to break a contract in the *client's* interest. It may be difficult to determine beforehand if an arguable refusal to perform will be found to be an actionable breach of contract. Indeed, a lawyer—without worrying about civil liability—may not only advise but even assist a client's breach of contract, by, for example, sending a letter stating the client's intention not to perform, or by negotiating and drafting a contract with someone else that is inconsistent with the client's existing contractual obligations. These same principles apply to interference with an existing contract.

Of course, a lawyer may be liable to *his client*, in malpractice, for failure to explain the possible ramifications to the client of breach of the client's obligations to a third party. And *if the lawyer personally benefits* from the breach or interference (e.g., because the client enters into a contract with an entity related to the lawyer as a result of the breach), then the lawyer can be as liable to the nonparty as would any non-lawyer.

Other legal issues raise further distinctions. Assume a client wishes to challenge the constitutionality of a law. The best way to challenge a law that forbids picketing in front of an abortion clinic is to engage in such picketing and then raise the constitutionality of the statute in defense of the criminal charge. The Rules specifically allow advice given to effectuate a good faith challenge to the constitutionality of the law. The lawyer "may counsel or assist a client to make a good faith effort to determine the validity, scope, meaning or application of the law,'' according to Rule 1.2(d).

What if, however, the lawyer advises the client to violate a law whose violation invokes a very small penalty? Assume that a county law forbids operating a department store on Sundays. A client (who wants to keep his store open because a competing store, just across the county line, remains open) asks his lawyer for advice. May the lawyer advise that the penalty for a violation is a $100 fine, but the fine is not imposed on each sale. Instead, each day of violation is treated as only one violation, so that it will make economic sense for the department store to remain open as long as the profits for that day are in excess of $100. The purpose of this advice is not to test the constitutionality of the law: the purpose of advice is to advise breaking the law.

Has the lawyer acted unethically? Unlike fraud, a violation of the Sunday closing laws is *malum prohibitum*, (*i.e.*, wrongful not as a matter of morality—*malum in se*—but merely because positive law makes it illegal). And the violation is open and notorious: unlike fraud, everyone knows that the client is open on Sunday, while the whole point in fraud is to make sure that the victim does not know that he is being defrauded.

In general, the ethics rules provide no easy litmus test for such cases. We know that the lawyer may present an analysis of the legal aspects of questionable conduct but may not recommend ''the means by which a crime or fraud might be committed with impunity." Rule 1.2, Comment 9. The lawyer may not suggest, for example, how the client might conceal his illegal purpose. Comment 10.

If a lawyer later discovers that she has been unwittingly assisting her client in conduct that the lawyer now learns is criminal or fraudulent, then the lawyer must stop assisting the client now that she has learned what is really going on. But must the lawyer resign? Yes, according to Comment 10 to Rule 1.2. On the other hand, Comment 9 specifically authorizes the lawyer to give "an honest opinion about the actual consequences that appear likely to result from a client's conduct."

Additional considerations apply if the lawyer learns that his client or a witness on behalf of his client has presented perjured testimony or false evidence before a tribunal, a topic that is considered later, in Rule 3.3.

RULE 1.3: DILIGENCE

Rule 1.3 requires that a lawyer "shall act with reasonable diligence and promptness in representing a client." Clients often accuse lawyers of dilatoriness, procrastination, and delay. The Model Rules acknowledge that criticism and their Comments warn that unreasonable postponements can cause "needless anxiety" to a client. Thus, in addition to the lawyer's affirmative duty to engage in reasonable communication with his client, the lawyer must not neglect a legal matter entrusted to him.

"Neglect" is an important concept in the law of ethics: it means a pattern of action or inaction, not just one instance of delay. If a lawyer on one occasion forgot to file an answer to a complaint in time because of inadvertence, he might be liable for malpractice if the client suffered damages, but he would not be guilty of the ethical violation of neglect. Neglect involves indifference and a *consistent failure* to carry out the obligations that the lawyer has assumed to the client, or a conscious disregard for the responsibility owed to the client. Clients resent "procrastination." Rule 1.3, Comment 3.

Thus, if a lawyer fails on one occasion to file a case within the statute of limitations because she does not know about the statute of limitations, she might be liable for malpractice *and* guilty of violating the ethical rule against *incompetence*, but she would not be guilty of *neglect*. Sometimes the same act may lead to both malpractice and legal discipline, or only malpractice, or only legal discipline.

Most ethics rules are for the protection of clients, who can usually waive them if they choose. However, some rules are not subject to waiver. Even a client's refusal to pay her lawyer's fee does not waive the rule prohibiting the lawyer from neglecting the client's case. If the client deliberately ignores his obligation to pay his attorney, the attorney may withdraw from representation only after taking reasonable steps to protect her client's interests. If the matter is before a tribunal, the lawyer may not withdraw unless the tribunal permits. In any event, until the lawyer withdraws in accordance with the requirements in the ethics rules, the lawyer may not neglect the client's case. Rule 1.17(d).

Nor does an attorney's heavy workload excuse her neglect of legal matters committed to her. It is her responsibility to control her workload so that each matter can be handled adequately. Otherwise, she is subject to discipline.

RULE 1.4:
COMMUNICATION

Clients who use lawyers a lot, such as corporations involved with many transactions and court matters, understand that they are unlikely to be in daily contact with their lawyer except during crucial phases of the representation. In fact, such clients often expect that, in many instances, their lawyers will simply take care of the matter, so that they need no longer be bothered by it. However, individual clients, particularly in the case of litigation that do not involve business transactions (divorce, family disputes and medical malpractice actions, among others) often act differently. They want frequent contact with their lawyer. One of the most common complaints of this type of client is that the lawyer should communicate with the client more frequently. Sometimes lawyers complain that "high maintenance" clients want constant contact.

The old ABA Model Code addressed this problem at the aspirational level by exhorting the lawyer to "fully and promptly inform his client of material developments in the matters being handled for the client," and to keep his client informed of relevant considerations before the client makes decisions. The Model Rules have gone further, by making clear that these requirements are not merely horta-

35

tory; to violate them is to violate either Rule 1.4(a)(1), which requires the lawyer to "promptly inform the client" of relevant matters and consult with the client, and/or Rule 1.4(b), which requires the lawyer to explain the matter to the extent necessary to permit the client to understand what is going on, so the client can make informed decisions.

Sometimes when clients complain that the lawyer has "neglected" their case, they really mean that the lawyer has failed to communicate with them. If the lawyer had kept them informed, they would have known that there had been no neglect of their case. Nonetheless, when lawyers keep their clients in the dark and unaware, without good reason, they are also violating the ethics rule requiring lawyers to communicate with their clients.

RULE 1.5: FEES

Rule 1.5 contains various provisions dealing with fees. Rule 1.5(a) requires that fees not be "unreasonable." Rule 1.5(b) advises that the basis for the fee shall be communicated to the client, "preferably" in writing. Rule 1.5(c) requires contingent fees to be in writing signed by the client, and Rule 1.5(d) prohibits certain types of contingent fees. Rule 1.5(e) places restrictions on fee division with lawyers who are not practicing in the same law firm.

1. Factors That Determine Whether a Fee Is Reasonable

In contemporary times, the two primary methods that lawyers use to determine their fees are the contingency fee (used primarily by plaintiffs' attorneys in personal injury actions), and billable hours (used by both plaintiffs' and defendants' attorneys in all other cases, ranging from corporate advice to litigation). In recent years, both types of fees have come under heavy criticism.

Because the lawyer is a fiduciary of the client, the lawyer is subject to discipline if the fees are not "reasonable." The Model Code used the term "clearly excessive," but that phrase really meant "unreasonable." It did not mean that the fee could be excessive as long as it was not "clearly" so. Both the Model Code and the Model Rules list the same eight factors that are relevant in determining reasonableness. The ethics rules do not limit the determination of reasonableness to these eight factors, but these factors represent typical components that the lawyer may consider in setting a reasonable fee:

- the time and labor required, the novelty and difficulty of the questions involved, and the skill requisite to perform the legal service properly;

- the likelihood, if apparent to the lawyer, that the acceptance of the particular employment will preclude other employment by the lawyer (what economists call "opportunity costs");

- the fee customarily charged in the locality for similar legal services;

- the amount involved and the results obtained;

- the time limitations imposed by the client or by the circumstances;

- the nature and length of the professional relationship with the client;

- the experience, reputation, and ability of the lawyer or lawyers performing the services;

- whether the fee is fixed or contingent.

While a lawyer may consider factors such as the novelty of the legal service, how much skill is needed to perform it, and so forth, for many lawyers the hourly rate is the most important—or often the sole—factor used to determine fees.

It is often said that "time is money." That is certainly true for hourly billing. The movement from fixed fees to hourly fees began in earnest in the 1950s. Various factors, including the explosion of pretrial discovery in civil litigation, explain this shift, which both clients and lawyers initially acclaimed. If a lawyer charges by the hour, instead of a fixed fee, then it would be dishonest to bill more time than the lawyer actually spent on a matter. However, she can engage in standard practice disclosed in the retainer agreement of rounding up minimum time periods such as quarter-hours, or tenths of an hour.

A lawyer basing her fee on hours expended obviously may not engage in goldbricking, that is, employing wasteful procedures in an effort to maximize the number of billable hours. Nor may the lawyer simply make up hours, that is, charge his clients for more hours than he actually worked. Alas, there is empirical evidence indicating that a few lawyers engage in this fraudulent practice.

Similarly, a lawyer may not double-count hours. If the lawyer agrees to bill a client by the hour, it would violate Rule 1.5 for the lawyer to bill several clients for the same hour (e.g., scheduling court appearances for two clients on the same day, spending two hours at the courthouse, and billing each client the full two hours), or for the same work product (e.g., spending 15 hours preparing a research memorandum for one client, which happens to be relevant to a second client, and then billing each client the full 15 hours). When the lawyer agrees to bill solely on the basis of time spent, one should consider the client's perspective and his expectation that the lawyer will only bill on the basis of hours actually expended. *ABA Formal Opinion* 93–379 (1993) considered these issues and concluded that a "lawyer who spends four hours of time on behalf of three clients has not earned twelve billable hours." If a lawyer is able to reuse old work product "he has not re-earned the hours previously billed and compensated when the work product was first generated."

In cases where the client agrees to be billed solely on the basis of hours spent, the lawyer may be able to secure a particularly favorable result after spending fewer hours than anyone might have expected. The lawyer may not retroactively charge for hours not actually expended. When the lawyer purports to bill only on the basis of hours expended, the lawyer should pass on to the client any efficiency that results in fewer hours being expended. Lawyers who are more efficient often charge more per hour. That is permissible, and part of the agreed-upon bargain with the client; charging phantom hours is not.

If the client alleges that his lawyer's fee is excessive, the court should normally look at the fee agreement as of the time that it was made, not with 20–20 hindsight. Consider, for example, a contingent fee case where the plaintiff wins a large award. A disgruntled client, after-the-fact, can always argue that the fee is excessive because the lawyer now knows that the plaintiff has won a huge award. But, the lawyer may not know beforehand that the client will win, nor will the lawyer know, beforehand, how much. After the fact, the risks inherent in a contingent fee agreement will disappear if the contingency has occurred. Thus, the court analyzes the contract as of the time it was made.

In determining what is reasonable, it is crucial to know if the attorney overreached, abused the relationship, or was not completely candid in discussing the elements of a fee or other relevant factors. For example, if the lawyer falsely told the client that lawyers in a particular area of law (e.g., filing in court to change officially one's name) were charging about $100, when the standard fee was really $50, the court should find the $100 fee unreasonable because the lawyer lied to the prospective client as to the fee customarily charged in the locality for similar services. On the other hand, imagine that Lawyer Alpha truthfully informs the prospective client that the standard rate is around $50, but that Lawyer Alpha will charge $100 because it is not worth his time to work on any case for less than $100. In this case the client—who is fully informed—is free to accept that higher fee, which would not be unreasonable. Alternatively, this client can decide to go elsewhere.

A lawyer's acceptance of one matter may well preclude her from taking other legal work. Thus, in setting her fee, the lawyer may consider what economists call "opportunity cost." To take one case deprives the lawyer of the opportunity to take another case. First, the lawyer only has a finite number of hours in any given period. Therefore if she takes one assignment, she may not have the time to take another one. Second, whenever a lawyer accepts one job, she creates conflicts that prevent her from accepting other work. If the client is not aware of this opportunity cost, the lawyer may want to explain. The issue of opportunity costs leads to the question of non-refundable retainers.

Sometimes lawyers charge a client a "non-refundable retainer." In a typical case, the retainer provides that the fee is earned when paid. The fee is payable before any work is begun and is not refundable if the work turns out to take little time or if the client later fires the lawyer. The client is paying the lawyer to retain her services and also for being on call and for not working for adverse parties.

Some commentators contest the validity of non-refundable retainers, and courts often scrutinize them with care. For example, *Matter of Cooperman* (N.Y.1994) suspended a lawyer for imposing non–refundable fees ranging from $5000 to $15000 on his clients. Cooperman, in effect, told the client that once he entered an appearance for them in their case, he would not return any part of the fee even if the client fired him (even if the firing was for cause). Non-refundable fees in this case violated the fiduciary relationship between lawyer and client and chill the client's right to fire an attorney who loses the client's trust, the Court of Appeals reasoned. The court reasoned that if the impugned fee structure were validated—

Instead of becoming responsible for fair value of actual services rendered, the firing client would lose the entire "nonrefundable" fee, no matter what legal services, if any, were rendered. This would be a shameful, not honorable, professional denouement. Cooperman even acknowledges that the essential purpose of the nonrefundable retainer was to prevent clients from firing the lawyer, a purpose which, as demonstrated, directly contravenes the Code and this State's settled public policy in this regard.

The court affirmed a two-year suspension from practice.

While a non-refundable retainer does not prevent the client from firing the lawyer, it certainly makes exercising that right more costly. Consequently, courts often have suggested that no retainer is truly non-refundable in all cases if a lawyer is fired for cause, because then she will quite often have to return non-earned fees regardless of any stipulation that a retainer was "non-refundable."

Courts vary in deciding whether any given nonrefundable retainer is excessive in the particular facts. In some cases, an attorney may incur real opportunity costs by taking a case. Assume, for example, that a client wants her lawyer to assure her that she will set aside the month of September to try a matter. She agrees to do so for a non-refundable fee of $20,000, her typical monthly billing. She then turns down opportunities to take other litigation because it will interfere with the

September trial. On August 31st, the client fires the lawyer without cause, at a time when she is unable to take the other cases that she earlier had turned down. In that case, the fee would not be per se improper and a court may approve the fee as reasonable under the circumstances.

The lawyer may also consider the fees customarily charged in the locality for similar legal services. It would be a violation of antitrust laws for the bar association to discipline a lawyer because he charged less than a minimum (or more than a maximum) fee. However, the mere fact that all lawyers of similar quality charge the same, or approximately the same, fee for similar services is not in and of itself proof that lawyers have conspired to fix prices. In fact, in a perfectly competitive economy, the prices for similar services tend to be about the same.

While lawyers and bar associations may not conspire to fix prices, the federal antitrust laws do not forbid the *state* from setting prices by statute or other law. Price-fixing by "state action" is exempt from the Sherman Act. In other words, if a statute sets a price for legal services, a lawyer does not charge an excessive fee or conspire with the state when he or she follows the statute. The lawyer merely complies with the law. While state-mandated fee schedules are unusual, in some cases they do exist.

Misunderstandings regarding fees are among the most frequent cause of clients' disputes with their attorneys. The Ethics 2000 Commission's Report recommended amending Rule 1.5 to require that all fee agreements be in writing, except when the client is a regular one and the matter a routine one for that client, or if the total bill would be less than $500. But the ABA House of Delegates rejected this proposed change and kept the "preferably in writing" language.

As to contingent fees, discussed below, the former Model Code urged that the agreement be reduced to writing, but the Model Rules go beyond that and flatly *require* a writing signed by the client. This writing must state how the fee is determined and whether expenses are deducted before or after the contingent fee is calculated. After the matter is concluded, the lawyer must also provide a detailed statement to the client.

2. Fee Disputes

If there are disputes involving the interpretation of the fee agreement, the court should construe the agreement as a reasonable person would in the circumstances of the client. An established rule of interpretation states that doubtful agreements are to be construed against the drafter. As a general proposition, the meaning of a written document, if placed in doubt, is construed against the party that wrote it, and the principle surely counts double when the drafter is a lawyer writing on his or her own account to a client. In setting fees, lawyers "are fiduciaries who owe their clients greater duties

than are owed under the general law of contracts."
Beatty v. NP Corp. (Mass.App.1991).

In any proceeding to collect a disputed fee, the
lawyer, and not the client, has the burden of persuasion. The lawyer must show the existence and
terms of the fee agreement. The lawyer also has the
burden of persuasion that the fee agreement is
reasonable. If the lawyer sues to collect his fee, he
should not be surprised if the client counterclaims
and argues that the lawyer was incompetent, the
fee was unreasonable, the hours were not sufficient-
ly documented, and so forth.

The ABA adopted *Model Rules for Fee Arbitration*
in 1995. These were part and parcel of the *Report of
the Commission on Evaluation of Disciplinary Enforcement* (the "McKay Commission") in 1992. If
the client requests arbitration, the model fee arbitration rules make the arbitration mandatory for
the lawyer. If the lawyer files a petition for arbitration, the arbitration may not proceed unless the
client files a written consent within 30 days of
service. The burden of proof is on the lawyer to
prove, by a preponderance of the evidence, that the
fee is reasonable. The proceedings are normally
confidential, thus protecting client confidences.

Mediation is appropriate when the dispute between lawyer and client does not allege that the
lawyer engaged in misconduct or, if there is only
relatively minor misconduct alleged, sometimes
called "lesser misconduct" in the jurisdiction's rules
of disciplinary enforcement. To fill this need, the

ABA has developed *Model Rules for Mediation of Client–Lawyer Disputes* (August 1998). Mediation may be helpful in resolving disagreements involving fees, but one should realize that mediation extends to disputes that go well beyond fee issues.

An allegation that a lawyer failed to return a client's file because of a fee dispute with the client is something that may be suitable for mediation. So also are disputes that involve the lawyer's release of her lien on a client's recovery in a case where a new lawyer has replaced the original lawyer, or a dispute that involves the alleged failure to return an un-earned portion of the fee, or an alleged failure to communicate the status of a matter, or a client's alleged failure to pay for costs (including expected future costs) or to communicate with the lawyer.

3. Contingent Fees

The Rules impose several important requirements on contingent fees. First, all contingent fee arrangements *must* be in writing, signed by the client. Previously, the Model Code merely *encouraged* a written agreement for contingent fees.

If a lawyer demands payment of an alleged contingent fee but there is no written contingent fee agreement, some courts allow attorneys a reasonable *quantum meruit* recovery, while many courts allow no recovery whatsoever. E.g., *Estate of Pinter v. Mc Gee* (N.J.Super.App.Div.1996). If the lawyer only accepts contingent fee arrangements, and that is contrary to the client's best interest, the client should go elsewhere. *The contingent fee, in short, should not be for the benefit of lawyers, but for the benefit of clients* who may wish to choose that type of arrangement.

A. Common Objections Raised Against Contingent Fees

Contingent fees by their nature raise potential conflicts of interest between the attorney and client. For example, the client may wish to settle litigation for a low, guaranteed amount while the attorney would want to press on, or (more likely) the opposite may be true. The ethics rules attempt to manage such conflicts, which are inherent with contingent fees, and have specific provisions—examined in the conflicts of interest section—dealing with contingent fees.

One basic point to remember is that the lawyer cannot ethically require the client to give up her right, under Rule 1.2, to settle litigation, and her right, under Rule 1.16, to fire her lawyer.

For example, assume that a client ("Client") agrees to compensate her lawyer ("Lawyer") by giving him a one-fourth interest in certain real property and mining claims. Ownership of these properties is disputed and the Lawyer defends the Client (and, indirectly, himself as well, given that the Lawyer's one-fourth interest is now involved). Then assume that Client becomes dissatisfied with Lawyer's services and tries to discharge Lawyer, who refuses to leave. In this hypothetical fact situation, Lawyer has violated Rules 1.8(i) and 1.16(a)(3) because he has refused to accept the client's discharge.

Opponents of contingency fees frequently claim that the lawyers who bill this way are "over-compensated." Contingency fee lawyers dispute that. Because the lawyer only receives remuneration if the client agrees to a contingency fee and if the case is successful, proponents of contingency fees argue that the fees cannot be "too high." Clients only accept the fees if they choose to do so, and the lawyers assume the risk of collecting no fee at all.

Contingent fee lawyers have a diverse portfolio of cases. The contingent fee client almost invariably does not have a diverse portfolio of law cases, only one. The law firm knows that its losses in one case are likely to be balanced by gains in another. The individual plaintiff's risk of losing is real; the lawyer's risk of losing an entire diversified portfolio of cases is statistically remote. One commentator has charged that plaintiffs' lawyers "find that playing the litigation lottery is profitable: they bring the same dubious multimillion dollar claim before many juries in the expectation that a few random victories will more than compensate for a larger number of losses. One attorney who only handles breast implant cases boasts that he 'tell[s] everyone I've got a license to gamble.' " David E. Bernstein, *The Breast Implant Fiasco*, 87 Calif. L. Rev. 457, 492 (1999).

Another objection to contingency fees is that the fee structure encourages lawyers to take frivolous cases. This argument appears counter-intuitive, because truly frivolous cases are losers, and the lawyer is only paid if his case is successful. On the other hand, contingency fees may encourage litigation of dubious (though not totally frivolous) cases involving sympathetic plaintiffs. The lawyer who takes on a portfolio of cases may be quite willing to take an individual case that is not likely to win if he or she thinks that the likelihood of all the cases being lost is small (given the fact that each severely injured plaintiff cuts a sympathetic figure when before a jury).

Some claim that a contingent fee case places the lawyer in a conflict of interest with respect to his or her client. The lawyer may be willing to cynically downplay or distort the plaintiff's chances of winning in a protracted suit, so as to settle the case very quickly, before much work has been done, and maximize his effective hourly income. On the other hand, as the case approaches trial, the lawyer (if he has fully prepared for trial) may be more interested in not settling because it is only by playing in the litigation lottery (by going to the jury) that the lawyer can now hope to hit the jackpot.

Lawyers who work for hourly fees are not immune to potential conflicts of interest. The lawyer may want to put in "too many" hours on the case or send two lawyers to cover a deposition instead of one. That does not mean that most lawyers engage in such practices; it only means that there are inevitable ethical problems when lawyers negotiate with their clients on fee matters (whether contingent fees or hourly fees) and that the ethics rules cannot eliminate these problems, but only endeavor to manage them.

B. When the Rules Prohibit Contingent Fees

The Model Rules forbid contingent fees in criminal cases. The rationale usually given in support of this prohibition is the lack of a *res* [*i.e.*, a "thing" or monetary gain] out of which the fee is to be paid. Contingent fees are often heralded in tort suits (where there *is* a *res*) as allowing the indigent to obtain counsel. Yet, in other areas of the law, for example in corporate derivative suits, litigation may produce no *res* and yet the attorney may still be paid only if successful. In criminal adjudication, if the client is indigent and cannot afford to pay, the court will provide free appointed counsel.

The reason for the rule prohibiting contingent fees in criminal cases today may rest on the self-interest of criminal defense counsel: criminal counsel typically prefer that their clients pay them in advance; the ethical prohibition thus gives lawyers a good excuse to reject the efforts of clients who might insist on a contingent fee if that alternative were possible.

It would be contrary to public policy for the state to hire a prosecutor on a contingency fee basis, i.e., a prosecutor paid only if he secures a criminal conviction. The rationale behind this prohibition is not difficult to find: the duty of a prosecutor is to do justice, not merely to convict. The state's interest in a criminal prosecution is not that it shall win a case, but that justice shall be done.

The former Model Code concluded that contingent fees in domestic relations matters are "rarely justified," but it did not raise this note of discouragement to the level of discipline. In contrast, the Model Rules flatly forbid fees in divorce matters contingent upon "the securing of a divorce or upon the amount of alimony or support or property settlement" achieved.

The Rules do not explain the purpose of the prohibition in divorce cases, but the reason behind it is easy to understand. Public policy does not encourage divorce, and the lawyer's fee arrangements should not encourage the lawyer to prevent a possible reconciliation of the parties: the lawyer who charged a contingent fee would place himself in a conflict situation, for if he encouraged reconciliation, he could lose his fee. Thus, a lawyer may not charge a contingency fee for the initial securing of the amount of support, because a reconciliation would deprive the lawyer of his fee. But, he may charge a contingency fee to secure the collection of support in arrears, because the reason for the rule against contingency fees does not apply in that situation. Similarly, the lawyer may charge a contingency fee to *enforce* an equitable distribution of property, though he could not ethically charge such a fee initially in order to *secure* an equitable distribution of property.

C. When the Rules Allow Contingent Fees

Contingent fees typically occur in personal injury litigation, but the ethics rules do not limit contingent fees to those cases. For example, it is permissible for a lawyer to charge a contingent fee in an administrative agency proceeding.

Contingent fees allow poorer litigants to hire competent lawyers and pay them out of the judgment won. However, the ethics rules do not limit contingent fees to poorer clients. In fact, they specifically allow contingent fees even when the client can afford a different fee arrangement. However, if there is doubt that a contingent fee is in the client's best interest, the lawyer should explain their implications. The Reporter's Notes for the ABA Ethics 2000 Commission to Rule 1.5 advises, ''If the contingent fee is reasonable, then lawyers need not offer an alternative fee nor need they inform clients that other lawyers might offer an alternative.'' Nonetheless, if a contingent fee is not in the client's (or prospective client's) interest, the lawyer (who has fiduciary responsibilities) should tell the truth and warn the client of that fact. If the client does not want to pay a contingency fee and the lawyer only works for a contingency fee, then the client can hire a different lawyer.

Clients who can afford an hourly billing may still prefer a contingent fee because of the special incentive it creates for their lawyer. A contingency fee system also makes it easier for clients to budget legal expenses.

Often, the civil liability of the opposing party is
not clear in a contingent fee case, but there is no
ethical rule that restricts contingent fees to that
type of case. The ABA has advised that the "mere
fact that liability may be clear does not, *by itself*,
render a contingent fee inappropriate or unethical."
ABA Formal Opinion 94–389 (Dec. 5, 1994) (emphasis added). Although liability may be clear, the
defendant may be of dubious solvency and the judgment may be difficult to collect; or the client may
wish to be assured that he need not pay until (and
unless) the money owed him is collected, and that
the fee will be no more than a certain percentage of
the money actually collected. The client, in short,
can decide to pay only for results. But, if the client
does not understand that liability is certain, the
lawyer must explain the pertinent facts in order to
secure the client's informed consent to the contingent fee arrangement.

The lawyer and client may agree that the lawyer
will charge a different contingent fee rate at different stages of a matter and may increase (or de-
crease) the percentage taken as a fee as the amount
of the recovery to the client increases. *Increasing*
contingent rates are well designed for cases where
liability is clear but where the *quantum* is hotly
debated. It is, after all, the last dollars of recovery,
not the first, that often require the greater effort.
So, if the client agrees, the lawyer may charge a
higher contingent fee if the recovery becomes larger, e.g., 20% of the first million, 25% of the next
million, and 30% of any amount over \$2 million.

In other cases, however, it is very hard to obtain any finding of liability. Once held liable, however, the defendant will likely be on the hook for a very substantial sum. In this type of case, a *decreasing* contingency rate would be appropriate. Thus, if the client agrees, the lawyer may charge a lower contingent fee for a higher recovery, e.g., 25% of the first million and 20% of any amount above $1 million.

There is no *per se* ethical objection to either type of arrangement, although particular facts may make each type of fee unreasonable in any given instance.

We do not often think of contingency fees for defense matters, but the ABA Model Rules do not preclude them. Rule 1.5(d) only prohibits contingent fees in divorce or criminal cases. Rule 1.8(i)(2), another ethical rule dealing with contingent fees, also does not limit them to actions brought by plaintiffs. It simply authorizes lawyers to contract with a client "for a reasonable contingent fee in a civil case." No ethical provision prohibits contingent fees in all defense cases.

While there is no per se ethical prohibition of contingent fees charged by defense counsel in civil cases, every fee agreement is still subject to the other requirements of Rule 1.5. In other words, a defendant's contingent fee must be reasonable and the lawyer must fully inform the client in order to secure a valid agreement to the fee arrangement. Often, the amount that plaintiff claims in a case is not readily determinable; an unliquidated tort damages complaint may claim a vague amount ("damages in excess of \$10 million''). If a plaintiff does not specify a liquidated dollar amount, then the negotiations between the defense lawyer and the client defendant will establish, at least initially, what should be a "fair dollar figure to attribute to plaintiff's claim." ABA Formal Opinion 93–373 (Apr. 16, 1993).

These fee negotiations may not be fair because the lawyer may know a lot more about the issue than what he reveals to his client. The reasonableness of the reverse contingent fee depends on the degree to which the possible reduction from conceivable liability is reasonably ascertainable and not based on speculation. There is some danger that an unscrupulous attorney might exaggerate the potential exposure, so as to inflate his own value when a lower plaintiff's verdict (or a defense verdict) is returned. A plaintiff might sue the defendant for tens of millions of dollars in punitive damages, when the lawyer knows that the realistic risk is exceedingly remote. If the defendant in this circumstance agrees to pay defense counsel one-third of what is "saved," the reverse contingent fee could be an unconscionable windfall for the defense lawyer: the defense counsel may have "saved" the defendant \$39 million because the plaintiff sued for \$40 million and the verdict was only for \$1 million, but, in reality, the defendant's realistic exposure was much more modest. To use the plaintiff's prayer for relief in an unliquidated tort damages claim as the sole basis to calculate a reverse contingent fee is unreasonable because the claim is purely speculative. ABA Formal Opinion 93–373 (Apr. 16, 1993).

4. Referral Fees and Sharing Fees

A. Basic Rules

For lawyers in the same law firm, the Model Rules do not regulate how legal fees are to be divided. The ethics rules simply do not concern themselves with intra-firm referrals. The "rainmakers" in the law firm (those who bring in a lot of the business) may delegate work to, and share fees with, other lawyers in the same firm—those who supervise and manage cases and those who do most of the detail work in cases, such as write the briefs, research the memoranda, and so forth. Often, firms distinguish sharply among these groups in terms of pay, with rainmakers commanding the highest share of firm profits. Some of those who supervise or who do the detail work may, in some firms, be called "partners" but they may not, in reality, have any equity interest in the firm. Sometimes they may work for an annual salary. All these issues are the object of intra-firm contract.

However, the ethics rules are *very* concerned with how lawyers divide the fees if they are in *different* law firms. Once lawyers are in different law firms, the ethics rules impose important limitations on the power of the lawyer to shift fees from one firm to another.

A division of a fee "is a single billing to a client covering the fee of two or more lawyers who are not in the same firm." Rule 1.5, Comment 7. Such divisions are commonly called "referral fees" or "forwarding fees." Several rationales explain historical concerns over fee splitting. If a lawyer may not handle a case because of a conflict, it seems reasonable to prohibit that lawyer from receiving part of the fee through a referral. In addition, the historical concerns for fee-splitting exhibit a general distaste towards commercial methods of obtaining clients. There was also a concern that some lawyers might simply be in the business of finding clients and referring them to other firms. Recall, however, that the Model Rules have no concern when such rainmakers, who find clients but rarely engage in law work, exist inside the same law firm.

The former Model Code allowed referral fees only if several restrictive conditions existed. The Model Rules also impose conditions, but with several important differences that make referral fees much easier to collect.

First, the Rules allow a referral fee if the fee division is in proportion to the services that each lawyer performs *or* if each lawyer assumes joint responsibility for the representation. This provision—allowing the lawyer to collect a referral fee even if the fee is not in proportion to the services he rendered, provided that the lawyer assumes joint responsibility—is what would automatically occur if the lawyers were in the same law firm.

The former Model Code required that any division of fees be made "in proportion to the services performed *and* the responsibilities assumed by each." For example, assume that Lawyer #1 referred a client to Lawyer #2 [in a different law firm], a person whom Lawyer #1 believed to be more competent to handle a particular matter. Under the old Model Code, Lawyer #2 could not pay Lawyer #1 a referral fee (e.g., one-third of Lawyer #2's contingent fee) because the extent of Lawyer #1's service was only to recommend Lawyer #2. The mere act of recommending Lawyer #2 did not entitle Lawyer #1 to a referral fee under the former Model Code. These restrictions did not give any financial incentive to Lawyer #1 to refer the case to Lawyer #2, even if the referral is in the client's interest. The Code allowed Lawyer #1 to avoid the restrictions of DR 2–107(A)(2) only through formal association with Lawyer #2. The Model Rules reject all of that.

Solo practitioners and practitioners in small law firms often complained that the Code discriminated against them as compared to large law firms, because the ethics rules imposed no restrictions on what might be considered "internal referrals"— intra-law firm referrals. The Rules correct this discrimination against small law firms or solo practitioners, while also seeking to aid clients by encouraging referrals to other (more competent) lawyers. Thus the Rules allow a division of fees if the division is *either* in proportion to services performed by each lawyer *or* if each lawyer assumes joint responsibility for the representation.

Joint responsibility "entails," for that particular matter, "financial and ethical responsibility for the representation as if the lawyers were associated in a partnership." Rule 1.5, Comment 7. May a lawyer who receives a referral fee fulfill his or her entire ethical responsibility merely by telling the new lawyers that they must comply with the Rules of Professional Conduct? The term "joint responsibility" must include more than that: to protect the client and to encourage referrals to competent attorneys, the assumption of joint responsibility also requires assumption of joint malpractice liability for the particular matter as if the lawyers were associated together. Requiring this assumption of malpractice liability will encourage the referring lawyer to pick with care the lawyer to whom the case is referred. The referring lawyer will have an added incentive to pick the most competent lawyer. Recall that the first rule of legal ethics, the prime directive, is competence.

The referring lawyer is therefore like a quasi-partner, part of an ad hoc partnership or joint professional venture, for purposes of the representation in question. As the Restatement of the Law Governing Lawyers concludes, the requirement of "joint responsibility" means that—

"each lawyer can be held liable in a malpractice suit and before the disciplinary authorities for the others' acts to the same extent as could partners in the same traditional partnership participating in the representation. Such assumption of responsibility discourages lawyers from referring clients to careless lawyers in

return for a large share of the fee." Restatement of the Law Governing Lawyers, Third,
§ 47 (Official Draft 2000), at Comment *d* (internal citation omitted).

Model Rule 1.5(e)(2) requires that the client
"agrees to the arrangement, including the share
each lawyer [in the different firms] will receive.... " This agreement must be "confirmed in
writing."

For shared contingent fees, the total fee charged
be reasonable. Rule 1.5(e)(3). Normally, this requirement is not difficult to meet because, typically,
referral fees are charged in contingent fee cases
where the referring lawyer gets back a percentage
of the fee finally collected and the total percentage
is not changed as a result. For example, if the
typical referral fee is one-third, the referring lawyer
may receive one-third of one-third; the client's total
fee is not changed because of the referral. If the
original fee is reasonable, it does not become unreasonable simply because the new lawyer rebates
some of the final fee to the referring lawyer.

In sum, a referral fee is proper under the Rules if
Lawyer #1 assumes joint responsibility with Lawyer #2 for the particular matter, the total fee is
reasonable, the Client agrees, and the agreement is
"confirmed in writing."

B. Comparing Referral Fees to the Sale of a Law Practice

It is interesting to compare the rules relating to
referral with those relating to partial or total sale of

a law practice. Rule 1.17—which governs the sale of
a law practice—refers only briefly to Rule 1.5(e),
which requires the referring lawyer to assume joint
responsibility for the representation. Rule 1.17,
Comment 5 notes that if a lawyer sells only an area
of law practice, he must "cease accepting any matter in the area of practice that has been sold, either
as counsel or co-counsel or by assuming joint responsibility . . . as would otherwise be permitted by
Rule 1.5(e)."

Rule 1.17, Comment 15 and Comment 5 specifically provide that that Rule 1.17 does not apply to
the transfer of legal representation unrelated to the
sale of a practice. That transfer is a referral, governed by Rule 1.5(e). However, one would think, as
a logical matter, that the responsibilities that a
lawyer selling an entire practice must assume under
Rule 1.17 should be no less than those that a
referring lawyer must assume pursuant to Rule
1.5(e). This view is consistent with the requirement
under Rule 1.17, Comment 11, that the seller has
the obligation to exercise competence in identifying
a qualified purchaser. While the seller—unlike the
lawyer who refers one case—cannot exercise continuing supervision (he has, after all, left the practice), it would not be unreasonable to make him also
share joint malpractice liability (as if the selling and
purchasing lawyers were partners) with the person
whom he has handpicked to buy his practice. Such a
rule would assure that the seller picks carefully,
and it is no more onerous than the burden already
imposed by Rule 1.5(e)(1). But Rule 1.17 does not

do that. Such a rule would, obviously, impose mal-practice liability on those leaving the practice, of law, something the Bar was apparently reluctant to do.

C.   Referral Fees and Hiring of Law–Temps

The issue of *law-temps* raises special fee-sharing problems. Sometimes a law firm has a short term need to hire lawyers for a specific project or staffing problem, or to offer special expertise on a particular issue. In such cases, the law firm typically hires a temporary lawyer, often called a "law-temp." The firm may either hire the law-temp directly or use the services of a placement agency.

The law-temp is treated, for purposes of Rule 1.5(e), the same as an associate who works under the supervision of other lawyers who are associated with the law firm. Therefore there is no need for the law firm to secure any special client permission before hiring law-temps, just as it does not secure client permission before hiring a new associate to work on the matter. It may even pay the law-temp a percentage of the firm's net profits.

On the other hand, if the law firm does not supervise the law-temp, and the law-temp engages in independent work for a client, the law firm must secure the client's consent, because the client, by retaining the law firm, "cannot reasonably be deemed to have consented to the involvement of an independent lawyer." ABA Formal Opinion 88–356 (Dec. 16, 1988).

If the firm treats the work of the law-temp as an expense item (that is, an expense over and above its regular fee), the ABA advises the firm to bill the client only for what the firm actually paid for the law-temp's services. The firm may not collect a surcharge, as it implicitly does for, say, associates' salaries that are built in to its regular fee structure. On the other hand, if the law firm bills for the law-temp as part of its normal overhead, not as a separate expense item, then its contractual terms with the client may implicitly incorporate a surcharge, as is the case with associates.

5. Hourly Fees

While contingent fees for plaintiff-lawyers are common in cases involving personal injury, in other instances, lawyers usually base their charges on hourly billing. Opponents of contingent fees sometimes favor hourly fees, but these can raise their own set of problems. Clients often express concern not only that law firms miscalculate hourly fees, but that hourly billing encourages law firms to overstaff a case (e.g., two or three lawyers to handle a routine deposition). Consequently, clients increasingly are auditing their lawyers' bills, and finding significant fault with the bills their lawyers send them. Law firms, in response, are auditing their own bills to catch embarrassing mistakes before the client does. As legal costs continue to rise (because of higher salaries as well as increased costs of computer and other support), clients are also demanding more efficient legal services and object to putting more lawyers on a matter than the client thinks necessary.

One difficulty is that the nature of the hourly fee makes it difficult for the client to budget legal expenses. Thus, while the hourly fee is still the overwhelming method of choice when lawyers charge for their services, clients and lawyers have been examining alternatives to the hourly fee.

Some of the most popular alternatives to a straight hourly fee include the following:

- *Fee limits or caps*. In this situation, the hourly rate is subject to an agreed maximum.

- *Discounted hourly rates and volume rates*. In this situation, the firm may agree to charge reduced hourly rates to the extent that the client gives more business to the law firm.

- *Unbundled fees*. The law firm may offer the client the option of not hiring the law firm to perform certain chores, and instead, hiring others to perform this separate, law-related work (duplicating, document indexing, messenger services). Larger corporate clients usually have in-house facilities that can perform these services relatively less expensively.

- *Variations on Contingency Fees*. The client and lawyer may agree that the law firm will charge less than its normal hourly fee, but that the client will pay a bonus for success in reaching particular goals or for achieving particular objectives, such as expeditious disposition of a motion or completion of a negotiation.

● *Task-Based Billing or Fixed Fees*. It sometimes makes good economic sense for a law firm to offer a client the option to pay a flat fee for its legal work. Flat fees shift the risks of the unknown—how many hours the law firm will actually have to devote to a case—from the client to the law firm, which typically has more knowledge and experience in this matter. The law firm is also the more efficient risk-spreader because it has, in effect, a diverse portfolio of cases.

6. Charging for Disbursements

Whether the lawyer charges a contingent fee an hourly fee, or some other form of fee, it is quite common for lawyers to charge separately for disbursements that lawyers have made on behalf of a client.

The Restatement of the Law Governing Lawyers, Third, § 38(3)(a) (Official Draft, 2000), states that, unless a contract construed in the circumstances indicates otherwise, "a lawyer may not charge separately for the lawyer's general office and overhead expenses. . . ." This provision does not *prevent* separate charges——it merely requires the lawyer to let the client know about them at the time of the retainer.

Charging for disbursements leads to the problem of how to value some types of "disbursements."

Some cases are easy. If the lawyer takes a $15 taxi ride, the firm will bill the client for $15. But other expenses are more difficult to value. The cost of a photocopy is not merely the cost of the sheet of paper, because the machine itself must be depreciated and serviced. And then there is the cost of the labor to use the machine.

Some firms have become imaginative in estimating the cost of such disbursements. A 1995 confidential survey of 30 major New York law firms indicated that many firms charged $2 per page for an outgoing domestic fax, a 50% mark-up on their cost of Westlaw® use, and so forth. A lawyer once told me that he considered the photocopy machine his silent partner. It did not speak up at meetings or take a quarterly draw, but it contributed to the bottom line like a real law partner. Note that the law firm could have out-sourced many of these expenses, charging only what it paid and therefore saving its clients considerable money. But then the law firm would not have been able to profit from these disbursements.

In addition to these typical legal expenses, some firms feel freer than others in determining when an expense is on behalf of the client. Just as a law firm may not charge a client for phantom hours it may not charge a client for phantom disbursements. If the lawyer sends a client's material to an outside photocopy service and receives a discounted rate, the lawyer must pass along that discount to the client. "The lawyer's stock in trade is the sale of legal services, not photocopy paper, tuna fish sandwiches, computer time or messenger services." ABA Formal Opinion 93–379 (Dec. 6, 1993). Is charging for some of these disbursements any different than a restaurant charging extra for heat and electricity on its meal tab?

Consider, for example, the cost of sending a one page fax. The piece of paper may cost a penny, and the long distance charge may be $1. Thus, the marginal cost of sending the fax may be $1.01, because the law firm already has already purchased the fax machine, and is already paying the fax operator a set monthly wage, whether he sends a fax or not. Under current rules the law firm can charge $1.01 for the fax (the marginal, or incremental cost), *or* it can charge the average cost, say $1.50 a page to take into account other expenses, such as the depreciation of the fax machine and the salary of the operator. The key is that the overhead may only include costs related to the fax operation. The law firm may not include in the fax charge the costs of the oil painting of the firm founder or the sky box at the local stadium in order to bring the price of the fax to "$5 per page plus long distance charges."

RULE 1.6: CONFIDENTIALITY OF INFORMATION

1. Introduction

The attorney's obligation to protect a client's confidential and secret information is based in part on the rules of evidence—the attorney-client privilege—and the rules of civil procedure—the work product doctrine. However, there is also an ethical duty (derived from the law of agency) that is broader than the contours of the evidentiary privilege. Model Rule 1.6, Comment 3.

The attorney is the agent of her client, who is the principal. It is a general rule of agency law that the agent must neither use nor disclose "information confidentially given to him by the principal or acquired by him during the course of or on account of his agency...." Restatement of the Law of Agency, Second, § 395. While an attorney is certainly subject to discipline for violating the attorney-client evidentiary privilege, she is also subject to discipline for violating the broader ethical duty of confidentiality. The ethical proscription "applies not only to matters communicated in confidence by the client but also to all information relating to the representation, whatever its source." Model Rule 1.6, Comment 3.

Consider an example to highlight the distinction between evidentiary and ethical obligations: the client ("Client") asks his lawyer ("Lawyer") to represent the client in a transaction. In the course of his representation, Client asks Lawyer to solicit certain business proposals from third parties. Lawyer does so and thereby uncovers secret information from these third parties, i.e., information not generally known to the world at large. Pursuant to a criminal investigation, a court later orders Lawyer to reveal this information to the grand jury on the grounds that lawyer learned it from non-clients, so the evidentiary privilege is inapplicable. Lawyer reveals this information in the grand jury room. Later, news reporters ask him: "Did you comply with the court order?" Lawyer answers: "Yes." Then they ask him: "What did you say to the grand jury?" If Lawyer responds, Lawyer will commit a disciplinary violation by revealing a client's secret. Although the lawyer told the grand jurors, that proceeding is not public, so one cannot argue that the information is no longer secret.

In other words, virtually all information obtained as part of the legal representation is initially within Rule 1.6. It is not necessary that the source of the information be the client; it is only necessary that the information is "relating to the representation...." While the information that third parties gave to the attorney in the example above was not within the evidentiary privilege—the judge required the lawyer to testify after ruling that the evidentiary privilege did not exist—the ethical obligation still protects it. The information remains secret because it was not generally known (it was disclosed only during the grand jury proceeding, which is secret).

The former Model Code divided client information into two types: ''confidence'' and ''secret.'' A ''confidence'' is any information protected by the attorney-client evidentiary privilege. A ''secret'' is any other information if: (1) the client has requested (expressly or by implication) that it be held ''inviolate;'' *or* (2) disclosure would embarrass the client; *or* (3) disclosure would likely ''be detrimental to the client.'' DR 4–101(A).

One would think that these three categories cover virtually all information obtained by the attorney. However, the Code's language—''information gained in the professional relationship''—is ambiguous. It allows the possibility that information is only protected when it is learned ''because of'' the client-attorney relationship. A broader interpretation would cover knowledge that the lawyer gained fortuitously, that is, during the course of, but not because of, the attorney client relationship. For example, the lawyer, at a cocktail party, may have learned from her client's loquacious banker, that the client is delinquent on a major loan and may face bankruptcy. Must the lawyer keep this information secret (assuming that it is not public knowledge), or may the lawyer treat it as gossip that he may pass on?

The drafters of the Model Rules thought that protections offered by the Model Code were not broad enough. Hence they drafted new language intended to provide broader protection for clients and to protect this cocktail party information.

Rule 1.6 initially protects all information ''relating to the representation,'' unless the disclosures are impliedly authorized, or fall within certain named exceptions, or the client gives informed consent. All information of consequence is, at least initially, protected. In the example considered above—during a cocktail reception the lawyer learns from her client's talkative banker that her client may be facing bankruptcy—the lawyer is not free to pass on the chatter about her client's bankruptcy problems, as long as the information relates to her representation and is not already publicly known.

The purpose of the broad protection of Rule 1.6 is to encourage the client to speak freely with the lawyer and to encourage the lawyer to obtain information beyond that offered by the client. Needless to say, this purpose is not furthered if a lawyer must treat as confidential information that has become a matter of general knowledge. If everyone already knows about this information, there is nothing to keep secret.

The Rules explicitly adopt this exception in Rule 1.9(c)(1), which allows a lawyer to use, to the disadvantage of a *former* client, information otherwise protected by Rule 1.6, if the information is ''generally known." The lawyer may not be able to make adverse use of such information against a *present* client's interest because of the duty of loyalty—but disclosure of generally known information in and of itself would not be an ethical violation.

2.   Inadvertent Disclosure

A client may inadvertently lose the attorney-client evidentiary privilege. For example, if the client voluntarily reveals a portion of a privileged communication with his lawyer, courts typically find that he may not withhold the remainder. One cannot open the door a crack; once the litigant has started to talk, he cannot slam the door shut.

Some courts are particularly unsympathetic and find a permanent loss of evidentiary privilege even if the client *or* lawyer *inadvertently* discloses part of a privileged communication. The attorney "must treat the confidentiality of attorney-client communications like jewels—if not crown jewels." *In re Sealed Case* (D.C.Cir.1989). Rule 1.6, Comment 15 makes clear that the lawyer "must act competently to safeguard information" from "inadvertent or unauthorized disclosure." Dean Wigmore was also antagonistic to the privilege and argued for automatic waiver even if the disclosure was inadvertent, or even when a thief stole confidential client documents. 8 John Henry Wigmore, Evidence § 2325 (J. McNaughton rev.1961). His approach is now in the minority.

The Restatement's position, which many courts now appear to accept, is that the client does not lose the privilege if the lawyer or client acted "reasonably" in protecting the privilege. "Waiver does not result if the client or other disclosing person took precautions reasonable in the circumstances to guard against such disclosure." Restatement of the Law Governing Lawyers, § 79, Comment *h*. Illustration 6 offers a useful example. Assume that Plaintiff threatened Defendant with suit unless Defendant persuades Plaintiff's lawyers that Defendant is free from fault. Plaintiff imposes a stringent deadline. Defendant authorizes Lawyer to produce a large mass of documents. Lawyer reviews the documents, but mistakenly includes a confidential memorandum from Defendant to Lawyer. The standard (and reasonable) procedure for lawyers in these circumstances would not have included reexamining the copies prior to submission. Lawyer's inadvertent disclosure did not waive the privilege. After discovering the mistake, Defendant "must promptly reassert the privilege and demand return of the document." See also, *SCM Corp. v. Xerox Corp.* (D.Conn.1976) (lawyer's failure to edit matters turned over in course of en masse copying does not constitute implied waiver if the lawyer previously had excised the privileged portions of documents but later failed to detect the lack of deletion in the substituted copies of documents because of production pressures).

A. The Case of the Inadvertent Fax

If a court is harsh on those who inadvertently disclose matters that are covered by the attorney-client privilege, that harshness is exacerbated by a simple fact of modern technology. With the touch of a finger, one can broadcast a fax to the wrong party or transmit an inadvertent email. The situation where a fax, containing confidential material, is sent to the wrong party is really a specific instance of inadvertent disclosure. Several ABA Formal Opinions deal with the issues that occur when a law firm receives a misdirected fax. ABA Formal Opinion 92–368 (November 10, 1992) was the first ABA Opinion that addressed the situation where a law firm inadvertently receives information from the opposing party that, on its face, appears to be covered by the attorney-client privilege or is otherwise confidential.

In a typical case, a clerk in a law firm mistakenly faxes a document to opposing counsel instead of faxing it to the client or to co-counsel. The ABA Opinion, while conceding that is there no satisfactory answer in the black letter Model Rules, seemed to conclude that a lawyer who receives the fax should refrain from reviewing the materials, notify the sending lawyer, and abide by that lawyer's instructions. In November 2005 the ABA issued Formal Opinion 05–437, clarifying and overruling 92–368. The new Formal Opinion is less constraining than the old one:

> "*A lawyer who receives a document from opposing parties or their lawyers and knows or reasonably should know that the document was inadvertently sent should promptly notify the sender in order to permit the sender to take*

protective measures. To the extent that Formal Opinion 92–368 opined otherwise, it is hereby withdrawn.''

ABA Formal Opinion 94–382 (July 5, 1994), argued that if an unauthorized source, e.g., a whistle-blower, *intentionally* sends secret information to counsel, then the receiving lawyer should either inform the adversary's lawyer and follow her instructions, or refrain from using the unsolicited material until a court makes a definitive resolution of the proper disposition of the materials.

The ABA officially withdrew (overruled) Formal Opinion 94–382 when it issued ABA Formal Opinion 06–440 (May 13, 2006). That later opinion belatedly recognized that Rule 4.4(b) ''requires only'' that the lawyer who receives the document notify the sender if the lawyer knows or reasonably should know that the sender sent the document *inadvertently*. ''The Rule does not require refraining from reviewing the materials or abiding by instructions of the sender.'' If the sender sent the materials *advertently*, *i.e.*, the sender is a whistle-blower, then Rule 4.4(b) does *not* even require the lawyer ''to notify another party or that party's lawyer of receipt'' of the material. The ABA withdrew Formal Opinion 94–383 because, it conceded, the Model Rules do not justify its conclusion.

If the misdirected fax from lawyer #1 causes his client to lose the evidentiary privilege (which is what some jurisdictions would rule), why should ethics rules prohibit lawyer #2 (the recipient of the misdirected fax) from using the faxed information? If lawyer #1 lost the attorney-client evidentiary privilege in any other situation, then lawyer #2 could take advantage of this difficulty, in the same way that he could take advantage of the circumstance where lawyer #1 mistakenly filed a complaint the day after, instead of the day before, the statute of limitations had run.

Rule 4.4(b), as amended in 2002, effectively narrowed the obligations of the receiving lawyer, stating that a lawyer who receives a document relating to the representation of the lawyer client and knows or reasonably should know that the document was *inadvertently* sent shall promptly notify the sender. Rule 4.4(b) thus only obligates the receiving lawyer to notify the sender of the inadvertent transmission promptly. ABA Formal Opinion 05–437 (2005) thus can allow use of the misdirected fax, albeit with advance notice. In other words, the sending lawyer can take ''protective measures,'' like seeking a court ruling on the evidentiary issue. If the court rules that the privilege is lost, the sending lawyer is out of luck. The other lawyer may ''accept the advantage of inadvertent, and even negligent, disclosure of confidential information by the other lawyer, if the effect of the other lawyer's action is to waive the right of that lawyer's client to assert confidentiality.'' Restatement of the Law Governing Lawyers, Third, 102 (Official Draft 2000).

If the sender is a whistle-blower and sent the materials on purpose, then Rule 4.4(b) does *not* even require the lawyer ''to notify another party or

that party's lawyer of receipt'' of the material. ABA
Formal Opinion 06–440 (May 13, 2006). This Formal Opinion, using the convoluted passive voice
that the ABA appears to favor, said: ''A lawyer
receiving materials under such circumstances is
therefore not required to notify another party or
that party's lawyer of receipt as a matter of compliance with the Model Rules.''

Of course, the simplest solution is for the lawyer
to avoid the problem by taking reasonable care to
ensure that faxes are not misdirected. The general
trend in the law is to hold that attorney-client
privilege is not waived by inadvertent disclosure *if*
the lawyer and client take *reasonable* precautions to
guard against inadvertent disclosure. What is ''reasonable'' depends on the circumstances, including
the sensitivity of the information.

If a lawyer receives a misdirected fax in a jurisdiction where the issue of waiver has not been decided,
the safest policy is for the lawyer receiving these
documents to notify the sender, who can then take
whatever protective measures are appropriate. The
lawyer receiving the misdirected documents may
also submit them to the relevant court, advise the
court that privilege may have been waived due to
disclosure (whether due to inadvertence, negligence,
or whistle-blowing) and ask the court if the lawyer
must return the documents. Then, the lawyer will

know what to do and not risk being sanctioned for violating ethical rules.

That is the conclusion of Rule 4.4(b), and Comment 2. They require the lawyer to promptly notify the sender ''in order to permit that person to take protective measures.'' That person will presumably go to court to secure a protective order. A decision of a court denying a protective order is also a decision that the material has lost its privilege. Hence, the lawyer may use the information from the misdirected fax, if the court allows it.

Comment 3 adds that it should be a matter for the lawyer's professional judgment (reserved to the lawyer, not the client) whether to return the document unread if the document was sent inadvertently. However, a lawyer who follows the old saw that ''gentlemen do not read other gentlemen's mail,'' will be at a competitive disadvantage to a lawyer who goes to court to have it decide if the material has lost its privilege. The client may not like using a lawyer who refuses to take advantage of the other lawyer's mistakes and may sue for malpractice.

Some courts have been unsympathetic of the lawyer or client who inadvertently discloses attorney-client material to the adverse party, even if the disclosure was not negligent. In other cases, courts have gone the other way and ordered that when lawyers receive inadvertently disclosed attorney-client material, they must return the documents and destroy all copies in their hands. This remedy— return of the documents to the original party and destruction of any remaining copies—is not difficult to implement. Moreover, this judicial relief will prevent the document in question from being introduced into evidence or used in a deposition. However, it is no panacea. It may not be possible for the lawyer to forget what she has reasonably read before concluding that the document was inadvertently sent to her.

Thus, some litigants have also sought an additional, more onerous remedy: they have asked the court to disqualify the lawyer who has received the material. Litigants have successfully pursued this remedy in the case of possibly corrupt (as opposed to innocent and inadvertent) disclosure of privileged material. See, *Maldonado v. New Jersey* (D.N.J. 2004), where the court disqualified two lawyers who failed to notify opposing counsel in an employment discrimination case about their unauthorized possession of a critically important privileged letter of defendant and instead used the letter in formulating their client's case. There was alleged misconduct by plaintiff in connection with the unexplained disclosure of defendants' privileged letter. A copy of the letter disappeared from the defendant's desk, and ''inexplicably'' turned up in the plaintiff's mailbox at work. The letter, an evaluation of the case written by two of the defendants to their attorney, somehow wound up in the workplace mailbox of the plaintiff, who turned it over to his counsel. The trial judge found the conduct of the plaintiff's lawyers in not adhering to the ''cease, notify, and return'' protocol required by professional conduct rules, cou-

pled with the high degree of prejudice from their
possession and use of the letter, justified removing
them as the plaintiff's counsel. En route to that
conclusion, the judge ruled that the unauthorized
disclosure of the letter did not waive the defendants' attorney-client or work product privileges.
Nor did it justify dismissing plaintiff's case.

The remedy of disqualifying the lawyer who receives inadvertently-disclosed material is tricky for
several reasons. First, court-ordered disqualification
will not affect the situation where the *client* has
also seen the document in question (as was the case
in *Maldonado*, for example). The court cannot disqualify an adverse party who received the misdirected fax! Second, the remedy of disqualification
would, in effect, punish lawyer #2 (and the client of
lawyer #2) because lawyer #1 (or the client of
lawyer #1) turned over material. Whether their
disclosure was negligent or a reasonable error, the
fact remains that it was the *other side* (lawyer #1 or
the client of lawyer #1) who is to blame for the
disclosure. The court may not wish to punish the
sending lawyer because of his error (particularly if
the error was not negligent), but neither should the
court reward him and punish the recipient by disqualifying him. Consequently, many courts have
refused to disqualify the receiving lawyer in this
situation.

It is a different situation when the lawyer who
received the unintended disclosure receives it because the courts finds that his client obtained it
improperly. For example, in *Lipin v. Bender* (N.Y.

1993), the client *stole* privileged documents from
defense counsel who had brought them to a hearing.
Plaintiff's lawyer then copied the documents and
used them against the defendant. The court dis-
missed the complaint as a sanction against the
plaintiff.

B. Using Insecure Modern Communica-
tions Methods

Some modern methods of communications may be
possibly vulnerable yet normally quite secure. Consider, for example, email and cellular telephone
calls. Federal Express® or UPS® are, in a sense,
not completely secure because the sender usually
signs a form release that allows the shipper to look
inside the package if necessary to secure its proper
delivery. Once the shipper looks inside, he or she
may read more of the document than you would
like. Yet, the shipper does not look inside on a lark,
and, in practice, one does not find the National
Enquirer publishing secrets from the vaults of Federal Express®.

That example illustrates an important issue: if a
method of communication is useful, common, and
usually secure, should the ethics rules nonetheless
prohibit its use? Most ethics authorities respond
''no.''

For instance, some have argued that law firms
should not use email when transmitting information that is protected by the attorney-client privilege, or the work product privilege, without first
securing the client's consent. Email is not secure in

the same sense that a sealed letter is secure. Knowledgeable persons can tap into email.

Yet, knowledgeable people can also tap into cordless telephones, analog cellular phones, and even land-based phones, though this snooping is not legal See U.S.C.A. §§ 2510, 2511 *et seq.* Consequently, most ethics opinions conclude that it is reasonable for lawyers to use unencrypted email to communicate with clients, and that use of email does not waive the attorney-client privilege. See, e.g., ABA Formal Opinion 99–413 (March 10, 1999). The client may, of course, insist that some forms of communication should not be used. In addition, *unusual* circumstances—involving very sensitive, top-secret information—may require increased security measures under pains of malpractice. Strong protective measures, notes the ABA Formal Opinion, "might include the avoidance of email, just as they would warrant the avoidance of the telephone, fax, and mail." In general, the basic rule is that the lawyer should take reasonable precautions, and that email is, in most instances, a reasonable method of communication.

The ethics opinions are more divided on the issue of whether it is reasonable for lawyers to use cordless telephones or cellular phones, even though federal law, since 1994, gives these phone communications the same legal protections given to land-based telephones. Commentators generally conclude that one has a reasonable expectation of privacy when using cellular and similar wireless phones, and ethics opinions should reach a similar conclusion in light of federal legal protections.

C. Metadata

"Metadata" is embedded information in email and other electronic documents. Such information may include the last time anyone accessed the document or saved it, the number of revisions of the document, the person who created the document, and so forth. Metadata may also include prior drafts and edits of the document. Sometimes the other party may find this metadata of great interest, because, e.g., a redlined change may suggest how much more the opposing party is willing to pay for a settlement. Or, the date that someone created a document may be important for discovery purposes. When lawyers seek discovery, or when they send electronic documents to each other, they may be sending relevant metadata whether or not they intended to do so.

ABA Formal Opinion 06–442 (August 5, 2006) advised that lawyers who do not wish to give metadata to their opponents should avoid creating the metadata in the first place (e.g., by not using the redlining function in a word processing program, or by not embedding comments in a document). Or, they may fax the document, or only provide a hard copy. Or, the lawyers can use computer software programs to scrub metadata from a document before they email it to their opponents. It is the duty of the lawyer to "safeguard information relating to the representation,'' Rule 1.6, Comment 16, quoted in ABA Formal Opinion 06–442.

Sometimes a document has forensic interest. In that case, ABA Formal Opinion 06–442 advised, in footnote 13: ''Of course, when responding to discovery, a lawyer must not alter a document when it would be unlawful or unethical to do so, e.g., Rule 3.4(a).''

Some state opinions have argued that a lawyer may not use computer technology to uncover metadata, but the ABA rejects that view. In general, Formal Opinion 06–442 concluded that the Model Rules ''permit a lawyer to review and use embedded information contained in e-mail and other electronic documents, whether received from opposing counsel, an adverse party or an agent of an adverse party.''

Rule 4.4(b) obligates a lawyer to inform the sender of the receipt of inadvertently sent information. However, Formal Opinion 06–442 announced that the question whether sending metadata is ''inadvertent'' is ''outside the scope of'' this Formal Opinion.

3. Lawyers Consulting with Other Lawyers (in Different Law Firms), When They Are Not Associated in a Matter

Lawyers #1 and #2 in the same law firm may routinely discuss with each other confidential matters involving a client. This rule applies even if the client hired Lawyer #1 and never anticipated that

Lawyer #1 would discuss anything with Lawyer #2. Lawyer #1 does not need to warn the client that he will discuss a matter with lawyer #2 in the same firm, but the client may take the initiative and instruct the lawyer that particular information be confined to specified lawyers. Rule 1.6, Comment 5.

In addition, with the client's express permission, a lawyer in one firm may associate with a lawyer *in a different firm* in order to handle a particular matter. Often, this association occurs when the lawyer in another law firm has special expertise to bring to a matter. In this case as well, lawyers in the two different law firms may freely consult with each other about client confidences related to that case.

A third type of consulting with another lawyer in a different firm does not involve the explicit prior consent of the client. Consider the case when lawyer #1 seeks legal advice from lawyer #2, when that second lawyer has a special expertise, or a more detached judgment on the issue *because* he is in a different law firm. Sometimes, for example, lawyer #1 may consult lawyer #2 on an ethics question to determine if a special action is required. Rule 1.6(b)(4) now specifically allows a lawyer to secure legal advice about the lawyer's compliance with the ethics rules. See also, Model Rule 1.6, Comment 9.

Of course, Lawyer #1 must be careful not to jeopardize or compromise the duty of confidentiality owed to his client when consulting with lawyer #2. For example, Lawyer #1 should avoid consulting with a lawyer likely to be representing an adverse party. Lawyer #1 may ask general legal questions, speak in hypotheticals, and should avoid discussing specific facts that would identify the client to lawyer #2. Lawyer #1 is impliedly authorized to disclose some information in this context if the disclosure does not compromise the attorney-client privilege and if it is not otherwise detrimental to the client.

ABA Formal Opinion 98–411 (August 30, 1998) concluded that there is no attorney-client relationship between lawyer #2 (the consulted lawyer) and the client of lawyer #1, but lawyer #2 may either ''expressly or impliedly'' agree to respect the confidentiality of any information that was disclosed. Unless there is such an express or implied agreement that the consulted lawyer not undertake representation adverse to the client of the consulting lawyer, the consulted lawyer may undertake such representation and has no duty of confidentiality under Rule 1.6 and no conflict of interest under Rule 1.7.

4. The Prospective Client

To protect legitimate client expectations, the ethics rules protect not only confidential information that the lawyer obtains from her clients but also secret information that she learns from a *prospective* client who sought to (but did not) retain her. This ethical principle is derived from the fact that information from a prospective client is also confidential. Model Rule 1.6 does not make this point explicitly, but it is acknowledged in the Preamble of the Model Rules. See Scope ¶ 17 (''some duties,'' such as confidentiality under Rule 1.6 attach ''when the lawyer agrees to consider whether a client-lawyer relationship shall be established'').

Until the 2002 revisions, there was no specific Rule dealing with the duties owed to prospective clients. Now, there is Rule 1.18, which deals specifically with the lawyer's duties to prospective clients.

The duty of confidentiality owed to prospective clients was nicely illustrated in *Barton v. U.S. District Court for the Central District of California* (9th Cir.2005). Plaintiffs sued GlaxoSmithKline, claiming injury from a drug called Paxil. Plaintiffs did not initiate contact with their lawyers by walking into the law office. Instead, the law firm posted a questionnaire on the internet, seeking information about potential class members for a class action the law firm contemplated. The questionnaire asked for extensive information about use of Paxil and symptoms. The law firm's presentation on the web did not say that those who answer the questionnaire are submitting themselves to the firm as potential clients. In order to email the questionnaire to the law firm, the person filling it out had to check a ''yes'' box, which acknowledged that the questionnaire ''does not constitute a request for legal advice and that I am not forming an attorney client relationship by submitting this information.'' The law firm acknowledged that it did not want to commit itself to an attorney-client relationship. It received many thousands of responses, and did not want to leave itself open to suits for malpractice to anyone who answered (e.g., for letting the statutes of limitations run).

The manufacturer sought the four plaintiffs' questionnaires in discovery "to juxtapose against what they are now claiming in discovery to determine whether or not the two fit and whether there's any information that provides for fertile cross examination at trial." The plaintiffs opposed production on the basis of the attorney-client privilege. The district court concluded that the plaintiffs' attorneys could not assert the attorney-client privilege against defendants when they insisted on "a disclaimer of confidentiality" to protect themselves, although the district court also stated that, "the four individuals submitted answers 'because they were seeking legal representation . . . .' "

The Ninth Circuit disagreed, holding that the law firm's disclaimer did not form an attorney-client relationship and did not act as a waiver of confidentiality because, while these people were not clients they were prospective clients. The questionnaire was ambiguous, "but the plaintiffs should not be penalized for the law firm's ambiguity. It is their privilege, not any right of the lawyers, that is at stake. A layman seeing the law firm's internet material would likely think he was being solicited as a potential client." As *prospective* clients these communications via the Internet were covered by attorney-client privilege regardless of whether the prospective client retained the lawyer. Rule 1.18(b).

5. The Former Client

A. Confidential Obligations to Former Clients as Creating Conflicts of Interest

The fact that a former client no longer employs a lawyer does not eliminate the lawyer's obligation to preserve the former client's confidences and secrets. Model Rule 1.6, Comment 18; Model Rule 1.9(c)(2). The primary rationale behind restrictions on the ability of a lawyer to sue or take a position adverse to a *former* client (discussed below in connection with Rule 1.9, dealing with conflicts of interest and duties to former clients) is the need to protect relevant and material confidences or secrets of the former client.

B. The Death of the Client

The duty of confidentiality, like the attorney-client privilege, usually survives the client's death. A dead client is a former client.

The client's death means that the lawyer's disclosure of the client's secret will not place the client in jeopardy. If the client were alive, the state could require the client to testify if the state offered immunity from further criminal prosecution. The client's death serves to give the client effective criminal immunity in life, no matter what the after-life offers.

This issue is the subject of much debate. The lawyer's silence in such a case may permit a grave injustice to be done. *State v. Macumber* (Ariz.1976) held that the trial judge in a murder case had properly excluded testimony by two attorneys that a third person, now deceased, had confessed to them that he had killed the people whom the state had charged the defendant with murdering. This third person confessed to the two attorneys who had represented him when he was tried in federal court for an unrelated murder. The state court ruled that attorney-client privilege prevented this disclosure. The dissent argued that when this third person died and there was no chance of his prosecution for other crimes, any purported privilege was merely a matter of property interest, which should not prevail over the constitutional right of the accused to introduce reliable hearsay declarations evidencing his innocence.

An early draft of the proposed Restatement of the Law Third, of the Law Governing Lawyers offered an illustration based on *Macumber*. At its May, 1989 annual meeting, various American Law Institute members objected to the *Macumber*. At its May, 1989 annual meeting, various American Law Institute members objected to the *Macumber* holding as "grotesque," "revolting," and "disgusting." It is not right, they said, that a lawyer may reveal privileged information in a fee dispute (see below) but may not reveal to prevent an innocent person from going to jail or worse. By the vote of 164 to 65, ALI members voted to strike the illustration. The ALI then rejected the rule espoused in *Macumber*. A comment in the Restatement now criticizes the case, and proposes a narrow exception, when a capital conviction would be imposed on an innocent person. See Restatement of the Law Governing Lawyers, Third, § 82, Comment *e*.

The United Kingdom explicitly recognizes an exception to attorney-client privilege and confidentiality when an innocent person risks being convicted of a crime (not just a capital offense, of which there are none in the U.K.).

While the academic commentary and the American Law Institute rejected *Macumber*, a divided U.S. Supreme Court followed *Macumber* in *Swidler & Berlin v. United States* (S.Ct.1998). The Office of Independent Counsel had subpoenaed notes of conversations between Vincent Foster (a senior White House aide) and his lawyer shortly before Mr. Foster's suicide. The Independent Counsel sought these notes as part of a criminal investigation of allegedly fraudulent activities by President Clinton.

The D.C. Circuit analyzed the case law and noted that, while cases often say the attorney-client privilege survives death, it is usually said in the context of finding an exception to the rule to assist in construction of a will. Thus, the D.C. panel concluded, it is reasonable to make another exception for communications significant to a criminal case, because the client's own criminal liability obviously expires when he departs from life.

The Supreme Court reversed, six to three. Chief Justice Rehnquist, for the Court, argued: "Knowing that communications will remain confidential even after death encourages the client to communicate fully and frankly with counsel." Justice O'Connor, joined by Justices Scalia and Thomas, dissented and argued: "In my view, a criminal defendant's right to exculpatory evidence or a compelling law enforcement need for information may, where the testimony is not available from other sources, override a client's posthumous interest in confidentiality."

Model Rule 1.6, as now amended, allows (but does not compel) revelation of confidential information "to prevent reasonably certain death or substantial bodily harm." Model Rule 1.6(b)(1). This provision, which will be examined more fully below, presumably allows revelation of a credible death-bed confession only when execution of an innocent convict is "reasonably certain"—unless, that is, wrongful incarceration (as opposed to execution) would be considered "substantial bodily harm." Note that new Rules 1.6(b)(2) and (3) do not change this result, since they only relate to disclosures to prevent reasonably certain damage to financial or property interests caused by client's crime or fraud, in furtherance of which client has used lawyer's services.

The new provision would not allow revelation of a secret for "compelling law enforcement" reasons. Thus, in *Matter of John Doe Grand Jury Investigation* (Mass.1990), prosecutors strongly suspected that Charles Stuart was responsible for the deaths of his wife and child, Carol and Christopher Stuart. Charles had talked with his lawyer for two hours on the day before his suicide, and the prosecutor surmised that he had admitted to the crimes at that time. If so, the state could stop looking for the author of those murders, and so it wished to compel testimony by his attorneys. The court held that attorney-client privilege did not end with Charles's death. The new Model Rule would not change this ruling. The American Law Institute, however, is less clear and may not embrace the ABA position. Restatement of the Law Governing Lawyers, 82, Comment *e*.

6. Co–Plaintiffs or Co–Defendants of a Client: Confidential Duties Owed to Persons Other than Clients or Former Clients

Under the law of agency, an agent of a principal (e.g., the lawyer-agent for a client-principal) may not reveal information about a third party if the principal [*i.e.*, the client] has a fiduciary obligation to keep that information confidential. The lawyer is not an agent of the third party, but she may be a sub-agent of a client who has a fiduciary obligation to keep information confidential. The lawyer's fiduciary duty comes from the law of agency, not the law of ethics, because the Model Rules impose no special ethical duties that the lawyer owes to these third parties, who are neither clients, former clients, nor prospective clients.

In a typical fact pattern, the lawyer (Lawyer) represents a client (Client) who is sued along with others. Each of the co-defendants is separately represented, and they decide to cooperate with each other because their interests are aligned. For example, the co-defendants may set up a joint defense consortium. Even though the Lawyer becomes privy to confidences discussed by the other members or lawyers in this consortium, it is clear that Lawyer is not representing any of these other co-defendants.

It is because of the existence of this joint defense consortium that the Client (under the law of agency) assumes certain fiduciary duties to the other co-defendants. If the Client, under the law of agency, assumes a fiduciary duty to third parties to keep certain information confidential, then the Lawyer (the sub-agent of Client) may not reveal information that the Client has an obligation to keep confidential. This duty comes from the law of agency.

Let us consider the example of the joint defense further. If Lawyer, in the course of representing his client (e.g., Company #1) acquires confidential information about other members of the joint defense agreement (e.g., Company #2, Company #3, etc.), Rule 1.6 imposes on the lawyer a duty to his client, Company #1, to keep this information confidential. Even if this information came from and relates to other companies, it is still information "relating to the representation" and thus protected under Rule 1.6, because of the duty that Lawyer owes Company #1.

However, Company #1 may waive its rights and consent to Lawyer using this information. Rule 1.6 imposes on Lawyer a duty to Company #1, but it imposes on Lawyer no duty to the other companies, who were never his clients, prospective clients, or former clients. Consequently, if Company #1 waives its rights under Rule 1.6, ethics rules do not bar

Lawyer from taking on a related representation adverse to one of the other companies, because doing so no longer violates any rights owed to Company #1. ABA Formal Opinion 95–395, July 24, 1995.

While the Model Rules therefore do not prevent Lawyer from suing Company #2 if Lawyer's former client, Company #1, waives any rights it may have under Rule 1.6, the ABA Ethics Committee has advised that the law of agency may impose a restriction. In the example we have been discussing, Company #1 [the client] was the agent of the co-defendants (Company #2 and Company #3) in the defense consortium, all of whom shared confidential information. The lawyer for Company #1 is therefore a subagent of this client who, in turn, was the agent of the co-defendants. The ABA Committee advised, "it is likely" that the joint defense agreement obliged Company #1 to "have its lawyer preserve such confidences, and so could not give such consent without exposing itself to liability to the members of the consortium whose confidences were involved." Formal Opinion 95–395. If so, the lawyer has a fiduciary obligation to other members of this defense consortium—and a court may disqualify the lawyer because of the law of agency, but not because of the law of ethics.

This subagency principle extends beyond joint defense agreements. For example, assume that Lawyer represents Hospital in several cases and, because of that representation, has access to Patient's medical records. Lawyer thereby learns confidential information about Patient (e.g., that Patient has an addiction to a controlled substance). Patient was not a party to the earlier cases. Now, Lawyer represents another party in a suit where Patient will be an adverse witness. It would be useful for Lawyer to be able to cross-examine Patient about his addiction and thus undermine his credibility. However, under the law of agency: "Lawyer may not reveal information about Patient that Hospital has an obligation to keep confidential." Restatement of the Law Governing Lawyers, Third, § 132, comment *g(ii)*, Illustration 7 (ALI 2000).

If a lawyer is disqualified under the rules of *ethics*, those rules often impute that disqualification to other lawyers in the same firm. However, in this case, the lawyer is disqualified under the law of *agency* because he is a subagent. Agency law does not normally impute disqualification. So, if the lawyer is disqualified, that disqualification would not prevent other lawyers in the same firm from engaging in the representation that was forbidden to the first lawyer. The law of agency *would* impose a "screen," which, as we shall see, the ethics rules usually do not allow. See Restatement, § 132, comment *g(ii)*.

7. The Law Firm's Supervisory Responsibilities Over its Agents Regarding Attorney–Client Confidences

Though a client may only deal with a few lawyers in a firm, the client in fact hires "the firm," rather than a particular lawyer in the firm. Partners and associates regularly discuss with each other the affairs of their clients and seek from each other advice regarding client affairs. Such intra-firm communication is one of the reasons for the rule regarding imputation of attorney disqualifications. See Model Rule 1.10, below. Consequently, unless the client otherwise directs, a lawyer may disclose to other lawyers in the firm confidential client information. Model Rule 1.6, Comment 5.

It is reasonable for lawyers to disclose client confidences to nonlawyer employees of their firm, such as secretaries, investigators and paralegals. These employees must treat this client information as confidentially as the lawyers treat it. However, the Model Rules have no jurisdiction directly over these nonlawyers. Thus, the ethics rules impose a requirement that the lawyers in the firm reasonably supervise these employees. It is part of a lawyer's professional responsibility to exercise reasonable care to prevent employees from violating the obligation regarding client confidences or secrets. Similarly, the lawyer may give limited information from his files to an outside agency for accounting or other legitimate purposes if the lawyer exercises due care in selecting the agency. See Model Rule 5.3, below. However, the lawyer may not transfer this information if the client forbids it. Model Rule 1.6, Comment 5.

8. Government Lawyers and the Attorney-Client Privilege

The obligations imposed by Model Rule 1.6 apply not only to lawyers in private practice, but also to attorneys for the government and lawyers for any other entity, such as a corporation or an association.

The general principle is that government and corporation lawyers have an attorney-client privilege for communications with their client, which is with the "government" or the "corporation," not with any particular individual. As Rule 1.13(a) points out, the lawyer for an organization, including a governmental client, represents the "organization" as an entity and not the individual flesh and blood agents who act for the organization.

Just as in-house corporate attorneys, discussed below, represent the incorporeal entity, so also do government lawyers represent "the government" and not any particular official in the government.

Government attorneys must assert the attorney-client privilege to third parties, but they may not validly assert it when it is the government itself that is seeking information about an official. Thus, a government lawyer cannot refuse to divulge information relevant to a criminal investigation of another official on the grounds that this other government official confided in her, because the government lawyer represents the government, not any official in his or her personal capacity. In short, a government lawyer may not assert the government attorney-client privilege of the government against the government.

Two of the decisions in this area, one from the 8th Circuit, *In Re Grand Jury Subpoena Duces Tecum* (1997), and one from the D.C. Circuit, *In re Lindsey* (1998), involve President Clinton. Both come to this conclusion—the government, not the official (not even the President) controls the attorney-client privilege for government attorneys. See also, *In re Witness Before Special Grand Jury 2000–2* (7th Cir.2002) (in context of a federal criminal investigation, no attorney-client privilege existed between state officeholder and state government lawyer).

To the contrary is *In re Grand Jury Investigation* (2d Cir.2005). The United States, investigating alleged bribery of state public officials and employees, moved to compel the former chief legal counsel in the Connecticut governor's office to reveal to federal grand jury the contents of private conversations she had had with governor and various staff members for purpose of providing legal advice. The court held that the state governor's office could invoke the attorney-client privilege against federal government's inquiries. The court relied on a state statute that preserved the privilege and used that statute against the federal government, notwithstanding the supremacy clause.

9. Client Waiver—Express and Implied

Clients may always waive confidentiality rights. If the lawyer wants the client to *expressly waive* rights to confidentiality, the client's consent to do so is effective only if it is *informed*, i.e., if the lawyer communicates to the client enough information to permit the client to appreciate the significance of the waiver.

Or, the client may "impliedly" waive in the sense that the client has implied authorized the lawyer to engage in the disclosure in order to carry out the representation. Rule 1.6(a). For example, the lawyer may disclose some information in order to conclude satisfactorily a negotiation, or the lawyer in litigation may admit a fact that "cannot properly be disputed." Model Rule 1.6, Comment 5.

10. Revealing Confidential Information without a Waiver: Some Special Cases

A. When Required or Permitted By Other Ethics Rules, Other Law, or a Court Order

Other provisions of ethics rules may permit or require disclosure in certain situations. For example, important rules discussed elsewhere [Rule 3.3(b), below], may require a lawyer to reveal client perjury. Rule 1.6 incorporates these other sections by including an explicit provision allowing lawyers to reveal secret information "to comply with other law or a court order." Rule 1.6(b)(6).

If a court orders the lawyer to reveal information the lawyer thinks is protected by the attorney-client privilege, the lawyer may either reveal the information or challenge any court order requiring his testimony. However, there is no ethical requirement that the lawyer must first suffer contempt before revealing client information in response to a court order. The lawyer may simply comply with the order and reveal the client confidences rather than violate the order and challenge the contempt.

The current Model Rules provide [Rule 1.6, Comment 13] that the lawyer should assert on behalf of the client all nonfrivolous claims that other law does not authorize the court's order compelling disclosure or that the information sought is protected (say, by attorney-client privilege). If the ruling is against the lawyer, then he must consult with the client about the possibility of an appeal. If there is no appeal, then the Model Rule permits compliance with the court order.

In short, the lawyer may challenge the court order or obey it; the ethics rules offer her no protection if she ignores the court order and the court holds her in contempt. While courts must uphold valid claims of the attorney-client evidentiary privilege, they will not protect what the Model Code called client "secrets," i.e., the more general duty of confidentiality, a duty that is broader than the evidentiary privilege. This is because "secrets" are a concept of the law of ethics; the law of evidence does not protect them as an evidentiary privilege. Thus, if information is protected by the law of ethics but not by the evidentiary privilege, the lawyer may not volunteer the information but would have to reveal it in a deposition or other compelled testimony.

Note that Comment 13 to Rule 1.6 alludes to final orders of a court "or by another tribunal or governmental entity claiming authority pursuant to other law." An arbitrator, for example, is a "tribunal" for purposes of the Model Rules. Rule 1.0(m) (Terminology Rule, defining "tribunal").

B. When Necessary for the Lawyer to Establish a Claim or Defense in a Controversy with the Client, When Necessary to Defend Against any Civil or Criminal Charge, and When Necessary to Secure the Lawyer's Fee

Rule 1.6(b)(5) lists several other important exceptions to the general rule on protecting client information. The lawyer may reveal otherwise confidential information if the lawyer reasonably believes it necessary "to establish a claim or defense on behalf of the lawyer in a controversy between the lawyer and the client, to establish a defense to a criminal charge or civil claim against the lawyer based upon conduct in which the client was involved, or to respond to allegations in any proceeding concerning the lawyer's representation of the client."

In general, the lawyer may reveal client confidences or secrets if necessary in order to establish or collect the lawyer's fee, or to defend herself against a suit that the client *or* a third party brings.

The lawyer need not wait until the complaining party files suit. Rule 1.6, Comment 10.

One purpose of this exception is to prevent the client, who is the beneficiary of a fiduciary relationship, from exploiting that relationship to the detriment of the lawyer-fiduciary. For example, the client ought not to be excused from a contractual obligation to pay a fee solely because the lawyer could not prove (unless he revealed a client confidence or secret) that services were in fact performed. The lawyer, in this case would be revealing confidences in order to establish that it was appropriate to perform the work for the client and that the work was, in fact, done.

Case law confirms that the lawyer may use client confidences to secure or collect the fee. In *Nakasian v. Incontrade, Inc.* (S.D.N.Y.1976), the lawyer secured a lien on his client's property after his fee went unpaid. He only knew about the existence and location of this property—a secret bank account— because of what his client had told him in confidence. It was acceptable for the lawyer to use this client confidence in order to collect his fee.

But this right to use confidences or secrets does not create a right to blackmail the client. The lawyer may only exercise the right to reveal client information to the extent that it is *reasonably necessary* to establish or collect the fee. There must not be any extortion or unnecessary disclosure. Thus, the court suspended a lawyer for six months for telling his client:

"You should understand that if we are forced to file suit [to collect attorneys' fees], you forego the attorney-client privilege and I would be forced to reveal that you lied on your statements to the IRS and to the bank as to your financial condition. This would entail disclosure of the tapes of our conversations about your hidden assets. There is a federal statute 18 U.S.C. § 1001 which provides for up to one year in jail for such perjury. The choice is yours." *In re Disciplinary Proceeding Against Boelter* (Wash.1999).

A lawyer may disclose client information if necessary to respond to an accusation of wrongful conduct. Originally, the ABA ethics rules limited this exception to the case where the "lawyer is accused *by his client....*" ABA Canons of Professional Ethics, Canon 37 (emphasis added) (ABA, 1908, as amended). When the ABA adopted the Model Code of Professional Responsibility in 1969, it did not include this limitation. The current version of the Rules agrees that revelation is permitted "to respond to allegations in any proceeding concerning the lawyer's representation of the client."

So the accuser may be someone other than the client—and the accusation need not be made in a formal complaint. The Comment is quite clear on this point:

"The lawyer's right to respond [to allegations of wrongful conduct] arises when an assertion of such complicity has been made. Paragraph (b)(5) does not require the lawyer to await the commencement of an action or proceeding that charges such complicity, so that the defense may be established by responding directly to a third party who had made such an assertion.'' Rule 1.6, Comment 10.

For example, assume that a newspaper editorial accuses Lawyer of having won an acquittal in an important criminal case a year earlier by suborning her client's perjury, which by the time of the editorial had become obvious to all. The Bar authorities respond by threatened to institute disciplinary proceedings against Lawyer. Consequently, Lawyer defends herself by revealing that her client had intentionally kept Lawyer in the dark about the perjury and that Lawyer never learned of it until after the acquittal, when the client confessed to Lawyer on his deathbed. Assume further that the client, at that time, also told Lawyer never to reveal the perjury. Lawyer also states that an associate in her office who was present during the conversation in question can confirm her version. Lawyer's disclosures are not disciplinable in these circumstances. As Rule 1.6, Comment 10 makes clear: ''Such a charge [against the lawyer] can arise in a civil, criminal, disciplinary or other proceeding and can be based on a wrong allegedly committed by the lawyer against the client or on a wrong alleged by a third person . . . .''

The Model Rules, in short, make clear that, first, the lawyer need not wait until a proceeding has been brought challenging the lawyer. Second, the

client need not be the person making the charge.
Finally, the lawyer can respond directly to a third
person making the charge. Case law and commentators agree with the Model Rules in allowing a
lawyer to disclose what otherwise would be client
secrets in order for the lawyer to defend himself
preemptively. To the criticism that this important
exception to the confidentiality rule is in the Model
Rules for self-serving reasons, my reaction is that of
the police commissioner in Rick's Bar: "I am
shocked, shocked, to find gambling going on in
Casablanca."

C. When the Client Intends to Commit a Future Crime, or When Death or Bodily Harm Is Reasonably Certain But Not "Imminent"

(i) The Basic Provisions

Rule 1.6(b)(1) says that the lawyer "may reveal
information relating to the representation of a
client to the extent the lawyer reasonably believes
necessary" to "prevent reasonably certain death or
substantial bodily harm." For example, if the lawyer knows that the client is about to kill someone,
the lawyer "*may*" reveal this information.

In the famous case of *Spaulding v. Zimmerman*
(Minn.1962), the defendant in a medical malpractice
suit knew of a brain aneurism of which his patient,
the plaintiff, was unaware. Under the current Model Rule, the lawyer may reveal this life-threatening
aneurism, even though the defendant would be benefited by its nondisclosure because its revelation

increases the amount of the plaintiff's known damages.

Some states reject the ABA formulation and *require* the lawyer to reveal such information, a mandatory disclosure rule that reflects existing tort law in several states. See, e.g., *Tarasoff v. Regents of the University of California* (Cal.1976) (involving a psychotherapist).

A proposed (but not adopted) draft of the 1983 Model Rules *allowed* disclosure of confidential information "to prevent the client from committing a criminal *or fraudulent* act that the lawyer believes is likely to result in death or substantial bodily harm, *or in substantial injury to the financial interests or* property of another." The ABA rejected this proposal in 1983, but some states adopted it and allow or require the lawyer to reveal secrets to prevent economic as well as physical harm. Finally, the ABA accepted this proposal in 2003.

The requirement of Rule 1.6(b)(1) that the bodily harm be "substantial" means that harm must be serious, such as life-threatening injuries or illnesses, "and the consequences of events such as imprisonment for a substantial period, and child sexual abuse. It also includes a client's threat of suicide." Restatement of the Law Governing Lawyers, Third, § 66 (Official Draft 2000), at Comment *c*.

The requirement of Rule 1.6(b)(1) that the death or bodily harm be "reasonably certain" means that it is not necessary that it be "imminent," the test of the Model Rule until 2002. For example, under the *post*–2002 formulation, the lawyer may reveal that a client's environmental law violation—the release of toxic substances into the city's water supply—will likely cause death to elderly people in the city. Rule 1.6, Comment 6. The harm need not be "imminent;" lingering or delayed death or substantial bodily harm still triggers the rule as long as the harm is "reasonably certain."

The Rules now authorize the lawyer to reveal client confidences even when the client is not the cause of the death or substantial bodily harm. And, the lawyer may reveal even if she learns of the information because of a non-criminal act of the client. For example, in some jurisdictions suicide and attempted suicide are not crimes, yet the lawyer may reveal the client's intention to commit suicide to prevent reasonably certain death.

(ii) When an Innocent Person May Be Convicted

Should there be exceptions to this rule when the client has personally confessed to her lawyer that she is guilty of a crime for which an innocent person is being punished? In that circumstance, the lawyer's silence will cause a grave injustice. The rules do not appear to provide for any disclosure, except that Rule 1.6(b)(1) states that the lawyer may reveal client secrets "to the extent the lawyer reasonably believes necessary: to prevent reasonably certain death or substantial bodily harm."

Assume, in a capital murder situation, that the client did not *cause* the state's faulty prosecution; the client did not frame the innocent defendant; the client committed a *past* crime but has no legal duty to come forward to admit it because the client has a constitutional right not to incriminate himself. Yet, the lawyer's silence will result in an innocent person's execution. Perhaps that language fits the hypothetical presented because the state-sanctioned execution will result in the death of the innocent defendant.

What if the court did not impose death as a punishment but life imprisonment, or a term of 5 years? Is incarceration "substantial bodily harm." If it is, then Rule 1.6(b)(1) may allow the lawyer to reveal the client's confidences, but that creates other problems because the right against self-incrimination and the attorney-client privilege may not be treated lightly.

A basic principle of agency law is that the agent is under no duty to keep secret information that the principal is about to commit a crime. But a confession of a *past* misdeed is no crime:

> "An agent is privileged to reveal information confidentially acquired by him in the course of his agency in the protection of a superior interest of himself or a third person. Thus, if the confidential information is to the effect that the principal is committing or about to commit a crime, the agent is under no duty not to reveal it. However, an attorney employed to represent a client in a criminal proceeding has no duty to reveal that the client has confessed his guilt."

Restatement of the Law of Agency, Second, 385, Comment *f* (ALI 1958).

In contrast, the Restatement of the Law Governing Lawyers regards "imprisonment for a substantial period" us substantial bodily harm, allowing disclosure Restatement, Third, § 66, at Comment *c* (2000).

(iii) The Crime–Fraud Exception in the Law of Evidence

The Model Rules create the *ethical* duty to keep client confidences. However, there is also the *evidentiary* attorney-client privilege. One should distinguish between the lawyer's limited right to disclose future actions under Rule 1.6(b)(1), and the loss of the evidentiary attorney-client privilege because of the past actions, under the crime-fraud exception to attorney-client privilege.

A client may not claim the evidentiary privilege for any communications with his lawyer that were in furtherance of a criminal or fraudulent transaction. Rule 1.6, after the 2003 changes, now has a specific exception for fraud, like the law of evidence.

It is not necessary for the lawyer to have known that he or she was part of a criminal or fraudulent transaction for the crime-fraud exception to apply. For example, if a client secures his lawyer's services in order to file a perjurious affidavit, the client's conversations with the lawyer with respect to this affidavit are not privileged, even if the lawyer did not know at the time that the client was committing perjury.

Thus Monica Lewinsky had no privilege for communications with her lawyer in 1998 that led to a false affidavit. *In re Sealed Case* (D.C.Cir.1998). The party opposing the privilege based on the crime-fraud exception has the burden of producing prima facie evidence of the existence of the criminal or fraudulent enterprise. Then, the burden of persuasion shifts to the party asserting the privilege to give a reasonable explanation of the conduct or of the communication. If the court does not accept the explanation, the privilege is lost. The court uses the preponderance of the evidence standard in weighing the evidence.

D. Tort Liability and the Lawyer's Discretion to Reveal

While Rule 1.6(b)(1) gives the lawyer ethical discretion to reveal client information, the ABA intends this discretion to be absolute and not subject to judicial review, so that, in the view of the ABA, a lawyer's decision *not* to reveal information is always within his discretion. Rule 1.6, Comment 15. But one wonders if the judiciary will recognize the purported nonreviewable discretion, in light of court decisions like *Tarasoff v. Regents of the University of California* (Cal.1976).

In *Tarasoff*, a psychotherapist knew his patient planned a murder and did not warn the victim. The court held that a cause of action in tort existed for wrongful death, against the psychotherapist.

"When a therapist determines, or pursuant to the standards of the profession should determine, that his patient presents a serious danger of violence to another, he incurs an obligation to use reasonable care to protect the intended victim against such danger. The discharge of this duty may require the therapist . . . to warn the intended victim or others likely to apprise the victim of the danger, to notify the police, or to take whatever other steps are reasonably necessary under the circumstances."

Given decisions like *Tarasoff*, the efforts of the ABA House of Delegates to grant lawyers unreviewable discretion may well be unsuccessful, at least in a tort case with the right set of facts. Rule 1.6, Comment 15 does concede that "other law" may mandate disclosure and thereby supersede Rule 1.6.

In other words, the lawyer is not subject to *discipline* for not revealing, but, he could well be liable in *tort* if the victim (or the victim's estate) sued the lawyer for damages for not revealing or warning the victim. The lawyer will argue that he did not have to reveal, but the plaintiff's lawyer will respond that nothing in the ethics rules prevented the lawyer from revealing, but he chose not to reveal and the result is that the victim was injured or killed. "May," in other words, can lead to "must" in the civil liability context because tort law may mandate disclosure the ethics rules do not forbid disclosure. Discretion not to reveal does not mean that one may abuse one's discretion.

E. Proposed Client Wrongdoing and a "Noisy Withdrawal"

The *previous* version of the Model Rules made clear that if the client intends to use a lawyer's services to further the client's "criminal or fraudulent conduct," then the lawyer must withdraw and may file a "notice of withdrawal." Former Rule 1.6, Comment 14 (2002 ed., *now repealed*).

The former Comment 14 which explicitly authorized a lawyer to file this *Notice of Withdrawal* even though its issuance may be a warning to all concerned that the former client is up to no good. Former Comment 14 stated the obvious, that the lawyer may not blow the whistle in many cases, but that she may in many cases wave a red flag.

Former Comment 14 (now repealed) provided, in relevant part:

> "If the lawyer's services will be used by the client in materially furthering a course of criminal or fraudulent conduct, the lawyer must withdraw, as stated in Rule 1.16(a)(1). After withdrawal the lawyer is required to refrain from making disclosure of the client's confidences, except as otherwise provided in Rule 1.6. *Neither this Rule nor Rule 1.8(b) nor Rule 1.16(d) prevents the lawyer from giving notice of the fact of withdrawal, and the lawyer may also withdraw or disaffirm any opinion, document, affirmation, or the like.*" (emphasis added).

Rule 1.8(b), referred to in this Comment, provides that the lawyer shall not use client information to the disadvantage of the client, unless the client consents. Rule 1.16(d) states that, after withdrawal, the lawyer must take reasonable steps to protect a client's interests. Neither of these Rules, nor Rule 1.6 itself, limited the power discussed in former Comment 14, which authorized the lawyer, in appropriate circumstances, to engage in a "noisy withdrawal."

Note also that *former* Comment 14, on Notice of Withdrawal, did not limit to whom the Notice of Withdrawal may be sent. The Notice could be sent to third parties, not merely the opposing side. See Rotunda, The Notice of Withdrawal and the New Model Rules of Professional Conduct: Blowing the Whistle and Waiving the Red Flag, 63 Oregon L. Rev. 455 (1984).

The 2003 revisions eliminated Comment 14 to Rule 1.6. Instead, Rules 1.6(b)(2),(3) simply allow the lawyer to reveal the information in order to prevent the fraud. Rule 1.3, Comment 4, makes a brief reference to a "notice of withdrawal," but it is only referring to a way of telling the client that the lawyer-client relationship no longer exists.

However, even after the 2003 revisions, two other sections, do approve of filing a noisy "Notice of Withdrawal." First, Rule 1.2, Comment 10 states:

"The lawyer is required to avoid assisting the client, for example, by drafting or delivering documents that the lawyer knows are fraudulent or by suggesting how the wrongdoing might be concealed. A lawyer may not continue assisting a client in conduct that the lawyer originally supposed was legally proper but then discovers is criminal or fraudulent. The lawyer *must*, therefore, withdraw from the representation of the client in the matter. See Rule 1.16(a). In some cases, withdrawal alone might be insufficient. It may be necessary for the lawyer *to give notice of the fact of withdrawal* and to disaffirm any opinion, document, affirmation or the like. See Rule 4.1.'' (emphasis added)

Rule 4.1, Comment 3 repeats the essential words of this Comment.

The lawyer, in short, may file a noisy Notice of Withdrawal even though its issuance may be a red flag that the client is up to no good.

Consider this hypothetical. Assume that Lawyer learns, on the eve of a deal's closing, that the limited partnership agreement Lawyer has prepared for Client is a criminal fraud under federal securities laws. Lawyer confronts Client, who states that he will go through with the deal and if Lawyer does not like it, Lawyer can resign. Lawyer then resigns, in compliance with the ethics rules. Under the Model Rules, she may do more than simply leave her position, accept the client's behavior, and silently slip away. Rule 1.6(b)(2) specifically authorizes her to reveal the information necessary to prevent her client from causing reasonably certain and substantial injury to the financial interests of another.

Rule 1.2, Comment 10, and Rule 4.1, Comment 3 also authorize the Lawyer to send a noisy Notice of Withdrawal to the other side and to the Securities & Exchange Commission. The noisy notice of withdrawal, under these provisions, does not describe exactly why she is withdrawing (though many states' rules do allow for this, or even require it). But the *noisy* notice effectively warns the other lawyers that something is afoot because she can say that she is withdrawing and disaffirming any documents or opinion letters that she earlier had prepared. Lawyers who are unwilling to exercise their power to disclose under Rules 1.6(b)(2) & (3) may determine to file a noisy notice of withdrawal.

The client cannot preclude the lawyer from filing a noisy withdrawal by firing the lawyer first. "Whenever circumstances exist that would otherwise require a lawyer to withdraw, disaffirmance [of the lawyer's work product] may be in order even if the client fires her before she has a chance to do so." So states ABA Formal Opinion 92–366 (Aug. 8, 1992).

The Opinion adds that, if the fraud is already completed and the lawyer knows or reasonably believes that the client does not intend to make further fraudulent use of the lawyer's services, the lawyer may (but is not required to) withdraw, but she may not file a noisy withdrawal. However, a lawyer follows this advice from the 1992 ABA Opinion at her peril, in light of the present-day Rule 1.6(b)(3), which gives lawyers a right to "mitigate or *rectify* substantial injury to the financial interests or property of another that is reasonably certain to result *or has resulted*'' if the client has used the lawyer's services to perpetrate a fraud. (emphasis added).

Lawyers have a greater obligation than merely considering future legal advice; those who sit on their hands in such a situation may find that the courts are less understanding than this old ABA Opinion. After all, a fraud, especially a securities fraud, is usually ongoing, with people relying on the earlier representations so that it is unclear if one can ever conclude that the fraud is "completed." Those who commit fraud do not like to be caught, so that the fraud will always be continuing, at least to the extent that the perpetrator keeps it covered up.

F. Offering False Evidence and the Rule of Candor Toward a Tribunal

If a lawyer has offered material evidence and later learns of its falsity, under Rule 3.3(b) the lawyer "must take reasonable remedial measures, including, if necessary, disclosure to the tribunal." This duty applies "even if compliance requires disclosure of information otherwise protected" by the confidentiality requirements of Rule 1.6, as Rule 3.3(c) makes clear.

The Model Rules obviously contemplate that a "noisy withdrawal" might not be sufficient to undo the fraud's impact on the case. Rule 3.3(a)(3). For example, the opposing party might drop the case or settle it, in reliance on a false deposition, in spite of the lawyer's noisy withdrawal. Consequently, direct disclosure, to the opposing party or to the court, may prove to be the only reasonable remedial measure in the client fraud situations most likely to be encountered in pretrial proceedings. Rule 3.3, Comment 10.

This issue is discussed in detail in connection with Rule 3.3, below.

RULE 1.7: CONFLICTS OF INTEREST—CURRENT CLIENTS

1. Introduction

A. The Basic Rationales

The rules governing conflict of interest derive, in large part, from two needs: to protect client confidences and secrets, on the one hand, and to assure clients that they have their lawyer's loyalty, on the other. The rules are found, primarily, in Rules 1.7 through 1.13 of the ABA Model Rules. See also the Restatement of the Law Governing Lawyers, Third, §§ 121–135 (Official Draft 2000). These Restatement sections, by the way, occupy nearly two hundred pages of the second volume of the Restatement. From this length, you can appreciate that this topic is complex, will only give you an introduction to this multifaceted and difficult area of the law.

As we have already seen, one of the lawyer's primary duties is to protect the client's confidential information. This duty survives the client-lawyer relationship, and even applies to conversations with prospective clients. Consider the case where a lawyer simultaneously represents Client *A* and Client *B* (or now represents Client *B* and previously represented Client *A,* or now represents Client *B* and Client *A* was a prospective client who imparted material confidential information to the lawyer when the client sought the lawyer's services). A conflict may develop because the lawyer may know secret information about Client *A* (the present, or former, or formerly-prospective client), and this information would be relevant, material, or useful to Client *B*, whom the lawyer is now representing. If the lawyer does not reveal the information to Client *B*, the lawyer would be violating her duty of loyalty to *B* because she would not be representing *B* vigorously. But if the lawyer does reveal this information to *B*, the lawyer would be violating her duty of confidentiality to *A*.

In the example just given, the conflict derives from the fact that the lawyer either divulges the secrets of one client (or a former client), or fails to represent vigorously the other client. However, there can be a conflict of interests even if there are not two conflicting clients. For example, assume that a lawyer for Client *D* is paid by the insurer of Client *D*. The insurer instructs the lawyer (who is defending *D*, the insured, in a tort suit) not to dispute Plaintiff's charge that *D*'s tortious conduct was in fact intentional. If the jury believes that *D* acted intentionally, the insurer will not be liable because the insurance policy excludes coverage for intentional torts. If the lawyer follows the insurer's instructions, she will be violating her duty of loyalty to *D*, her client.

Given these needs, the rules distinguish various types of conflicts: between the client and the lawyer's (business or personal) interests; between the interests of one client and of another present or former client; and between the interests of a client and of a person who may be paying for the client's legal assistance. This section and subsequent ones will analyze and discuss these various categories of conflicts.

Rule 1.7 deals with conflicts between current clients. Rule 1.8 revisits that subject, with specific rules to govern particular problem areas. Rule 1.9 turns to conflicts between present and former clients. Rule 1.10 presents the general rule for imputing the conflicts of one lawyer to other lawyers in the same firm. Rule 1.11 presents some special rules that apply when the client is a current or former government lawyer. Rule 1.12 deals with the lawyer who is a former judge or mediator or arbitrator. Rule 1.13 deals with the rules applicable when the client is a non-corporeal organization such as a corporation, a partnership or another aggregate of individuals. Rule 1.18 governs duties to prospective clients.

First, let us turn to Rule 1.7, which focuses on the conflicts of interest between current clients.

Rule 1.7(a) announces the general prohibition against concurrent representation of clients whose interests are conflicting. The rule prohibits a lawyer representing a client if that representation ''will be directly adverse to another client,'' or if ''there is a significant risk that the representation of one or more clients will be materially limited by the lawyer's responsibilities to another client, a former client or a third person or by a personal interest of the lawyer." This Rule offers no test to distinguish "*directly adverse*" from "*materially limited*."

Rule 1.7(b) narrows the blanket prohibition of 1.7(a), by specifying cases in which the ethics rules conclude that the clients may consent or waive concurrent conflicts. This Rule is intended to allow, *inter alia*, concurrent representation of codefendants or coplaintiffs in the same litigation, or of several parties on the same side in negotiation. In such cases, when representation of multiple clients in a single matter is undertaken, each party must give informed consent to the concurrent representation. The Rule requires the consent to be confirmed in writing. The client need not sign the writing. Rule 1.0(n) & Comment 1.

B. Consent: The General Principle

The general rule is that the lawyer must explain to two prospective clients who seek to have the lawyer represent both of them that, if these two clients engage the same attorney to represent them in a matter, and each on occasion communicates separately with the attorney, then as between the two clients there are no confidences. The general evidentiary rule is that each client, knowing that the attorney represents the other party also, would not intend that the facts communicated should be kept secret from the other co-client. But lawyers should explain this evidentiary rule because clients often do not know it. The lawyer should explain to them that if either co-client wants to keep relevant information from the other, each should obtain separate counsel.

Rule 1.7(b) specifies that, in principle, clients may *consent to* concurrent conflicts, but that some conflicts are not *consentable*. Sadly, the rule offers no litmus test. Nonetheless, we can envision several classes of cases where the law of ethics would not allow the clients to consent to a concurrent conflict. When a conflicts rule is designed to protect only the client, little reason exists to prohibit a lawyer from engaging in concurrent representation when a competent and informed client desires to waive that protection. In contrast, if the conflicts rule is designed to protect a systemic interest—an interest of the justice system—client waiver should be ineffective.

Rule 1.7(b)(3) makes clear that it does not allow client consent where the lawyer wishes to represent adverse parties in the same litigation or other proceeding before a tribunal. In other words, Lawyer cannot represent both P and D in the law suit of P v. D—even if both P and D voluntarily consent and want to waive the conflict. The system of justice is based on the assumption that the opposing parties in litigation will be represented by opposing counsel. The parties, having filed suit against each other, cannot waive what is inherent in litigation.

In other cases, clients may consent to concurrent conflicting representation, assuming that some other law does not preclude consent. Rule 1.7(b)(2). Yet even then, the lawyer must satisfy two other provisos before the waiver is effective.

For a waiver to be valid, under Rule 1.7(b)(1), the lawyer must *reasonably* believe that she can represent each client competently and diligently.

Second, under Rule 1.7(b)(4), each client must knowingly consent *in writing*.

With respect to the different types of conflicts, we will consider why a client may desire to waive and under what circumstances that waiver will be effective. But first we turn to a related issue, the question of *implied* waiver.

The ethics rules do not provide for implied waivers of conflicts by a client. They set out a procedure for a waiver, and that procedure is explicit. The client should be able to rely on the lawyer, on whom the Rules place the obligation to secure informed consent.

However, the case law sometimes recognizes implied waiver: in cases not involving lawyer discipline, a court may conclude that—while the lawyer has not complied with Rule 1.7—the court, in deciding whether to disqualify a lawyer, may rule that the petitioning party has nonetheless *impliedly* waived her right to object to the representation. Thus, the court might argue that the petitioning party waited too long to bring its motion. When the court reacts negatively and says that there is an ''implied waiver,'' the more correct term would be ''forfeiture by laches.'' For litigation purposes (as opposed to discipline purposes), when some courts find a forfeiture of a right, they call it an implied waiver.

It is a different story when a party does not timely raise a conflict simply because she did not know the relevant facts. If the lawyers do not secure a valid consent from their client, the burden should be on the lawyers to give promptly to the client the information needed to effectuate a valid waiver. Clients, who are not expected to know the Rules of Professional Conduct, normally trust their lawyers, their former lawyers and their prospective lawyers. The client may know certain facts (*e.g.,* ''I trusted my lawyer with confidential information and now she is representing another party against me'') but the client may not know the significance of those facts (*i.e.,* that the lawyer must disqualify herself unless the client voluntarily relinquishes the right not to have confidential information used against her).

As discussed in detail below, the Model Rules typically *impute* one lawyer's disqualifying conflict to other lawyers in the same firm. Because imputation applies even when the law firm is very large, with branch offices in different states, the firm must adopt reasonable procedures, appropriate for the size and type of firm and practice, to determine whether there are actual or potential conflicts, in both litigation and transactional matters. The lawyer must institute reasonable conflict-checking procedures so that other lawyers in the firm know if they are representing clients with adverse or potentially adverse interests. See Rule 1.7, Comment 3. The lawyer may not benefit from her own ignorance: if the lawyer does not know that there are clients with adverse positions simply because the law firm has not created reasonable conflicts procedures, then the lawyer has not complied with Rule 1.7(b)(1).

Because many conflicts are imputed, it becomes very important to figure out which lawyers have conflicts because they can infect all the other lawyers in their firm, like a computer virus infects an entire network.

2. Simultaneous Representation of Multiple Clients in Related Matters

Very often a lawyer represents two or more clients in the same matter. For example, a client may ask the lawyer to set up a small corporation, or a husband and wife may ask the lawyer's help for a real estate closing, or the driver and owner-passenger of a car may ask one lawyer to represent them when both are sued for injuries arising out of an automobile accident.

It is often in the best interests of such clients to share the same lawyer. Joint representation may reduce legal fees and save time. Public policy does not require two different lawyers if one will do. The mere possibility of conflict does not itself preclude the representation. On the other hand, such an arrangement does create the potential for conflict, so the lawyer must weigh carefully the possibility that his judgment may be impaired or his loyalty divided if he accepts or continues the employment. Model Rule 1.7, Comment 8.

The potential conflict when representing multiple clients exists whether the representation involves litigation or counseling. However, there is more case law dealing with conflicts of interest in litigation, and courts are more likely to find a conflict in litigation than in transactional work because the lawyer in litigation acts primarily as an advocate, while in counseling, his advocacy role is more muted. Moreover, in litigation, courts can disqualify a lawyer, but when lawyers represent their clients in counseling, the more realistic remedy is either discipline before the bar discipline authorities or damages for malpractice if there is a client disgruntled enough to sue his former lawyer.

The clearest non-consentable conflict is that the lawyer in litigation may not represent both Client *A* and Client *B* in the case of *A v. B*. Rule 1.7(b)(3). On the other hand, practice varies in cases that are denominated "litigation" but are really uncontested. If two parties are involved in an uncontested divorce, with neither party making any claim against the other, they may wish to have one lawyer represent both, where the lawyer's job is simply to draw up the papers and put into writing the divorce settlement, if the two parties fully understand the consequences and they agree.

However, even then, most lawyers would be unwilling to take such a case because of the risk that one of the parties will later become disgruntled and claim the lawyer favored the other spouse. Many jurisdictions flatly prohibit this sort of multiple representation. Restatement of the Law Governing Lawyers, Third, § 128, Reporter's Note to Comment *c* (2000).

If a lawyer represents multiple clients in litigation or in negotiation who are all on the *same* side—all co-plaintiffs, or all co-defendants, or several people who want the lawyer to draw up a contract where the parties are not contentious—Rule 1.7(b) applies, and clients may consent to potential conflict. Comments 29–33 to Rule 1.7 detail the factors a lawyer should mention to his prospective clients in seeking informed consent to this joint representation. A lawyer "cannot undertake common representation of clients where contentious litigation or negotiations between them are imminent or contemplated." Rule 1.7, Comment 29.

3. Simultaneously Representing Adverse Clients in Unrelated Matters

As the previous section explained, the lawyer may not represent Clients *A* and *B* in the case of *A v. B*, because the lawyer would be representing adverse parties in the same matter. However, Rule 1.7(b)(3) also provides that a lawyer may not sue *A* on behalf of *B* while simultaneously representing *A* in "other proceeding[s]," i.e., in a *completely unrelated* matter.

For example, assume Lawyer represents Wife in a divorce suit against Husband while simultaneously representing Husband in a worker's compensation claim. Those are the facts of *Memphis & Shelby County Bar Association v. Sanderson* (Tenn.App. 1963), in which the court disbarred the lawyer (for this and several other instances of unprofessional conduct, including representing the plaintiff in a divorce action alleging grounds of adultery committed by the opposing party and a paramour who turned out to be the attorney's own wife).

Although the two cases—the divorce and the worker's compensation claim—are seemingly unrelated, there is still a breach of the lawyer's duty of loyalty. When an attorney represents one client in a suit against another, some adverse effect on the lawyer's exercise of independent judgment on behalf of a client may arise because of the lawyer's adversarial posture towards that client in another matter. For example, in the attorney's effort to please his long-standing client there may be a diminution in the rigor of his representation of the client in the matter where he is suing the long-standing client. The lawyer might not—or it might appear that he might not—fight as vigorously for one of his clients as he otherwise would. Rule 1.7, Comment 6.

The ineffectiveness of client consent is illustrated by *Matter of Kelly v. Greason* (N.Y.1968). Two lawyers, Kelly and Whalen, were partners. Whalen was also employed as an insurance adjuster for Nationwide Insurance Co. Whalen had no access to any Nationwide files other than those of claims assigned to him. Nonetheless the firm handled some claims *against* Nationwide. There was no proof that any settlements with Nationwide were unreasonable or unfair to either the insurance carrier or the claimants. Nonetheless, the court held that "it was, prima facie, evidence of professional misconduct for the partnership to represent claimants, whether assured of Nationwide or not, in their claims against the carrier, while at the same time Whalen was also the carrier's employee." The court's broad dictum found that discipline was appropriate perhaps even if the lawyer had secured consent from both clients after full disclosure.

A conflict exists only in cases of truly adverse interests. If a lawyer represents a corporation, he or she may ordinarily represent another corporation in a matter that is unrelated, even though one enterprise is generally competing with the other. Assume that the lawyer represents a major auto company on a securities matter while representing another, competing major auto company on a different, totally unrelated securities matter. Although *A* and *B* generally compete with each other, the lawyer is not suing either *A* or *B*. Nor is the lawyer giving legal advice to *A* that is to be used against *B* (or vice versa). Nor is there any violation of client confidences or secrets. There is no real risk of the lawyer's diminution of the rigor of his representation of either auto company.

In the vague words of the Model Rules, *A* and *B* are only competing enterprises who are not "*directly* adverse." Or, as Rule 1.7, Comment 6 explains: "simultaneous representation in unrelated matters of clients whose interests are only economically adverse, such as representation of competing economic enterprises in unrelated litigation, does not ordinarily constitute a conflict of interest and thus may not require consent of the respective clients."

By contrast, if the lawyer were suing General Motors on behalf of Ford in one matter, the lawyer may not simultaneously represent GM, on a different matter, even if the two matters are completely unrelated.

4. Securing Consent

A. Full Disclosure

Before a lawyer may represent clients who are— or are reasonably likely to be—in conflict, the lawyer must secure each client's consent, unless the conflict is non-waivable as discussed above. In order for the clients' consent to be informed, the lawyer must provide full disclosure. In some cases, however, "full disclosure" may require revealing confidences or secrets protected under Model Rule 1.6. In such situations the lawyer cannot secure informed consent from Client *A* without violating her duty to keep confidential the secrets of Client *B*. Rule 1.7, Comment 18.

When the lawyer cannot secure adequate consent without violating his duty to keep confidential the secrets and confidences of each client, that lawyer may not take on such representation, because there is no valid waiver. Thus, if a lawyer has two clients, one of whom is a defendant in a murder case, and if the other client informs the lawyer that he, not the accused client, committed that murder, the lawyer must withdraw from the murder case representation. To effectively represent that defendant, she would have to use the other client's confidential declaration. *Lettley v. State* (Md.2000) (conviction reversed because trial court's refusal to allow counsel to withdraw).

B. Prospective Waivers

If a client can consent to a conflict, she may do so prospectively, *if* the prospective waiver meets all the requirements for waiving a present conflict of interest. The lawyer relying on this prospective waiver must show that it "reasonably contemplated" the future conflict so that the client's consent is reasonably viewed as fully informed when it was given. However, even a prospective waiver does not extend to disclosure or use of client confidences against the client, unless the client explicitly agrees to such disclosure or use.

In other words, a client may waive prospectively, a conflict based on loyalty, but it may not normally waive, prospectively, a conflict based on breach of confidences, because—at the time of the prospective waiver—a client cannot normally know what those confidences might be or their significance. *Westinghouse Electric Corp. v. Gulf Oil Corp.* (7th Cir.

1978): "Disqualification based on the potential for abuse of confidential information, however, involves different considerations which preclude the effectiveness of consent, particularly a vague, general consent given or implied prior to the threat of disclosure or adverse litigation."

For example, a Corporation [Client #1] located in Los Angeles might hire the local office of a national law firm to negotiate and draft a lease on a Los Angeles building. The law firm asks Client #1 to waive any objections to the Chicago office of that law firm representing the mortgagor, a Chicago bank [Client #2] in negotiating mortgages on Chicago property. Client #1 may waive, prospectively, its objections to this possible conflict of loyalties. [The law firm must also secure consent from Client #2.]

This prospective waiver would not normally include a waiver of confidences, though. For example, assume that the law firm later learns certain secrets about Client #1 that would be relevant to its negotiation of the mortgage (*e.g.,* its dire need to obtain a mortgage and its willingness to pay a higher than normal interest rate because of internal plans). The prospective consent to the representation would not normally include consent to the adverse use of confidential information. At the time Client #1 consented to the prospective waiver, it did not know that the law firm would later learn information—about its willingness to pay a higher rate of interest—that would be relevant to the negotiations.

Assume that a large client (''Alpha'') gives a little business to a lot of different firms. Alpha now asks a law firm to represent it in a specific matter. Later, that law firm may ask Alpha for permission to withdraw from representing Alpha in this given manner and then ask for permission to represent a new, conflicting client in matters where there would be no danger of any revelation of Alpha's confidences or secrets. One should not be surprised if Alpha refuses consent. Indeed, one reason that Alpha may retain a large number of extremely capable firms may be to preempt possible adversaries from hiring those firms. What law firms should do, if they wish to reduce such opportunity costs, is to ask for consent *before* accepting Alpha's initial retention. The courts will not accept open-ended waivers to future conflicts, just as courts do not routinely accept the parking garage's sign purporting to affirm, ''parking in this lot signifies your consent to waive all tort damages.'' But carefully drawn waivers should meet judicial approval if well-informed clients agree to them, at least where the client is not asked to waive, in advance, its confidences or secrets.

Prospective waivers are more likely to be effective if the client is giving informed consent to types of conflicts that are familiar to the client. For example, consider the case of a law firm that represents Client in collecting commercial claims though Law Firm's New York office. Law Firm's Chicago office also gives tax advice to many companies with which Client has commercial dealings. ''Law Firm asks for

advance consent from Client with respect to conflicts that otherwise would prevent Law Firm from
filing commercial claims on behalf of Client against
the tax clients of Law Firm's Chicago office. If
Client gives informed consent, the consent should
be proper as to Client." This law firm must also
"obtain informed consent from any tax client of its
Chicago office against whom Client wishes to file a
commercial claim, should Law Firm decide to undertake such representation." Restatement of the
Law Governing Lawyers, § 122, at Comment *d*
(2000), illustration 2.

The ABA amended Rule 1.7, in February 2002, to
permit a lawyer to obtain effective informed consent
to a wider range of future conflicts than would have
been possible under the Model Rules prior to their
amendment. ABA Formal Opinion 05–436 (May 11,
2005).

If the client agrees to consent to a particular type
of conflict with which the client is already familiar,
then the consent will ordinarily be effective with
regard to that type of conflict. But if the consent is
general and open-ended, then the consent ordinarily
will be ineffective, because it is not reasonably
likely that the client will understand the material
risks involved. On the other hand, if the client is an
experienced user of the legal services involved and
is reasonably informed regarding the risk that a
conflict may arise, such consent is more likely to be
effective, particularly if *the client is independently
represented* by other counsel in giving consent and

the consent is limited to future conflicts unrelated to the subject of the representation.

That situation—independent representation—is likely to occur in cases where a corporation has in-house counsel, who advises it to consent in advance when hiring outside counsel for a particular matter. The general rule is that the more comprehensive the explanation of the types of future representations that might arise and the actual and reasonably foreseeable adverse consequences of those representations, the greater is the likelihood that the client will have the requisite understanding to consent in advance. ABA Formal Opinion 05–436 (May 11, 2005).

In short, some conflicts are common and familiar to the client, and the client may wish to waive these conflicts in advance. If the lawyer fully informs her client of any risk that the client might thus face, the client may waive such conflicts in advance. If the circumstances or the reasonable expectations that formed the basis of the client's consent materially change, the lawyer must bring these new factors to the attention of the client and secure new consent. Rule 17, Comment 22.

5.   The Hot Potato Doctrine

In general, if a law firm finds itself simultaneously representing two adverse clients in two different law suits, it may not avoid the problem simply by dropping the disfavored client like a "hot potato" and trying to convert the present client into a former client. Absent special circumstances, if the parties do not consent to the conflict, the law firm must withdraw from representing *both* parties in the two cases.

The basic conflicts rule, discussed above, is that, unless the clients knowingly consent and the consent is waivable a lawyer may not sue Client *A* on behalf of Client *B* while simultaneously representing *A*, even in a completely unrelated matter. This rule exists in a world where law firms are ever changing. When a law firm undergoes metamorphosis by merger or acquisition, its client list may suddenly contain two clients directly adverse to each other. Some law firms erroneously conclude that the firm can pick one of the clients (typically the client who pays the most fees) to continue representing and withdraw from representing the other. However, the general rule is that, if the firm withdraws from further representation of Client *A*, it still may not ethically represent Client *B*. As Rule 1.7, Comment 29 states: "Ordinarily, the lawyer will be forced to withdraw from representing all of the clients if the common representation fails."

This is what is often called the "hot potato" problem—a phrase that probably derives from *Picker International, Inc. v. Varian Associates, Inc.* (N.D.Ohio 1987). In that case, a large national law firm merged with a smaller firm based in Chicago. When the newly-created firm compared the client lists, it turned out that the merged firm was representing opponents in current litigation and that it was now in the position of suing a client. (The larger firm was suing *B* on behalf of *A*, its longtime client; the smaller firm (now part of the larger law firm) was representing *B* in various matters, though not in the case of *A v. B.*)

The newly merged firm sought to withdraw from representing the smaller firm's client and to continue representing the longtime client of the larger firm. The firm, in short, sought to make one of the clients a *former* client (instead of a concurrent one) in order to avoid the rule against suing concurrent clients. The federal trial court held that the firm could not do that without the consent of all affected clients. Failing such consent, the new firm had to withdraw in the case of A v. B from representing *both* parties: "A firm may not drop a client like a hot potato, especially if it is in order to keep a far more lucrative client." From such colorful images the law of conflicts develops. The principles that the *Picker* court articulated are not unusual, and courts generally follow *Picker*.

Hot potatoes not only burn law firms that have restructured. Say a potential client comes along with interests adverse to an existing client. The firm views the new business favorably and considers withdrawing from further representation of its preexisting client in order to free itself to work for the newcomer. The firm wants to convert the preexisting client to a former client, and then accept the new client. Is this "preemptive" dropping of the "hot potato" permissible?

Courts do not view preemptive withdrawal favorably, and typically treat this situation as a hot potato, because the law firm drops the preexisting client *with the specific intent* of taking on the new client. That is disloyal. This situation is an illustration of the fact that clients impose an opportunity cost on lawyers, measured in part by the new clients the firm cannot accept while representing the original client. The cost is magnified because the firm may not remove it by the simple expedient of "firing" the current client to subsequently accept a new one.

When there is a question of whether the client the firm wishes to drop is a present or a "former" client (about which, more below), courts tend to resolve the facts against the law firm if it is reasonable for the client to think that it is a continuing client. Consequently, law firms should seriously consider sending out letters of disengagement so that both client and law firm know where they stand.

Courts are sometimes willing to allow withdrawal if the conflict occurred through no fault of the law firm. *Gould, Inc. v. Mitsui Mining & Smelting Co.* (N.D.Ohio 1990), illustrates this point. Jones, Day was representing Gould suing various defendants who had allegedly misappropriated Gould trade secrets. One of these defendants was Pechiney. In 1989, Pechiney acquired IG Technologies (IGT), a company that Jones, Day represented in an unrelated matter. Consequently, Jones, Day found itself in a conflict between Gould and IGT's parent. The court refused to disqualify Jones, Day from representing Gould against Pechiney. The court decided to adopt a "less mechanical approach" because of the "explosion of merger activity by corporations during the past fifteen years." The disqualification would cost Gould a great deal of time and money, and delay the case. The "conflict was created by Pechiney's acquisition of IGT several years after the instant case was commenced, not by an affirmative act of Jones, Day." The court concluded that the law firm had to discontinue its representation of either Gould or IGT, and erect a "screen" around the lawyers who had worked for the party whom the firm dropped. Accord, Rule 1.7, Comment 5.

Though some lawyers may think less about loyalty than they should, new factual contexts create complex scenarios, and the ethical standards that govern these scenarios still have loyalty as their touchstone. Let us turn to a few special problem areas.

6.   Special Problem Areas

A.   Estate Planning

Conflicts may occur in the course of estate planning and estate administration. The same basic conflicts rules apply. Comment 27 to Rule 1.7.

There are several basic conflicts issues to keep in mind. First, several family members, such as the husband and wife, may call on the same lawyer to prepare wills. The lawyer must make sure that there are no conflicts among these family members, and that there are no secrets that one member has that he or she does not want revealed to other members. For example, assume a husband wants to leave money to his illegitimate son and he does not want his wife to know that he has an illegitimate offspring and that he is providing for him in his will. The wife, in turn, wants to know exactly how her husband's will is drafted. If the husband and wife use the same lawyer to draft the will, the lawyer has a conflict because the same lawyer cannot keep a secret on behalf of one client while keeping that information secret from the other client.

In estate administration, there may also be an ethics issue in determining exactly who the client is because in some jurisdictions, the client is the beneficiary. In other jurisdictions, the client is the estate or trust, including its beneficiaries. Comment 27 advises the lawyer to "make clear the relationship to the parties involved."

There is a malpractice issue regarding the lawyer's duty to the beneficiaries of a will (nonclients) when the lawyer negligently drafts a will for his client, the testator. In *Osornio v. Weingarten* (Cal. App.2004), a lawyer drafted a will that included a gift to the testator's caregiver. Under state law, the gift to the caregiver was presumptively invalid, and ultimately failed because the lawyer negligently failed to advise the testator to follow the necessary procedure to insure the gift would stand up. The California appeals court held that the intended beneficiary could sue the lawyer for negligence. The court argued that the lawyer owed a duty to the presumptively disqualified beneficiary to use the lawyer's best efforts to ensure the intended gift would stand.

As matter of legal ethics, the general rule is that there is ordinarily no conflict of interest when a testator hires a lawyer to disinherit a beneficiary even though the lawyer represents the beneficiary on unrelated matters, unless doing so would violate a legal obligation of the testator to the beneficiary, or unless there is a significant risk that the lawyer's representation of the testator will be materially limited by the lawyer's responsibilities to the beneficiary. ABA Formal Opinion 05–434 (Dec. 8, 2004).

See also, ABA Formal Op. 02–428 (Aug. 9, 2002), concluding that a lawyer may, on the recommendation of a person who is a potential beneficiary, draft the testator's will, assuming that the lawyer complies with Rule 5.4(c) and secures any informed consents that other rules may require. If the person recommending the lawyer also agrees to pay or assure the lawyer's fee, the lawyer must also secure the testator's informed consent and satisfy the other requirements of Rule 1.8(f). If the person recommending the lawyer is a current client of the lawyer, the lawyer should obtain clear guidance from that person and the testator as to the lawyer's use or revelation of protected information of each of them in representing the other.

B. Examining a Present Client as Adverse Witness

Assume a lawyer (Attorney Alpha) represents Client *A* in a matter. Alpha, in the course of litiga-

tion, examines another individual, *B* (who happens
to be another client of the same firm), as an adverse
witness. Or, Alpha conducts discovery of Client *B* as
an adverse witness. In either case, if Client *B* is a
material witness, Alpha will ordinarily face a conflict of interest that is disqualifying unless there is
appropriate client consent, *even if the law firm's
representation of Client A is unrelated to the law
firm's representation of Client B.* This is because,
when the lawyer cross-examines a current client as
an adverse witness, or conducts third party discovery against a current client, there is a tension
between the lawyer's own pecuniary interest in
continued employment by the client-witness and the
lawyer's ability to effectively represent the litigation
client. ABA Formal Opinion 92–367 (Oct. 16, 1992).

The 2002 revisions added language to take account of this situation. Rule 1.7, Comment 6 now
says: "a directly adverse conflict may arise when a
lawyer is required to cross-examine a client who
appears as a witness in a lawsuit involving another
client, as when the testimony will be damaging to
the client who is represented in the lawsuit."

If the conflict arises or becomes foreseeable only
after both representations are underway, withdrawal from one of the cases may not be possible, under
the hot potato rule. Alternatively, it may be possible
for the client to retain another lawyer solely for the
purpose of examining the client of the principal
lawyer. In *United States v. Jeffers* (7th Cir.1975)
then-Judge Stevens of the Seventh Circuit suggested this alternative, though it was not the issue

before the court: "there is nothing in the record suggesting any reason why he [the lawyer] could not have made an offer to have some other lawyer retained for this limited purpose...."

C. Multiple Representations in Criminal Cases: The Problem of Constitutionally Adequate Representation

If a party in civil litigation waives a conflict, the court rarely raises conflicts issue *sua sponte*. In criminal cases, however, the court must ensure that the defendant has had adequate representation by counsel, a right that the Sixth Amendment guarantees.

In some cases, a defendant will base his appeal on a claim that his counsel's representation of multiple defendants resulted in a conflict of interest that deprived him of his Sixth Amendment right of effective assistance of counsel. The prosecutor may also challenge defense counsel's multiple representation because he has an interest in securing (1) convictions of only people who are guilty and (2) valid convictions, that is, convictions consistent with the Sixth Amendment.

The leading case dealing with general claims of ineffective assistance of counsel is *Strickland v. Washington* (S.Ct.1984). The Court created a high hurdle for the criminal defendant. To justify a reversal of his conviction, the defendant must show that his lawyer's acts or omissions are "outside the wide range of professionally competent assistance" *and* that the ineffectiveness caused "actual prejudice." "It is not enough for the defendant to show that the errors had some conceivable effect on the outcome of the proceedings."

Strickland does not end the discussion, because the Supreme Court earlier generated a special conflicts of interest principle in *Holloway v. Arkansas* (S.Ct.1978). The *Holloway* Court held that a criminal conviction must be reversed if a trial judge requires joint representation in a criminal case although the defendant entered a timely objection to the joint representation. In that case, such a joint representation is presumed prejudicial.

Holloway recognized that a conflict may "prevent an attorney from challenging the admission of evidence prejudicial to one client but perhaps favorable to another, or from arguing at the sentencing hearing the relative involvement and culpability of his clients in order to minimize the culpability of one by emphasizing that of another." In addition, the defense lawyer's joint representation may preclude him from exploring possible plea negotiations, or from considering the possibility of an agreement to testify for the prosecution in exchange for a lesser charge or in exchange for a favorable sentencing recommendation.

In *Holloway* the defendant had made a timely objection to the multiple representation. In contrast, in *Cuyler v. Sullivan* (S.Ct.1980), no party lodged any timely objection to multiple representations. *Cuyler* promulgated a new rule for that situation. If the court knows, or reasonably should know, that a particular conflict of interest exists, it must initiate an inquiry into the propriety of multiple representation. Thus, under *Cuyler*, in order to establish a Sixth Amendment violation because of multiple representation, if the defendant raised no objection at trial, the defendant must demonstrate that there was an actual conflict of interest that adversely affected the adequacy of his lawyer's performance.

D. Representing Government Entities and Private Clients Simultaneously

Sometimes the government retains a private law firm to represent it on a particular matter. That law firm also continues to represent private clients, some of whom may take positions adverse to the government. For example, the lawyer may represent a private party suing the state in the court of claims to recover on a contract, while defending the state before the court of claims in a personal injury tort on state-leased land.

The general principle is that the lawyer must first determine if the client is the government as a whole or a smaller entity, such as a particular agency or department. Initially, the identity of the client for conflicts purposes is established by agreement between the lawyer and the client when the client (in this case, the government official authorized to speak for the client) retains the lawyer. If there is no express agreement, one should look at the reasonable expectations of the client, such as how the government entity is funded, how it is legally defined, and whether it has independent legal authority on the matter for which it hired the lawyer.

Rule 1.13, Comment 9 advises: ''Defining precisely the identity of the client and prescribing the resulting obligations of such lawyers may be more difficult in the government context and is a matter beyond the scope of these Rules.''

Assume that two government agencies or departments are treated as different entities, so that the lawyer will not be opposing her client. She will be representing one client (the private client) while opposing a government entity that is not her client. The lawyer must still decide if her representation of the government entity will be adversely affected— ''materially limited'' in the words of Rule 1.7— because of the relationship between the two government entities. If so, she must disclose the situation and obtain valid consent from both her private client and the government client.

E. Job Negotiations Between Lawyer for One Party and Lawyer for Adverse Party

Sometimes a lawyer employed at one law firm explores employment opportunities with a law firm representing an adverse party (or, with that adverse party directly). Law careers used to be like our grandparents' marriage, typically for life. Now, when a lawyer joins a firm, it is more like modern marriage, not necessarily for life.''

ABA Formal Opinion 96–400 (January 24, 1996) concluded that discussions involving a change in employment should be considered under Rule 1.7, as something that may "materially" limit the lawyer's representation of a client. The general rule is that a lawyer in one law firm negotiating for employment with another firm with interests adverse to the interests of a client of the first law firm must take appropriate steps to protect client interests. These steps include consulting with the client, or with a supervisory lawyer, *before* the point when such negotiations are reasonably likely to interfere materially with the lawyer's professional judgment, and withdrawing from further representation.

What about *imputation*? A literal reading of Rule 1.10 before the 2002 revisions would appear to impute to the other lawyers of the firm the disqualification of the job-seeking lawyer "even after he himself had withdrawn from the matter." The 2002 revisions to the Model Rules added Comment 10 to Rule 1.7, to make clear that there is no imputation. After recognizing that "when a lawyer has discussions concerning possible employment with an opponent of the lawyer's client, or with a law firm representing the opponent, such discussions could materially limit the lawyer's representation of the client," it then advises that this is a "personal interest conflict" and thus should not normally be imputed to other lawyers in the firm. See Rule 1.10(a) ("personal interest" conflicts not imputed).

F. Idiosyncratic Personal Interests of a Lawyer

Consider the prospective client who asks Lawyer Alpha to sue Dr. Smith for medical malpractice.

Alpha happens to know Dr. Smith, who is her good friend and neighbor, and consequently she does not wish to take the case. Alpha should not take the case if she believes that her close personal friendship will adversely interfere with her own interests. She does not want to create a sore point with her neighbor, and this reluctance might inhibit her zealous representation of the client.

Given Alpha's decision not to sue her neighbor because she feels that there is a conflict, should that conflict be imputed to everyone else in Alpha's law firm? What if the neighbor is not a good friend, but Alpha just thinks that it is bad policy to sue her neighbor because neighborly relations may materially limit her representation? Alpha can always turn down the case, but may another lawyer in her firm (Beta) accept the representation?

What if Alpha is only a low-level, junior associate and will exercise no influence over the case? She may not want to represent a certain client (*e.g.*, her neighbor, or a company manufacturing tobacco, or an accused rapist), and the depth of her feelings may be such that she is in a conflict within the meaning of Rule 1.7. But must the entire law firm be disqualified by imputation in this situation, pursuant to Rule 1.10?

The most natural reading of the Model Rules, *prior* to the 2002 revisions, appeared to require imputation in these types of cases because there was no exception to the general rule regarding imputation for what are best termed idiosyncratic, or very personal, or eccentric conflicts.

However, the Model Rules since 2002 indicate that the conflict based on depth of a lawyer's personal feelings is not automatically imputed to the entire firm. Rule 1.7, Comment 10 refers us to Rule 1.10, and Rule 1.10(a), in turn, tells us that the Rule does not impute a prohibition based on personal interest unless there is a "significant risk" that the prohibited lawyer's conflict will "materially" limit the firm's representation of the client in question. If the senior partner has only a modest personal opposition to the client, there is little chance his views might influence young associates.

On the other hand, if it is reasonable to believe that the individually disqualified lawyer will adversely *affect* the representation by other lawyers in the law firm—perhaps, given her depth of feeling and power within the firm she may affect the ability of other lawyers to fight zealously—then this situation is different and the disqualification should be imputed to the law firm. In that setting, the individually disqualified lawyer's removal from the case has not removed her ability to affect it.

G.   Lawyers as Members of Unions

When a law firm employs personnel, it is, in general, subject to the same laws as other employers, such as laws forbidding discrimination on the basis of race, sex, or age. Similarly, bar associations may not promulgate minimum fee schedules under the antitrust laws, *Goldfarb v. Virginia State Bar*

(S.Ct.1975), and lawyers may not join in conspiracies in an effort to obtain higher compensation, *F.T.C. v. Superior Court Trial Lawyers Association* (S.Ct.1990). However, the situation may be more complex when ethics rules coexist with generally applicable laws regulating collective bargaining.

Consider the case where lawyer-employees join a union, which represents them in collective bargaining with the employer, who is also the client. In these circumstances, a third-party (the union) is in a posture that is adversarial to the client (typically a government agency or perhaps a corporation). The negotiations with the union typically involve the terms and conditions of employment, including discipline, discharge, work assignments, hours, and so forth. Legal ethics may also govern these issues.

The Model Rules do not discuss this issue directly, though Rule 1.7(a)(2) warns lawyers that they violate ethics rules if their representation of a client is "materially limited" by the lawyers' obligations "to a third person," which could include another organization such as a union.

The Restatement of the Law Governing Lawyers, Third, § 56, Comment *k* (2000) acknowledges that lawyers who employ others (whether lawyers or nonlawyers) are subject to laws governing antidiscrimination, unjustified discharge, and labor relations. However, it "remains to be decided whether some such laws, for example, the National Labor Relations Act, are subject to implied qualifications that accommodate the professional obligations of lawyers."

Only a few cases discuss this issue. *Santa Clara County Counsel Attorneys Association v. Woodside* (Cal.1994) concluded that a state statute (which did not exclude management or confidential employees from its coverage) allowed government employees who are lawyers to unionize, but that a lawyer would be subject to discipline if she "violates actual disciplinary rules, most particularly rules pertaining to the attorney's duty to represent the client faithfully, competently, and confidentially.... An attorney, in pursuing rights of self-representation, may not use delaying tactics in handling existing litigation or other matters of representation for the purpose of gaining advantage in a dispute over salary and fringe benefits." Once the union employees announced their intention to sue, the appellate court held that the trial court acted properly in upholding the right of the county to exclude these lawyers from confidential meetings with the county.

H. The Lawyer as Director of the Corporate Client

If a law firm does a substantial amount of work for a particular corporate client, it is not uncommon for one of the partners of the firm to be invited to join the corporation's board of directors. This dual role invites significant conflicts. For example, the lawyer on the board may witness certain events, and then be asked to be both a witness and an advocate in litigation. The corporate client may be confused as to when the lawyer is giving business advice (in her capacity as a director) or legal advice (in her capacity as counsel). If the corporation is sued, the lawyer who is also a director is more likely to find herself a named defendant or a witness.

Some corporations like to have outside counsel sit in on board meetings. However, one does not have to be a member of the board in order to attend its meetings. It is also true that some lawyers like to be members of the board. For one thing, it makes it less likely that their corporate client will wander off and decide to retain a different law firm.

The ABA Model Rules acknowledge the issue of the lawyer serving simultaneously as a director of, and counsel to, the corporate client. The Rules do not impose a *per se* prohibition on this dual role, and they offer little guidance besides advising that the lawyer should not wear these two hats if "there is material risk that the dual role will compromise the lawyer's independence of professional judgment . . . " The lawyer should also advise board members that the lawyer's firm may have to disqualify itself or refuse to undertake representation because of a conflict of interest, and that some matters discussed in board meetings while the lawyer is present in his capacity as a director might not be covered by the attorney-client privilege. Rule 1.7, Comment 35.

The Restatement of the Law Governing Lawyers, Third, § 135, at Comments *d* & *e* (Official Draft, 2000), also proposes no *per se* prohibition. The ethical duty of a lawyer serving an "entity" is "generally consistent with the duties of a director or officer." Comment *d*. However, if the obligations or personal interests of the lawyer as director are "materially adverse" to the obligations or personal interests of the lawyer as corporate counsel, then the lawyer must withdraw from representation unless the corporate client gives informed consent to the representation. *Id*.

For example, assume that Lawyer serves as director, inside counsel, and corporate secretary of the Company. The Company proposes to give bonuses to its five highest-paid officers, including Lawyer. Lawyer's status as director and potential recipient of the bonus creates a risk that his interests as counsel will be "materially adverse" to his interests as director. Hence Lawyer should withdraw from the representation unless the board consents. Neither the lawyer-director nor a partner of the lawyer-director can participate in making the decision to consent to the conflicted representation. Restatement of the Law Governing Lawyers, Third, § 135, illustration 3 (2000).

Conflicts can also arise when the lawyer-director no longer serves in *either* capacity. For example, if a former lawyer-director had served on the board of a hospital extensively evaluating and approving certain policies, both that former lawyer-director and his law firm are later disqualified from representing the plaintiff in a medical malpractice case against that hospital involving policies that the lawyer-director had earlier approved and implemented.

I.   The Insurer and the Insured

When the insurer pays the lawyer to represent
the insured, various conflicts issues may arise when
the insurer and the insured have differing interests.
For example, the insured may want to settle the
case for the policy maximum and avoid the time and
risk of a trial, while the insurer thinks that the
settlement offer is too high and wants the trial. Or,
the plaintiff may be suing for an amount in excess
of the policy coverage and the insured is worried
that the insurer is devoting insufficient resources to
the case. Or, the insurer may have a defense to the
insurance policy that will relieve it of liability (the
policy may exclude intentional torts), but the insured does not want the insurer to know facts that
support the policy exclusion.

On the one hand, these matters might be considered under Rule 1.7(a)(2). The lawyer's responsibility to the client may be materially limited by the
lawyer's responsibilities to a third person, namely
the insurer. On the other hand, insurers sometimes
argue that they are also clients, so that the alleged
conflict comes under Rule 1.7(a)(1) (representation
of one client directly adverse to another client).
However, Rule 1.8(f) deals specifically with the situation where the lawyer accepts compensation from
one person (the insurer) to represent another (the
insured), so we discuss this issue under Rule 1.8(f),
below.

There is an issue that does come under Rule 1.7,
not Rule 1.8(f). May a lawyer who is representing a

liability insurer as a named party in a civil action also represent a plaintiff in a separate civil action against a defendant when the insurance company is providing that defendant's defense? Rule 1.7 governs this question. ABA Formal Opinion 05–435 (Dec. 8, 2004) considered this issue and concluded that, in general, there is no conflict. However, these would be a "directly adverse" representation under Rule 1.7a)(1) if the liability insurer is a *named party* to the action brought by the lawyer's plaintiff-client, or the lawyer was taking testimony or discovery from the liability insurer. Otherwise, the normal rule is that the representations are "not directly adverse" so there is no concurrent conflict of interest because the lawyer represents the insurer in the other action.

However, a concurrent conflict may arise if there is "a significant risk the representation of the individual plaintiff will be materially limited" because of the lawyer's responsibilities to the insurer. For example, there may be cases where it would be to the advantage of the plaintiff for the lawyer to reveal or use information relating to the representation of the insurer. If there is a concurrent conflict of interest, the lawyer may seek the informed consent of each affected client, confirmed in writing, to waive the conflict.

J. Positional Conflicts

A lawyer may represent Client *A* in the case of *A vs. X* seeking a particular legal result (e.g., that the statute of limitations for tort should be tolled until the malpractice could reasonably have been discovered) and, at the same time, represent Client *B* in a completely different matter, the case of *Z vs. B*, concerning the same general issue. May the lawyer, on behalf of *B*, defend a position *contrary* to the one he advocated (or is advocating) on behalf of A?

The Model Rules raise this question but provide little guidance in answering it. Comment 24 to Rule 1.7 allows lawyers to advocate antagonistic positions on the same legal question in different cases unless "there is a significant risk that a lawyer's action on behalf of one client will materially limit the lawyer's effectiveness in representing another client in a different case."

The Restatement of the Law Governing Lawyers, Third, § 128, Illustrations 5 and 6 (Official Draft, 2000), recognizes the possibility of positional conflicts, but the conclusions in two illustrations read like *ipse dixit*. Illustration 5 allows an attorney to represent Client *A* and Client *B* in two separate cases brought in two different federal district courts, where the lawyer will seek to introduce certain evidence in one trial and argue against its admissibility in the other trial. Even though "there is some possibility" that the court's ruling in one case "might be published and cited as authority in the other proceeding," the lawyer "may proceed with both representations *without obtaining the consent* of the clients involved." *Id.* (emphasis added).

In Illustration 6, the facts are the same, except both cases are now before the U.S. Supreme Court, which will decide the evidentiary question by hearing both cases (though apparently without consolidating the two appeals). Illustration 6 concludes that now there is a conflict, and it is so great that "even the informed consent of both Client *A* and Client *B* would be insufficient to" permit the lawyer to represent each client before the Supreme Court.

These two examples tell us that the lawyer may represent both clients in Illustration 5, without securing consent from either, but may not represent either client in Illustration 6, even with consent from both. One would think that, at some point, the lawyer would have to advise the clients of what is going on, and both clients would probably prefer to know at the trial level, when there is time to do something about the problem, but the Restatement leaves that issue untouched.

Comment 24 to Rule 1.7 parallels these two Illustrations, and is equally unhelpful. It presents two potential situations. In one, advocating Client A's position "might create precedent adverse to the interests" of Client B who the lawyer represents in an unrelated matter. That alone, the Comment says, does not create a conflict. In the second situation, there is a conflict if there is a "significant risk" that the lawyer's action for one client "will materially limit the lawyer's effectiveness" in representing another client.

These tests are a bit vague. What do they mean in practice? Comment 24 tries to offer a concrete example. If the lawyer has successfully advanced Client A's position, and the resulting decision *"will create* a precedent likely to *seriously weaken* the position" taken on behalf of Client B, there is a conflict. (Emphasis added).

Comment 24 acknowledges the complexity of the issue without providing a definite standard for resolving it. It does provide a list of factors relevant to determining when the representations create a conflict so that a lawyer must inform her two clients. These factors include "where the cases are pending, whether the issue is substantive or procedural, the temporal relationship between the matters, the significance of the issue to the immediate and long-term interests of the clients involved and the clients' reasonable expectations in retaining the lawyer."

Any disqualification based on positional conflicts is magnified by the fact that the concept of positional conflicts is found in Comment 24 to Rule 1.7, and Rule 1.10 imputes disqualifications under Rule 1.7. Nowadays, when it is not unusual for firms to have hundreds of members scattered among various cities, there may well be positional conflicts, like those discussed in Illustration 5, occurring regularly. It would be difficult for a "conflicts check" to uncover all these positional conflicts because legal arguments change all the time, even within the same case. Perhaps a lawyer would argue that the "positional conflict" is "personal" under Rule 1.10(a) and thus not imputed, but one would have to concede that the Rule itself has no such blanket exception for positional conflicts.

A different type of conflict occurs when lawyers take conflicting positions in two different cases regarding a particular item of property, the same *res*, or the same facts. This type of conflict is much easier to deal with, because the conflict is more obvious. A good example of this type of conflict is found in *Fiandaca v. Cunningham* (1st Cir.1987).

In *Fiandaca*, the New Hampshire Legal Assistance (NHLA) represented women prisoners objecting to overcrowding. The state, in response, offered to move some of the prisoners to another facility that the state was using as a hospital for the mentally retarded. But NHLA also represented the retarded persons in that hospital, so it objected to the state's offer because it would adversely affect their other clients, the mentally retarded. The First Circuit held that NHLA was in conflict when it urged declining a settlement for one client because that settlement would adversely affect clients in a different case. Hence, the trial court should not have certified New Hampshire Legal Assistance as the class counsel for the female prisoners.

Fiandaca is not a case of conflicting abstract legal positions, because the lawyers' two clients had conflicting positions regarding the same piece of property, the hospital. However, one can draw from *Fiandaca* a legal principle that is useful in analyzing all positional conflicts: is the lawyer (and, by imputed disqualification, the law firm) likely to modify, soft-pedal, temper, or adjust arguments in one case in order to benefit the other client?

K. Motions of One Lawyer to Disqualify the Opposing Lawyer

If conflicts develop during litigation, counsel may petition the court to disqualify opposing counsel. If the conflict is such that it taints the fact-finding process or fairness of the trial, the court should grant the motion. For example, if the conflict occurs because the conflicted lawyer is privy to confidential information of his former client, and this information would be relevant in the lawyer's representation against his former client, the conflict will taint the fact finding process. If the conflicted lawyer may reduce the vigor of his representation or pull his punches on behalf of client #1 because he is simultaneously representing client #2 in another matter, the conflict will taint the fact-finding process.

If the alleged ethical violation does not affect the fact-finding process or the fairness of the trial, then the court should leave any enforcement of the alleged violation to the disciplinary process. For example, a claim by defendant that plaintiff's lawyer improperly solicited plaintiff will not taint the fact-finding process. By drawing this distinction between alleged ethics violations that taint the fact-finding process and alleged ethics violations that do not, the court will make it less likely that counsel will be able to use a disqualification motion as a technique of harassment.

RULE 1.8: CONFLICT OF INTEREST—CURRENT CLIENTS: SPECIFIC RULES

1. Rule 1.8(a)—Business Dealings with the Client

Rule 1.8 considers various specific conflicts issues. The Rule recognizes and implements the general principle that lawyers are fiduciaries of their clients, but that these fiduciaries may also be involved in commercial and other relationships with their clients.

Rule 1.8(a) deals with the lawyer entering into a business transaction with a client, or acquiring a pecuniary interest that may adversely affect the lawyer's ability to represent the client. In general, there is a conflict if these interests are significant and material enough to affect the lawyer's judgment. The lawyer in such cases should not accept the case unless the lawyer *reasonably* believes that the representation will not be adversely affected, *and* the client gives *informed consent* in writing.

If the lawyer deals with the client in a business transaction, the lawyer may overreach or get the better of the client, who may be relying on what the client thinks is the lawyer's independent legal judgment and loyalty. The Model Rules allow client business dealings with the lawyer if: (1) the transaction is fair and reasonable to the client; (2) the terms of the transaction are given to the client *in writing* so that the client can understand them; (3) the client is given a reasonable opportunity to consult another lawyer (whether or not the client actually exercises that opportunity); and (4) the client consents *in writing*. The client must sign this writing. Rule 1.8 does not specifically forbid the lawyer from seeking to invest in the client's enterprise, but such investment would be subject to these requirements.

It is not the duty of the client, even the sophisticated client, to recognize such a conflict. Rather it is the duty of the lawyer to bring the matter to the client's attention and to explain the significance of what is happening in a way the client can understand. If the lawyer represents a client in a transaction, and also receives a personal benefit in addition to the fee, then the lawyer's ethical obligation is not always fulfilled by merely disclosing the lawyer's personal stake, explaining the potential consequences, and obtaining consent. The lawyer "must always ensure that his or her personal interest does not interfere with the unfettered exercise of professional judgment the client is entitled to expect under the circumstances. The best way to achieve this, of course, is to see that the client has independent advice." *Matter of Breen* (Ariz.1992).

2.   Rule 1.8(b)—Using Client Information

The Rules forbid using client secrets or confidences to the disadvantage of the client. This prohibition applies equally to protect a former client, if the information has not become "generally known." See Rule 1.9(c)(1).

Note that a lawyer may violate this rule of confidentiality even if she does not disclose the information to anyone. She can violate this rule by using the information to the client's detriment. The rationale for this rule is that the freedom of communication that should exist between principal and agent would suffer if the law permitted the agent to use confidential information to the detriment of the principal.

For example, assume that Lawyer learned in confidence that Client is planning to renew the lease on the building Client presently uses. Lawyer then secretly visits Lessor and acquires the lease on Lawyer's own account, without revealing to Lessor any Client information. Lawyer plans to raise the rent because she learned that this location is more important to Client than Lessor suspects. Lawyer has committed a sanctionable violation. She has not *revealed* secret information to anyone, but she has *used* it to Client's detriment. Rule 1.8, Comment 5.

Under basic provisions of the law of agency, unless the principal consents, the agent may not use a client confidence or secret for the agent's own advantage (or a third person's advantage), whether or not the principal suffers any detriment. Under the law of agency, no agent, whether or not a lawyer, may use the principal's secret information to the agent's advantage even if there is no detriment to the principal and even if using the information does not require revealing it. The remedy in the law of agency for this breach of trust is that the agent must disgorge any profits to the principal. The agent cannot profit from using or selling the principal's secrets.

For example, where "a corporation has decided to operate an enterprise at a place where land values will be increased because of such operation, a corporate officer who takes advantage of his special knowledge to buy land in the vicinity is accountable for the profits he makes, even though such purchases have no adverse effect upon the enterprise." Restatement of the Law of Agency, Second, § 388, Comment *c* (1958). This rule is not applicable if the information is a matter of general knowledge. But if it is secret, the lawyer may not sell it or use it to the lawyer's own advantage unless the client consents.

The former Model Code, DR 4–101(B)(3), precisely covered this point. In contrast, current Rule 1.8(b) seems to negate the possibility that the Rules could be interpreted to incorporate this principle. Comment 5 advises: "For example, if a lawyer learns that the client intends to purchase and develop several parcels of land, the lawyer may not use that information to purchase one of the parcels *in competition with the client....*" [Emphasis added]

The negative implication is that there is no ethical problem if the lawyer's purchase of the land and use of the client's confidential information does not harm the client. The next sentence of the Comment says broadly: "The Rule does not prohibit uses that do not disadvantage the client." The client may always argue that the lawyer's use of the information caused detriment. E.g., the lawyer's purchase of the property signaled the market that there was more interest in that area of town.

Under the law of agency the client has a right to collect the lawyer's profits from using the secret client information, even if that use did not harm the client and therefore even if Model Rules have not been violated. Moreover, many jurisdictions have opted to keep the formulation of the older Model Code (forbidding the lawyer from "using or revealing" secret client information).

The Restatement of the Law Governing Lawyers follows the Restatement of the Law of Agency and rejects the implied Model Rules approach. The Restatement prohibit a lawyer's self-dealing in confidential information, whether or not there is prejudice to the client. If the lawyer does engage in such self-dealing, the client can force a disgorgement of profits. The Restatement takes no position on the question of discipline, however. Restatement of the Law Governing Lawyers, Third, § 60(2) (Official Draft 2000).

If the lawyer uses his client's inside information in the course of buying or selling stock, he will find that he is subject to criminal prosecution as well. *United States v. O'Hagan* (S.Ct.1997) makes that clear. In that case, a lawyer not working on the matter purchased securities on the open market after receiving favorable inside information. The SEC prosecuted the lawyer criminally for securities fraud under the so-called "misappropriation theory," *i.e.*, he defrauded both his law firm and its client, persons to whom he owed a fiduciary duty, by taking their information and using it to benefit himself. The Supreme Court upheld the application of the misappropriation theory to Rule 10b–5 cases and found that the lawyer's use of the information is inherently "deceptive," and the fraud is "consummated" when the information is used "in connection with the purchase or sale of [a] security." Compare Rule 8.4(e) (lawyer may not engage in deceit).

Rule 1.8, Comment 5 does not prevent the lawyer from using information that does not cause detriment to the client *and* that is *not* "secret" information of the *client*. As the Comment explains: "a lawyer who learns a government agency's interpretation of trade legislation during the representation of one client may properly use that information to benefit other clients."

3.   Rule 1.8(c)—Accepting Gifts From Clients

Because of the danger that the lawyer may take advantage of the client and abuse the fiduciary relationship, there are important ethical restrictions that a lawyer should observe when accepting gifts from the client. Some gifts do not involve the drafting of any instruments. A typical case involving no legal instrument occurs when the client, happy with the lawyer's work, decides to bestow a gift, which may be nominal (a basket of fruit) or substantial (e.g., an expensive gold watch).

The Rules prohibit the lawyer from soliciting *substantial* gifts. They also bar the lawyer from preparing any legal instrument substantially favoring the lawyer or a relative of the lawyer, even if the lawyer did not solicit that favor. For instance, if the client wants to make his lawyer a beneficiary of his estate, someone else must draft the will, a legal instrument.

The Rules make clear that the lawyer may not prepare this instrument, even if she had no undue influence on her client. *Attorney Grievance Commission v. Brooke* (Md.2003), held that "Rule 1.8(c) is absolute—an attorney may not prepare an instrument designating himself as legatee under the circumstances presented herein. Deterrence of such conduct and the public confidence in the legal profession can only be preserved by protecting against this behavior." This court also held that evidence of a lack of undue influence is irrelevant when considering the appropriate sanction for a lawyer who drafts a will including a large gift to himself; the court suspended the lawyer indefinitely. *Attorney Grievance Commission v. Stein* (Md.2003)(same).

If a client offers the lawyer a substantial gift, not requiring the preparation of a legal instrument, Rule 1.8(c) does not prohibit the lawyer from accepting it. However, the gift "may be voidable by the client under the doctrine of undue influence, which treats substantial client gifts as presumptively fraudulent." Rule 1.8, Comment 6.

4.   Rule 1.8(d)—Publication Rights

Consider a situation where the lawyer negotiates with the client for publication rights to a particular matter before that matter has ended and while the lawyer is still in the employ of the client. There is a danger that the lawyer, in bargaining with the client, will overreach. For example, the client, needing the lawyer's services, may feel pressured to waive attorney-client privilege, so that the attorney can later write a more interesting book. Also, the lawyer, in his representation of the client, may be consciously or unconsciously influenced to enhance the value of his publication rights to the prejudice of his client's case.

Hence, Rule 1.8(d) prohibits acquiring such rights "[p]rior to the conclusion of representation of a client. . . ." Once the representation has ended, the lawyer has no special powers or advantages in negotiating any publication rights from her former client. The lawyer would be in no better bargaining position than any other person who wanted to write a book on the client's legal adventures.

These provisions exist not simply to protect the client but also to protect the interest of the judicial system in competent representation. If a lawyer decides to forego a certain motion because it would reduce the publicity value of the media rights, it is not only the criminal defendant who is hurt, but the system of justice. Even if the defendant wishes to waive rights, and is competent and informed enough to do so, the system of justice has an interest in making sure that innocent people are not convicted falsely. Therefore, the Rules do not provide for client waiver of these restrictions. However, some jurisdictions (notably, California) have taken a different view of this issue [Maxwell v. Superior Court of Los Angeles County (Cal.1982)].

If the lawyer represents the client in a dispute or other transaction concerning the literary property itself, *e.g.*, a copyright claim, the lawyer may contract for a reasonable contingent fee, that is, a reasonable share of the ownership of the literary property, assuming no other rules are violated. The prohibition on acquiring publication rights is not meant to cover this situation. This situation does not raise the problem that Rule 1.8(d) was intended to solve. The lawyer is simply seeking a percentage of the *res*, or recovery. In some cases, the recovery may be a parcel of land. In other cases, it may be a sum of money. In a case involving a copyright dispute, it may be the value of the royalty.

5. Rule 1.8(e)—The Lawyer's Financial Advances to the Client

Rule 1.8(e) provides that, when representing a client in a matter involving litigation the lawyer may not provide financial assistance to the client, but may advance the expenses of litigation, such as the expenses of a medical examination.

Originally, the ethics rules placed several important limitations on financial advances. The Model Code had a specific requirement (DR 5–103(B)) that the client must remain "ultimately liable" for these expenses, but also advised (inconsistently) that the lawyer should not normally sue to collect his advances except to prevent fraud or gross imposition, and that lawyers should charge less fortunate clients a smaller amount or nothing at all.

The Model Rules are more straightforward on this point and better reflect what lawyers do in practice. The Rules eliminate the requirement of client reimbursement and also allow the lawyer to pay directly an indigent's litigation expenses and court costs without the client remaining even contingently liable.

Rule 1.8(e), in short, forbids the lawyer from providing financial assistance to a client in connection with pending or contemplated litigation (*i.e.*, giving the client a loan for living expenses), but has two major exceptions. First, the lawyer may advance court costs and the expenses of litigation (deposition costs, transcripts, expert witness fees, etc.), and the lawyer can agree that the client's obligation to repay these amounts is contingent on the outcome of the matter. In other words, if the plaintiff loses the case, the lawyer is stuck with the expenses and the client has no obligation to reimburse the lawyer. Second, if the lawyer represents an indigent, the lawyer may pay court costs and expenses of litigation on behalf of the indigent client. This rule helps indigents who have suits where they are unlikely to collect a monetary amount because, e.g., they are defendants, or because the relief sought does not result in a monetary payment.

The historical aversion to lawyers assisting clients financially is based on what the common law called "maintenance," "champerty" or "barratry."

Maintenance occurs when a lawyer improperly finances a lawsuit so as to "encourage a client to pursue lawsuits that might otherwise be forsaken." The English common law objected to improperly stirring up litigation and made maintenance a common law crime, abolished by statute in 1967.

A close kin of maintenance is *Champerty*, which occurs when one person assists a litigant in maintaining the lawsuit and, in exchange, receives from the litigant a promise to have a share in the recovery.

And a kissing cousin of maintenance is *Barratry*, which involves a person who urges another to file or continue a lawsuit. At common law, a cause of action could not lie without three instances of barratry.

Model Rule 1.8(e) does place some limits on loans by attorneys to clients. Rule 1.8, Comment 10 explains that lawyers may not "subsidize" lawsuits by making or guaranteeing loans to their clients for living expenses. But even this restriction does not prohibit lawyers from advancing court costs and the expenses of litigation, repayment of which may be contingent on the outcome of the litigation. Similarly, to the extent that the law firm agrees to a maximum cap on expenses, it is not part of an improper effort to engage in champerty or maintenance. It does not prevent the client from settling the case if she wants to do so. The fee cap is not unethical because it comes with no improper strings attached.

Rule 1.8(e) does not bar class action lawyers from advancing the full costs of litigation, repayment of which may be contingent on the outcome of the matter, so that the clients are not liable for the costs if the action is unsuccessful. *In re WorldCom, Inc. Securities Litigation* (S.D.N.Y. 2003) refused to apply New York ethics rule, DR 5–103, which required the client to be ultimately responsible for repayment of expenses, because the "strong federal interests require that the repayment of expenses provision" should in be disregarded in light of Rule 23 of the Federal Rules of Civil Procedure, governing class actions.

6. Rule 1.8(f)—Accepting Money From a Non–Client as Compensation to Represent a Client

A. The General Issue

Sometimes a third party pays the lawyer to represent the client. Parents may pay a lawyer to represent their child charged with a crime. An employer may pay a lawyer to represent an employee sued for matters within the scope of employment. A legal aid office may pay a private lawyer to represent an indigent client. If someone other than the client pays for the client's legal services, the lawyer's obligations are still to the client.

Rule 1.8(f) makes clear that the lawyer may not allow this third party to interfere with the lawyer's professional judgment. The client must also know about and consent to the lawyer accepting compensation from the third party. Indeed, the lawyer must not agree to represent someone when a third party pays compensation unless she determines that there will be no interference by that third party with the lawyer's independent professional judgment.

This arrangement must also respect the client's right to confidentiality. The third party payer may want to know matters about the client that are confidential. The lawyer may not reveal this information, even if the third party insists, unless the client gives informed consent.

Insurance companies fit within the contours of Rule 1.8(f). Liability insurance companies are contractually obliged to pay the lawyer to represent an insured sued in tort. Sometimes this arrangement leads to questions of alleged conflict of interests, which may also be considered under Rule 1.7, although we discuss the issue here.

B.   The Insurer and the Insured

The insurer, in a typical liability insurance policy (*e.g.,* automobile coverage), agrees to pay any liability within the policy limits, *and* to pay for a lawyer to defend the interests of the insured.

Under the typical liability insurance contract, the insured agrees to cooperate with the insurer in his defense. Ordinarily the insured and the insurer have a community of interest because both wish to defend vigorously against the claim brought by the plaintiff against the insured. However, conflicts may arise when, for example, the suit is for more than the policy limits. Or, the insurer and the insured may disagree as to whether the claim is covered by the policy. Or the insurer may wish to spend less on lawyers' fees to defend the lawsuit than the insured prefers. In some cases the insured may be seeking to defraud the insurance company. These and other scenarios are ripe for conflicts problems.

The case law is not entirely consistent, but the trend is to consider the lawyer in such cases to owe a duty of loyalty to the insured, and to treat only the insured as the client. This makes eminent sense. Usually, the lawyer will be filing a notice of appearance in court on behalf of the insured, not the insurer. While Louisiana allows a tort plaintiff to file a tort action against the insurance company directly, the purpose of such direct actions is not to change the law of ethics but to let the jury know that the defendant is insured and the insurer will have to pay the judgment up to the policy limits.

Model Rule 1.8(f)(2) supports the view that the lawyer represents only one client, the insured, when it states that, if another person pays the lawyer to render legal services for another, the lawyer may not permit that other person to interfere with the lawyer's professional judgment.

Of course, the insurer is no stranger to the relationship between the lawyer and the insured because the contract between the insured and insurer gives the insurer certain significant rights. That contract will govern when the insured has, for example, pre-authorized the insurer to settle within policy limits. The lawyer, though not a party to that contract, then should follow the contract (except to the extent that it violates the Rules).

The Restatement of the Law Governing Lawyers concludes: "It is clear in an insurance situation that a lawyer designated to defend the insured has a client-lawyer relationship with the insured. The insurer is not, simply by the fact that it designates the lawyer, a client of the lawyer." Restatement of the Law Governing Lawyers, Third, § 134, Comment *f* (2000).

The insurance carrier has legitimate interests to know how the defense is going, to evaluate if a particular defense expense is cost-effective, to sue for malpractice if the lawyer for the insured is incompetent, and so forth. The insurer does not have to be called a "client" to have these rights.

As a matter of insurance law, the insurer's duty
to defend the insured and its duty to pay any
damage award are separate duties. In other words,
a policy may provide coverage of defense costs even
though the insurer may have a valid defense (for
example, a contract exclusion) against paying the
ultimate judgment rendered against the insured.
When there is a dispute between the insured and
the insurer as to the extent of policy coverage, the
insurer frequently provides a defense to the insured
under a "reservation of rights." This "reservation"
announces that the insurer is not, by providing
representation, impliedly waiving any defenses it
may have against the insured under the policy, as
concerns ultimate liability.

These disputes frequently are connected with
charges of a violation of legal ethics. In one typical
line of cases, the insured complains that the lawyer
purporting to represent the insured is really working against the insured and on behalf of the insurer,
in violation of his duty of loyalty and his duty to
protect client secrets. For example, it is improper
for the lawyer to defend the insured and at the
same time secretly investigate and report on the
failure of the insured to give timely notice of the
accident involved as required by the insurance policy. In *Allstate Insurance Co. v. Keller* (Ill.App.1958),
the attorneys assigned to represent the insured
deposed him to gather evidence that he was not the
driver of the vehicle at the time of the accident. The
court agreed that the insured's initial false statements that he was the driver were a breach of the

cooperation clause, but it held the insurer's defense of non-cooperation was invalid in these circumstances. After the insured's assigned attorneys "became aware of a conflict of interest" between their client, the insured, and their employer, the insurer, they had to disclose "this information or its significance" to the insured. Failure to deal with this conflict in a way that assured the insured had loyal, independent representation, resulted in loss of the policy defense.

Disputes sometimes arise between the insurer (who is paying the lawyers' fee and other expenses of defending the law suit) and the insured as to how much to spend to defend the suit.

The insurance contract, to which the insured consents, requires the insured to cooperate with the insurer, which retains certain rights over litigation strategy. However, the lawyer may not accept the insurance company's contractually mandated direction as to litigation strategy if so doing would result in the lawyer performing incompetently, for this would breach the lawyer's obligations under the Rules.

Consider this example from the Restatement of the Law Governing Lawyers, Third. Plaintiff sues Policyholder for claims that are within the policy and its monetary limits. Insurer retains Lawyer to defend the action. Lawyer believes that doubling the number of depositions taken, at a cost of $5,000, would somewhat increase Policyholder's chances of prevailing; Lawyer informs both Insurer and Policyholder of this. If the insurance contract authorizes Insurer to make such decisions about the expense of defense, and Lawyer *reasonably believes* that the additional depositions can be forgone without violating the standard of care that Lawyer owes Policyholder, Lawyer may comply with Insurer's direction that taking these further depositions would not be worth the cost. Restatement of the Law Governing Lawyers, Third, § 13, Illustration 5 (Official Draft, 2000).

On the other hand, the lawyer may not accept this direction from the insurer *if* that means that the lawyer is performing incompetent service. Thus, ABA Formal Opinion 01–421 (Feb. 16, 2001), concluded that insurance companies may not exercise their contractual rights so as to preclude competent legal representation of the insured.

7. Rule 1.8(g)—Aggregate Settlements

The lawyer, on behalf of her multiple clients, may negotiate an aggregate settlement of the civil claims, or an agreement of guilty or *nolo contendere* pleas covering multiple clients in a criminal case. "An aggregate settlement or aggregated agreement occurs when two or more clients who are represented by the same lawyer together resolve their claims or defenses or pleas." ABA Formal Opinion 06–438 (Feb. 10, 2006). Aggregate settlements may arise in separate cases. For example, a lawyer may represent several homeowners suing for breach of warranties against a home builder. Each lawsuit involves different home, perhaps different breaches, perhaps even separate subdivisions, but the builder offers to settle all of them at once.

In such cases, Rule 1.8(g) provides that each client must give informed consent, which must include disclosure of "the existence and nature of all the claims or pleas involved and of the participation of each person in the settlement." Rule 1.2(a) protects each client's right to have a final say in accepting or rejecting a settlement offer.

Assume, for example, that Attorney Alpha represents 18 individual plaintiffs who entered into a prior agreement that majority rule would govern acceptance of a settlement. Defendant offered $155,000 for distribution to the group, which voted 13–5 to accept it. Notwithstanding the prior agreement, plaintiffs have a right to agree or refuse to agree once the settlement was made known to them. *Hayes v. Eagle–Picher Industries, Inc.* (10th Cir.1975). Alpha obviously must disclose the settlement offer to each of his clients, and any of them can reject it. Needless to say, the lawyer's retainer agreement should specify that if this occurrence would represent a breach of contract as among the co-clients, that the lawyer could not act to enforce or defend any suit arising from such breach.

Rule 1.8(g) "empowers each client to withhold consent and thus prevent[s] the lawyer from subordinating the interests of the client to those of another client or to those of the lawyer." ABA Formal Opinion 06–438 (Feb. 10, 2006). Hence, each client can vie to be the holdout, seeking more money before the others can settle as an aggregate.

Because of this problem, one might think that the lawyer could fully inform the clients of this problem and allow them, if they so desire, to bind themselves in the future. For example, if there are a dozen clients suing the homebuilder, they could agree to bind themselves by an aggregate settlement as long as the lawyer informs every one of all the facts of the settlement and 9 of the 12 (or 10 of the 12) agree. In corporate law, for example, parties can bind themselves by use of a voting trust. The common law used to be wary of voting trusts, but now state statutes "uniformly recognize the validity of voting trusts and they have received a more hospitable judicial reception." Robert W. Hamilton, The Law of Corporations in a Nutshell 199 (3d ed. 1991).

But, ABA Formal Opinion 06–438 does accept that modern view. Instead, it announces, "the informed consent required by the rule generally cannot be obtained in advance of the formulation of such an offer or demand," citing *In re Hoffman* (La. 2004)(per curiam). In *Hoffman*, the court suspended the lawyer and then conditionally deferred the suspension if the lawyer committed no professional misconduct within one-year post judgment period. The court found, in that case, that the "respondent did not first obtain the informed consent of each of his clients to such representation." In a will dispute, the lawyer failed to obtain the informed consent, from all the siblings/legatees, of acceptance of

an aggregate settlement offer and division of settlement proceeds among the siblings/legatees. The
court went on to say that the "lawyer must confer
with all clients directly, rather than communicating
with one client and expecting that client to confer
with the other clients."

8.   Rule 1.8(h)—Limiting the Lawyer's Liability for Malpractice

A.   Prospective Limitations of Liability

The general rule is that a lawyer may not attempt
to limit his liability for his future legal negligence.
Rule 1.8(h) & Comments 14–15. For example, a
lawyer violated this provision when he inserted a
provision in his attorney fee contract requiring his
client to contest the sufficiency of his work within
ten days or waive any malpractice claim. "The ten-
day provision substantially limits the time in which
a client can bring a legal negligence action against"
the lawyer. *Iowa Supreme Court Attorney Disciplinary Board v. Powell* (Iowa 2007)(Court imposed a
six-month suspension).

However, there is an exception. The client may
waive his right, prospectively, to sue his lawyer for
malpractice *if* another lawyer independently represents the client in making such an agreement. The
rationale behind this principle is that there is a risk
that the lawyer will be able to overreach the client
unless a second (non-conflicted) lawyer independently represents the client in making the decision
to waive malpractice liability prospectively.

One might think that, as a practical matter, it will be the unusual case where an individual will hire a second lawyer to represent him in negotiating an employment agreement with his first lawyer under which the second lawyer advises the client to waive his first lawyer's malpractice liability prospectively. In such cases, once the client visits the second lawyer, we should not be surprised if the second lawyer advises the client that there is no need to waive malpractice, for the client need only hire the second lawyer to perform the task and this second lawyer will not request a waiver in advance of malpractice liability.

However, the typical case to which this rule applies would likely not involve individual clients. Rather, it would involve corporations represented by their own inside counsel. When inside counsel hires outside counsel on behalf of the corporation, the corporation might find it reasonable to waive malpractice liability in some instances. Rule 1.8(h) would allow that prospective waiver because the client (the corporation) is separately represented by its own inside counsel.

The corporation, for example, may wish to hire the outside counsel to perform a specific, limited task, such as drafting a particular contract. The outside lawyer may argue that he has to perform an extensive overview of the problem and independently evaluate the tax implications before he can be certain that the contract can competently be written in that limited way. The corporation, to limit its legal costs, can assure the lawyer that everything is in order and that the lawyer should only perform a specific legal task and not be worried about malpractice liability for not investigating the tax implications of the contract.

Or, the corporation may hire an outside lawyer and retain her to draft a contract based on certain legal research that the in-house counsel has already prepared. The outside lawyer may be concerned that she should not rely on legal research that was prepared by someone who did not work under her supervision. Once again the in-house counsel can allay her fears by advising the corporation to waive any malpractice claims it has against the outside lawyer for relying on the legal research prepared by the corporation's in-house legal staff.

May a client agree in advance to arbitrate disputes with a lawyer? May the lawyer, in other words, ask the client to waive a judicial forum for a future malpractice claim? The general rule is that arbitration agreements are not in conflict with the prohibition on advance waivers of malpractice liability. The arbitration agreement simply provides a different forum to determine if there is liability and, if there is, what the remedy should be. Arbitration goes to remedy, not to the right to find liability. Thus, a lawyer dealing with a new client may propose an arbitration clause as part of the retainer agreement without violating any fiduciary obligations.

The restriction on the lawyer's ability to reduce his malpractice liability is limited to cases regarding his personal incompetence. Thus, a lawyer in a professional legal corporation may limit his vicarious liability for the malpractice of his associates, if other applicable law permits, i.e., if a statute or regulation or provision other than the ethics rules permits the lawyer to limit his imputed liability. ABA Formal Opinion 96–401 (Aug. 2, 1996). Otherwise, the normal tort rule is that a partner in a partnership is vicariously liable for the negligence of his or her partners and (via *respondeat superior*) associates.

The ABA has developed Model Rules for Fee Arbitration (Feb. 23, 1995). These Rules provide that proceedings are normally confidential, thus protecting client confidences. If the client requests arbitration, then the program makes the arbitration mandatory for the lawyer. If the lawyer petitions for arbitration, it does not proceed unless the client files a written consent within 30 days of service.

B. Subsequent Limitations of Liability

Let us say that a current or former client ("Disgruntled Client") has filed, or contemplates filing, a malpractice claim against his attorney (Attorney). If a separate, independent lawyer does not already represent Disgruntled Client on this claim, Rule 1.8(h) requires Attorney to advise Disgruntled Client that independent representation is appropriate. Unless Attorney provides such advice, Attorney may not settle the dispute with Disgruntled Client. The Rules specify that the lawyer's advice regarding the appropriateness of independent representation must be in writing. Even if Disgruntled Client is also a member of the State Bar, Rule 1.8(h)(2) requires the lawyer to advise the client to see the advice of independent legal counsel. *Connor v. Statewide Grievance Committee* (Conn.Super.2002)(unpublished). It is not necessary that Disgruntled Client that hire independent counsel, only that Attorney advise him of that right.

In some cases, if a lawyer sues a client for unpaid fees, the client counter sues for malpractice. A lawyer can ethically settle the fee claim and, at the same time, insist upon a waiver of what is often seen as a frivolous malpractice charge, *if* the client is advised that independent counsel should be obtained prior to negotiating such a settlement or release. Rule 1.8(h)(2). A client simply threatening such a countersuit may choose not to consult with a new lawyer, of course, but that is his decision.

9. Lawyers Related by Blood or Marriage

Assume that Lawyer *A* represents *P* who is suing *D*. Lawyer *B* represents *D*. Conflicts of interest may arise if Lawyers *A* and *B*—practicing law in different firms—are married to each other, or are related as parent, child, or sibling.

Until the 2002 revisions, the Model Rules had an explicit provision prohibiting such representations unless the client consents. See former Rule 1.8(h)(i). The 2002 revisions eliminated this prohibition, which was not imputed to the other members of either *A*'s or *B*'s firm.

However, that does not mean that the Model Rules do not address this issue. Instead, we must turn to Rule 1.7, Comment 11, which advises us that there may be problems when lawyers who are closely related by blood or marriage personally represent different clients in the same matter or in a substantially related matter. There might be a significant risk of revealing client confidences, or the lawyer's family relationship may interfere with loyalty and independent professional judgment. The lawyer-wife representing the criminal defendant may be less likely to accuse the lawyer-husband prosecutor of misconduct. This Comment advises that each client is entitled to know of the existence and implications of the relationship between the lawyers before the lawyer agrees to undertake the representation. Normally, a lawyer related to another lawyer, e.g., as parent, child, sibling or spouse, "may not represent a client in a matter where that lawyer is representing another party, unless each client gives informed consent."

But, this Comment advises, the disqualification arising from a close family relationship is "personal" and therefore is ordinarily *not imputed* to members of firms with whom the lawyers are associated. Hence, Lawyer *A* can represent Client *P* even though Lawyer *X* another lawyer) represents Client *D*. Assume that Lawyer *X* is a member of a law firm where Lawyer *B* is a partner or associate and Lawyer *B* is the husband of Lawyer *A*. There is no conflict and so need to secure consent simply because Lawyers *A* and *B* are married.

10. Rule 1.8(i)—Acquiring a Propriety Interest in the Client's Cause of Action

Rule 1.8(i) limits the lawyer's ability to acquire a propriety interest in a client's cause of action or the subject of the litigation. This rule is designed to avoid giving the lawyer an ownership interest in the subject of the representation such that it would be difficult for the lawyer to be discharged by her client. However, two important exceptions serve to limit substantially this restriction. First, lawyers may use liens to secure fees or expenses. Secondly, lawyers may contract with their clients for contingent fees in some civil cases.

A. Liens

First, let us turn to liens. Rule 1.8(i)(1) permits liens that are otherwise authorized by law. There are two basic types of liens, *retaining liens* and *charging liens*. Most states allow a lawyer a retaining lien, which gives the lawyer a possessory interest in the client's papers and funds in the lawyer's possession. She can use this lien to secure payment of her fee. In other words, the lawyer will not return papers and other property of her client that the lawyer possesses if the client has not paid the lawyer. This corresponds to the black letter law in the majority of jurisdictions, to the Restatement of

the Law of Agency, Second, § 464 (1958) and to the
Restatement of Security, First § 62(b)(1941).

On the other hand, the Restatement of the Law
Governing Lawyers adopts the minority view. Restatement of the Law Governing Lawyers, Third,
§§ 36(1), 43 (Official Draft 2000). The position it
embraces is that the lawyer should not acquire a
nonconsensual lien on property in the lawyer's possession or recovered by the client through the lawyer's efforts. As § 43, Comment *b* explains, a
"broad retaining lien could impose pressure on a
client disproportionate to the size or validity of the
lawyer's fee claim." The client and lawyer may
agree that the lawyer should have a security interest in the client's property. Otherwise, the Restatement does not recognize retaining liens on client
property. It argues that the lawyer's use of the
client's papers against the client is at war with the
lawyer's fiduciary responsibility to the client. If the
client does not pay the lawyer for her work in
preparing particular documents, then the Restatement does allow a lawyer to retain "unpaid-for
documents." However, even here, the "lawyer may
not retain unpaid-for documents when doing so will
unreasonably harm the client."

Most states also allow a lawyer a "charging lien."
This lien is non-possessory. It gives a lawyer who
gives notice to the person paying the settlement or
judgment a right to have any recovery in the case
applied to the payment of her fees. After the lawyer
has given her notice, the person or entity paying the
amount in settlement or judgment is liable for the

lawyer's fees if that person pays the amount directly to the client. Typically, the check is made out to
both lawyer and client, to protect the lawyer and
the paying party.

Unless a statutory scheme provides otherwise, the
Restatement articulates two requirements for a valid charging lien. First, the client must have agreed
in writing to the charging lien. Lawyers will often
make this writing part of their standard fee agreements. Second, the third party against whom the
lien will be enforced "must have been afforded
notice of the lien as required by law." Restatement
of the Law Governing Lawyers, Third, § 43 (Official
Draft 2000).

B. Contingency Fees as Proprietary Inter-
ests

Rule 1.8(i)(2) provides that the lawyer may "contract with a client for a reasonable contingent fee in
a civil case." Thus, a lawyer can acquire a proprie-
tary interest in the cause of action or subject matter
of litigation (that is what a contingent fee is, after
all), *but the lawyer's interest in the case cannot be
that of a co-plaintiff.* In other words, the client may
not assign to the attorney part of his cause of action
in a way that would allow the lawyer to prevent
settlement.

For example, assume that Client agrees to compensate Lawyer by giving her a one-fourth interest
in certain real property and mining claims. Ownership of these properties is disputed and Lawyer
defends Client. Client becomes dissatisfied with

Lawyer's services and tries to discharge Lawyer, who refuses to leave. Lawyer has violated the ethics rules by refusing to accept the client's discharge.

Opinion 95 of the District of Columbia Bar (1988) argues that a lawyer who prosecutes a patent application may not take an interest in the patent as security for payment of the fee. Because a patent application is technically "litigation," the Opinion claimed that this arrangement would necessarily constitute taking an interest in the subject matter of litigation. This Opinion seems contrary the contingent fee exception. Rule 1.8(i)(2) allows a lawyer to take a contingent fee in a patent case, as long as it is not excessive under Rule 1.5.

11. Rule 1.8(j)—Sexual Relations with Clients

Lawyers violate their fiduciary obligations to their clients if the lawyer unfairly exploits the fiduciary relationship. During the course of the representation, if the lawyer enters into a sexual relationship with the client that often impairs the lawyer's ability to act competently. The client's consent may not avoid the ethical problem because the lawyer's potential undue influence and the client's emotional vulnerability serve to vitiate meaningful consent. Hence, Rule 1.8(j) prohibits a sexual relationship with a client unless a consensual sexual relationship existed before the client-lawyer relationship began.

A sexual relationship between client and lawyer involves: (1) a potential abuse of the fiduciary relationship between that lawyer and a vulnerable client, (2) a loss of emotional distance between the client and lawyer, which can adversely affect the lawyer's need for objective, detached professional judgment, (3) potential conflicts of interest between the lawyer and client, and (4) a confusion between which communications are made in a professional relationship (therefore protected by attorney-client privilege) and which are personal and unprotected.

These problems can be especially pronounced in the context of divorce representation, because a sexual relationship with the client could destroy chances of a reconciliation of the parties. Where property division and child custody are at issue, "the attorney may himself become the focus of the dissolution or custody proceedings, be called as a witness, and thereby inflict great harm on the client." *People v. Zeilinger* (Colo.1991).

This is precisely what happened in *Oklahoma Bar Association v. Downes* (Okla.2005) where an attorney's consensual sexual relationship with a divorce client "added even more hostility to an already acrimonious divorce." When the client's husband learned of the his wife's affair with her attorney, the attorney was put in the position of a potential witness, and withdrew from the representation after failing to comply with discovery requests for admissions concerning his relationship with the client. The court suspended the lawyer for one year for this and other violations.

Rule 1.8, Comment 18 advises that there is less cause for concern if the sexual relationship *predates* the professional relationship, because the lawyer has not abused the unequal lawyer-client relationship to begin the affair. The lawyer should nonetheless consider whether or not his professional judgment will be impaired by the existing relationship, under Rule 1.7(a)(2).

The prudent lawyer should recognize that even if the emotional relationship predates the attorney-client relationship, the sexual partner can always hire a new lawyer: there is no need for the lawyer to represent someone who is also a boyfriend or girlfriend, and because of the lack of emotional detachment, there is always the risk that the lawyer's judgment may be clouded. The lack of emotional detachment that can adversely affect the lawyer's judgment is something that exists whether the emotional relationship predates or postdates the legal-professional relationship.

Comment 19 to the Rule clarifies that, when the client is a corporation or other organization, the prohibition on initiating sexual relations prohibits the attorney (whether he is inside or outside counsel) from beginning a sexual relationship with any "constituent [i.e., employee or other representative] of the organization who supervises, directs or regularly consults with that lawyer concerning the organization's legal matters."

RULE 1.9: DUTIES TO FORMER CLIENTS

1. An Introductory Note on the Distinction Between Rule 1.9 and Rule 1.10

Rule 1.9 governs conflicts that arise out of the fact that a particular lawyer previously represented one client and is now representing a different client in a matter adverse to his former client. Rule 1.9 governs the situation where the lawyer is personally disqualified, *i.e., individually* disqualified. Rule 1.10 focuses on when the law *imputes* an individual's conflicts of interest to other lawyers in that individual's firm. This section analyzes Rule 1.9 while the next section turns to Rule 1.10.

The general tenet of Rule 1.9 is that, unless there is a proper waiver by the client, a lawyer should be disqualified from taking a matter adverse to his former client if the lawyer acquired *confidential* client information from the former client that is *material* to the new representation. Rule 1.9 disqualifies the lawyer if he now represents a person in a matter that is "the same" or "substantially related" to the past representation of another client, and the new client's interests are materially adverse to the interests of the former client. The lawyer, for

195

example, may not switch sides, by (i) defending the criminal defendant at trial and then arguing the appeal on behalf of the state, or (ii) drafting a will for the deceased and then seeking to have the will declared invalid on behalf of a disgruntled heir.

While Rule 1.9 deals with an individual lawyer's disqualifications, Rule 1.10, discussed below, deals with *imputed* disqualification. If one lawyer in a law firm is disqualified, others associated with the affected lawyer may be automatically disqualified. Some disqualifications are imputed and others are not. Rule 1.10 lays out the basic rule regarding imputation.

However, Rule 1.10 always imputes to all members of a law firm all of the disqualifications of Rule 1.9. Thus, Lawyer X may be disqualified because he has actual confidential knowledge about the former client that is material to the present situation. As long as Lawyer X is with a given law firm, that law firm is also disqualified, because of Rule 1.10(a), which governs imputation of conflicts. If Lawyer X (by hypothesis, the only person with confidential knowledge) leaves that law firm, Lawyer X is still disqualified (because of Rule 1.9), but X's former law firm is no longer disqualified, since the only reason the original law firm was disqualified is because of the knowledge of Lawyer X, who is no longer there, as Rule 1.10(b) explains.

2. Rule 1.9(a)

Rule 1.9(a) is fairly straightforward. If a lawyer used to represent a client in a particular matter but no longer does so, that lawyer is still disqualified from representing a new client *in that same matter* if that new client has interests "materially adverse" to the former client. The lawyer, in short, may not switch sides. The lawyer also may not take a matter adverse to the former client if the new matter is "*substantially related*" to the former matter. Only the former client's written informed consent can allow the subsequent representation to take place.

The "substantially related" rule is originally a judicial creation, developed in the leading case of *T.C. Theatre Corp. v. Warner Brothers Pictures, Inc.* (S.D.N.Y.1953).

Rule 1.9 builds on this case and recognizes two distinct interests that must be protected: (1) loyalty and (2) client confidences. As a matter of loyalty, because the lawyer, in the case of *A vs. B*, learned from Client *A* secret or confidential information, that particular lawyer cannot now "switch sides" in the *same* matter and represent Client *B*. Thus, "a lawyer could not properly seek to rescind on behalf of a new client a contract [he had] drafted on behalf of the former client." Rule 1.9, Comment 1.

If the lawyer is involved in a "specific transaction," then switching sides is a direct breach of loyalty, and a conflict exists in the subsequent representation. If the matter is not exactly the same, the lawyer still may not "switch sides" if the matters are "substantially related." Whether the matters are so related is a question of degree.

Thus, if the matter was a "type of problem," the lawyer may represent a new client "in a factually distinct problem of that [general] type even though the subsequent representation involves a position adverse to the prior client." Comment 2. The touchstone, in determining if matters are "substantially related" is—

"if they involve the same transaction or legal dispute or if there otherwise is a *substantial risk that confidential factual information* as would normally have been obtained in the prior representation would materially advance the client's position in the subsequent matter." Rule 1.9, Comment 3 (emphasis added).

Consider this example: Lawyer has represented several auto dealerships over the years in judgment collection matters. However, a year ago she resigned from representing any auto dealerships, although she still practices in the same locality. A debtor now asks her to represent him in a collection matter that one of the lawyer's former auto dealerships is bringing against the debtor. Lawyer, by hypothesis, has stopped representing any of the auto dealerships. Assume that the new collection suit is a matter totally unrelated to his previous employment, i.e., no confidential information learned in the previous representations would be relevant to this case. In this circumstance, her former clients may not prevent the new representation. Lawyer does not have to secure the consent of her former clients.

Information gained through representation sometimes may have a limited shelf life. That is, the length of time between the end of the lawyer's former and current representations may render information obtained in the former representation obsolete and no longer material or relevant. The length of time "may be relevant to determining whether two representations are substantially related." Rule 1.9, Comment 3.

However, mere length is not dispositive if the information is still relevant, and courts have disqualified attorneys from serving as counsel or expert witnesses against former clients when matters were separated by more than ten years. *See, e.g.*, *Brand v. 20th Century Ins. Co.* (Cal.App.2004) (twelve years between matters); *River West, Inc. v. Nickel* (Cal.App.1987) (thirty years between matters). So long as the two matters are substantially related (i.e, the information is still secret and relevant), the mere passage of time will not eliminate a conflict.

3. Rule 1.9(b)

Rule 1.9(b) provides that if the lawyer was with a former law firm, and that firm had previously represented the client in a matter, the lawyer may not ethically represent a new client with interests adverse to the client of the former firm *if* the lawyer had acquired secret information about this former client, *i.e.*, information protected by Rules 1.6 or 1.9(c). The former client can waive his or her rights, but only by informed consent and in writing.

Assume that lawyer Alpha is a member of Firm *#1*. Firm *#1* represents Client *P* in a suit against Client *D*. Alpha herself was not involved in any representation of Client *P*, and Alpha has not acquired any secret or confidential information from Client *P* or from Firm #1 members that is relevant to Client *D*. Alpha now leaves Firm #1 and joins Firm #2, which represents Client *D*. Note that *P*'s and *D*'s interests are materially adverse to each other *and* Firm #2 (Alpha's new firm) is representing *D* in a matter that is the same as (or substantially related to) the matter in which Firm #1 (Alpha's old firm) is representing *P*. Nonetheless, both Firm #2 and Alpha may properly represent *D* against *P* because Alpha acquired from Client *P* no material information protected by Rules 1.6 or 1.9(b).

Now assume the same facts in the previous hypothetical except that Alpha *personally* worked for *P* in the case of *P v. D* while Alpha was with Firm #1. Let us assume that Alpha did not acquire any material client secrets or confidences, but that she did work on that particular case. For example, she filed an appearance in court and asked for a continuance.

Unless the former client consents, Rule 1.9(a) *personally* disqualifies Alpha. Rule 1.9(a) provides that if Alpha formerly represented a client in a matter, she may not thereafter represent another person in the same or a substantially related matter, if that other person's interest is materially adverse to the interest of the former client (unless, or course, the former client consents). This is the very same law suit.

The next question is whether Alpha's disqualification is imputed to the other lawyers in Firm #2. Rule 1.10 is the general rule on imputation, and subsection (a) in principle imputes conflicts under *all* of Rule 1.9, not just Rules 1.9(b) and (c). Thus, it appears that Rule 1.9(a) disqualifies Firm #2, unless the firm obtains a written consent.

It is true that Rule 1.10(a) does have an exception: "unless the prohibition is based on a personal interest of the prohibited lawyer *and* does not present a significant risk of materially limiting" the client's representation by remaining lawyers in the firm. However, "personal" interest refers to matters such as the lawyer's political beliefs, not to the problem of Alpha's disqualification because she earlier represented the adverse party in the "same matter." Rule 1.10, Comment 3.

4. Using Client Information to the Client's Disadvantage

The Rules forbid using client secrets or confidences to the disadvantage of the client. This prohibition applies equally to protect a former client, *unless* the information has become generally known. Rule 1.9(c)(1). A lawyer violates Rule 1.9(c)(1) even if the lawyer does not disclose the information to anyone. What is relevant is that she *uses* the information to the client's detriment.

Suppose that Lawyer learned in confidence that Client is planning to renew the lease on the building that Client now uses. Lawyer then secretly visits Lessor and purchases the lease for Lawyer's own account but does not tell Lessor any Client information. Lawyer plans to raise the rent because she learned, in confidence, that this location is more important to Client than Lessor suspects. Lawyer has committed a disciplinable violation.

This rule is not applicable if the "information is a matter of general knowledge." Restatement of the Law of Agency, Second, § 388, at Comment *c*.

Rule 1.9(c)(2) separately prohibits the lawyer from *revealing* the former client's secrets unless other rules allow or require revealing the information.

5. Waiver

A. Bringing Home to the Client the Significance of the Information Communicated Regarding the Waiver

Rules 1.9(a) and 1.9(b) allow a former client to waive the conflicts of interest. If there is a conflict, an otherwise disqualified lawyer may represent a new client against the former client *if* the former client gives informed consent, confirmed in writing. Rule 1.9(c) allows for waivers as well, as confirmed by Comment 9.

In some cases, a court may conclude that there has been an *implied* waiver of a conflict contemplated by Rule 1.9. For example, the court may refuse to disqualify a lawyer on the grounds that the party waited too long to bring its motion after learning certain facts. A party raising the conflict may play fast and loose with the court—for example, by making a calculation not to raise a conflict until later, so that disqualification of the offending attorney will impose a greater financial burden on the other party. It is not difficult to understand why the court might refuse to disqualify because of *estoppel*, which the court may call an "implied waiver."

On the other hand, a party does not waive a conflict simply because it did not initially grasp the significance of relevant facts. The burden is on lawyers to promptly provide the client all information needed to effectuate a valid waiver. Clients— who are not expected to know the ethics rules governing their lawyers—presume that they can trust their lawyers and former lawyers.

While the client may be aware of certain facts ("I trusted my lawyer with confidential information and now she is no longer representing me but an adverse party"), the client may not understand the significance of those facts (that the lawyer must disqualify herself unless the client voluntarily relinquishes a known right).

B. Prospective Waivers of Rule 1.9 Conflicts

If a former client may waive a conflict, she should also be able to waive her objections *prospectively*, if the prospective waiver meets all the requirements required when the former client grants consent to a present conflict of interest. The lawyer relying on this prospective waiver must show that it "reasonably contemplated" the future conflict so that the client's consent is reasonably viewed as fully informed when he gave it. In other words, the lawyer must give the client (or former client) the information in a way that this client or former client will appreciate the significance of the waiver that is being sought. Otherwise the consent is not "informed."

As one court explained in the course of analyzing the validity of a prospective waiver:

> "future directly adverse litigation against one's present client is a matter of such an entirely different quality and exponentially greater magnitude, and so unusual given the position of trust existing between lawyer and client, that any document intended to grant standing consent for the lawyer to litigate against his own client must identify that *possibility, if not in plain language, at least by irresistible inference including reference to specific parties, the circumstances under which such adverse representation would be undertaken, and all relevant like information*." *Worldspan, L.P. v. The Sabre Group Holdings, Inc.* (N.D.Ga.1998) (emphasis added).

It is unlikely that a court would uphold a waiver that purports to allow disclosure or use of client confidences against the client, unless the client very explicitly agreed to such disclosure or use. In other words, it is much easier for a client to waive, prospectively, a conflict based on loyalty, but it is harder to waive, prospectively, a conflict based on breach of confidences, because a client cannot normally know, at the time of the prospective waiver, what those confidences might be or what their relevance and significance will be at some point in the future. ABA Formal Opinion 05–436 (May 11, 2005).

A client's (or a former client's) prospective consent to his lawyer's representation of another client with adverse interests "does not amount to either consent to breach of confidential disclosure or the use of that information against the consenting party. . . ." Clients endowed with ordinary business sense and experience would not normally agree to such remarkably prejudicial arrangements. We would not expect a former client to "willingly and freely consent" to give to his adversary the "weapons with which to contest, and, possibly defeat, his valuable rights. . . ." *Westinghouse Electric Corp. v. Gulf Oil Corp.* (7th Cir.1978). Even if the lawyer has secured a prospective waiver of conflict, "the attorney must request a second, more specific waiver, 'if the [prospective] waiver letter insufficiently disclosed the nature of the conflict that subsequently arose between the parties.'" *Concat LP v. Unilever, PLC* (N.D.Cal.2004).

If the client validly consents to future conflicts, a material change in circumstances (perhaps caused by the passage of time) may make the consent no longer valid. In that case, the lawyer will have to secure a new informed consent. Restatement of the Law Governing Lawyers, Third, § 122, comment *d*. If the new conflict is not consentable, then the lawyer may not proceed.

RULE 1.10: IMPUTATION OF CONFLICTS OF INTEREST

1. Introduction

The general rule in disqualification cases that if a lawyer is required to decline employment or to withdraw from employment, no partner or associate, or any other lawyer affiliated with him or his firm may accept or continue such employment. One attorney's disqualification is usually imputed to all. And if the lawyer personally disqualified as to a particular case moves to a new firm, his disqualification is usually imputed to all the lawyers of the new firm.

When a client hires a private law firm, it is generally understood that the client expects to benefit from the expertise of the various lawyers in that firm. The client expects loyalty and confidentiality from the entire law firm. Though a client may only deal with a few lawyers in a firm, the client hires "the firm." Partners and associates regularly discuss with each other the affairs of their clients and seek from each other advice regarding client affairs. Such intra-firm communication is one of the reasons for the rule imputing attorney disqualifications.

Model Rule 1.10 lays out the general rule for imputed disqualification. The disqualification bans of Rule 1.10 are more extensive than those provided by Rule 1.11. Rule 1.11, discussed below, deals with the special problems of government lawyers and former government lawyers. See Rule 1.10(d).

The government is subject to different rules because of the special governmental interest in recruiting lawyers not unduly burdened in seeking later private employment because of their former affiliation with the government. Similarly, because of the government's unusually broad legal relationships, it should not be unduly hampered when it recruits a lawyer from the private sector. Other policy reasons also justify this distinction between lawyers in government versus lawyers in private practice. The partners and associates in private law firms and similar private associations of lawyers have an economic incentive to work for the economic good of the entire partnership. The lawyer for the government has no similar financial incentive.

2.   Waiver and "Screening"

Any affected client protected by the principles of Rule 1.10 may waive an imputed disqualification *if* each client consents after consultation, and this consent is confirmed in writing, and each lawyer involved *reasonably* believes that his or her representation will not be adversely affected. Rule 1.10(c).

But if there has been no waiver, and if a lawyer is disqualified and this disqualification is imputed to other members of the firm, Rule 1.10 does not provide for screening as a method of curing the disqualification. See Rule 1.0(k) & Comment 8.

Rule 1.10 (unlike Rule 1.11) nowhere refers to a screen to wall-off the affected lawyer. A client can of course decide to waive on the condition that the law firm institute a screen—sometimes called a "Chinese Wall"—around an affected attorney. But Rule 1.10 by itself does not approve or validate a screen and, in fact, does not provide for the use of a screen as a device to cure a conflict.

The Restatement, of the Law Governing Lawyers, Third, § 124(2) (Official Draft, 2000) has proposed a narrow role for screening. Section 124, titled: "Removing Imputation," provides that a law firm is not disqualified from suing a party simply because a lawyer in that firm learned relevant confidential information about that party when representing that party in an earlier matter, *if* the disqualified lawyer is screened, all parties are given notice of the screening, and "any confidential client information communicated to the personally prohibited lawyer is *unlikely to be significant* in the subsequent matter." (emphasis added).

Thus far, only a few cases have ever referred to section 124(2), and the case law has tended to reject the Restatement's proposed new rule and instead to impute disqualification. Of course, an individual state may decide to change its version of the Model Rules and provide for a screening mechanism. As of 2007, 11 states (Delaware, Illinois, Kentucky, Maryland, Michigan, North Carolina, Oregon, Pennsylvania, Tennessee, Utah and Washington) had adopted rules that permit screening in certain circumstances, typically when a newly associated lawyer has material information. The majority of states' rules do not allow screening, even though a few cases in these states have allowed a firm to overcome an imputed conflict where there is evidence of "effective" screening (e.g., Indiana), or where the parties would be overly prejudiced by imputing the conflict (e.g., Nevada). See *Lennartson v. Anoka–Hennepin Independent School District No. 11* (Minn.2003); Morgan & Rotunda, Selected Standards on Professional Responsibility 165–67 (Foundation Press 2007).

Clearly, the Model Rules do not accept a screen. Several reasons may account for this fact. A trial judge ruling on the disqualification motion cannot normally decide if the prior "confidential client information" is "unlikely to be significant" in the present case unless he knows what that confidential information is. Once the judge is told, the cat is out of the bag, and the matter is no longer confidential. In addition, a judge may not be able to determine if a matter is "unlikely to be significant" unless he knows the full theory of the case, and that might not happen until the trial is nearly over. Even lawyers deeply involved in a case often do not know the full theory until discovery is completed. In addition, the theory of the case changes as the discovery and trial proceeds. Facts that may appear insignificant on the first day of trial take on a new complexion as the case evolves.

When the Restatement uses the phrase, "is unlikely to be significant in the subsequent matter," it is possible to interpret that language to mean, "is irrelevant or immaterial to the subsequent matter." If that is what the Restatement provision means, it means very little, because Rule 1.9(b) already allows a lawyer to represent a party adverse to a former client if the confidential information about the former client is immaterial to the matter. If the lawyer's information is truly immaterial, as Rule 1.9 requires, then even the individual lawyer could handle the matter, because there is nothing from which to screen him: the information is immaterial.

3. Rule 1.10(a): Lawyers Currently Associated in a Firm

A. Defining the "Firm"

Rule 1.10 applies to lawyers associated together in a law "firm," a term intended to encompass not only private law firms but also corporate legal departments and legal service organizations. Because the purpose of this rule is to protect client confidences and client loyalty the definition of "firm" may vary. Rule 1.0(c), defines "firm" or "law firm" to signify a lawyer or lawyers in a law partnership, professional corporation, sole proprietorship or other association, or in a legal services organization or the legal department of a corporation or other organization.

Consider the way the law treats a legal aid office with offices in several locations compared to the differing treatment of a law firm that has offices in several cities. While "firm" includes a legal aid office, it does not *necessarily* include lawyers employed in separate units of the same legal aid organization. Even if public defender lawyers are in the same office, the need to protect confidences of clients is lessened because the lawyers do not have the same financial incentives that lawyers in a private law firm would have to talk about the case. As Rule 1.0, Comment 4 points out: "Depending upon the structure of the [legal aid] organization, the entire organization or different components of it may constitute a firm or firms for purposes of these Rules."

The definition of "firm" for this purpose may also include co-counsel who are not members of the same commercial enterprise but who are representing the same party, *if* co-counsel have exchanged confidential information.

In determining whether two or more lawyers should be treated as a "firm," it is relevant to know if the lawyers have mutual access to information concerning the clients that they serve. Thus, courts have not always disqualified an entire prosecutor's office, and have not treated the government prosecutor's office as one "firm" if care has been taken to make sure that the personally disqualified lawyer with the confidential information is so separated from the other lawyers as to be in another "firm."

Similarly a "law firm" may include lawyers who, in fact and in law, only share office space, but they imply to the public that they are a partnership. If lawyers "present themselves to the public in a way that suggests that they are a firm," then these lawyers are acting *as if* they are partners, and the application of Rule 1.10 is necessary to protect client expectations of loyalty. Rule 1.0, Comment 2.

B. The Ethics Rules Implicated by Rule 1.10(a)

Rule 1.10(a) is the basic imputation rule for lawyers *while* they are currently associated in the same firm. If there is imputation, it exists only while these other lawyers are currently associated in the same firm as the disqualified lawyer. Rule 1.10(a) does *not* impute to all the lawyers in the firm the disqualification of all the other lawyers in the firm. Rather it imputes only those disqualifications specifically mentioned.

Rule 1.10(a) imputes conflicts under all of Rules 1.7 and 1.9. For transactions prohibited by Rule 1.8, that Rule itself resolves the issue of imputation of conflicts. See Rule 1.8(k), which imputes conflicts under Rule 1.8(a) to 1.8(i).

Assume New Client asks Lawyer *A* to sue one of his current clients. Lawyer *A* says: "I am conflicted out, but my partner *B* can help you." If this occurs, then Lawyers *A* and *B* have each violated Rule 1.10(a) because they are practicing law in the same firm, as a single entity.

However, Rule 1.10(a) is *not* applicable to situations where one lawyer—either the one with the actual disqualification, or another lawyer with the imputed disqualification—*leaves the first firm* and joins another firm. Rule 1.10(b) and Rule 1.9 govern those situations. For example, assume that Lawyer *A* leaves the firm and joins a different law firm. When New Client makes the same request, Lawyer *A* says: "I cannot draft the will but my good friend and *former* law partner, Lawyer *B* can." Assuming that no confidences have been shared, lawyers *A* and *B* have not violated Rule 1.10(a) because they are no longer currently associated in the same law firm. See below for a discussion of Rule 1.10(b).

C. Lawyer Temps or Temporaries

A law firm may hire temporary lawyers (sometimes called "law temps") for a specific project expected to last for only a limited period of time, or to meet a short-term staffing need, or to supply a special proficiency on a particular problem. The firm may hire the temporary lawyer either directly or use the services of a placement agency. This lawyer may work on a single matter or on several different matters in the same firm. In addition he may work part-time for one law firm while simultaneously working on other matters for other firms. The use of temporary lawyers raises standard conflicts of interest issues that occur whenever a "law temp" moves to another law firm.

ABA Formal Opinion 88–356 (Dec. 16, 1988) analyzed conflicts issues related to temporary lawyers and concluded that Rules 1.7 and 1.9 should govern. For example, a temporary lawyer, under Rule 1.7, may not personally work simultaneously on matters for clients of different firms if the representation of each is directly adverse to each other. If a temporary lawyer works on a particular matter for a client, that temporary lawyer—just like any other lawyer whose relationship with the law firm is expected to be longer—"represents" that client for purposes of Rule 1.7 and Rule 1.9.

The more difficult question is whether temporary lawyers are "associated" in a "firm" for purposes of the imputed disqualification sections of Rule 1.10. The ethics rules should protect legitimate client expectations, but it is also true that an overly broad disqualification rule would impose significant costs on the law-temp, resulting in a radical curtailment of the opportunity to move from one practice setting to another and of the opportunity of clients to change counsel. A legitimate client expectation is that the ethics rules will protect client secrets, and a prime purpose of the imputation rules in this context (where the law-temp is not in the partnership track, has no special loyalty to any particular law firm, and is not in a situation where other lawyers in the law firm freely discuss matters involving other clients) is also to protect client confidences and secrets.

Consequently, ABA Opinion 88–356 concluded that the answer must be determined by a functional analysis of the facts and circumstances involved:

Ultimately, whether a temporary lawyer is treated as being "associated with a firm" while working on a matter for the firm depends on whether the nature of the relationship is such that the temporary lawyer has access to information relating to the representation of firm clients other than the client on whose matters the lawyer is working and the consequent risk of improper disclosure or misuse of information relating to representation of other clients of the firm.

For example, if the law-temp works on only a single matter for a particular law firm, and does not have access to information relevant to the representation of the law firm's other clients, then the law-temp should not be treated as "associated" with the law firm for purposes of Rule 1.10. The law-temp and the law firm in this case are treated as two separate and independent law firms who temporarily join forces and collaborate on a particular project or case.

On the other hand, if the law-temp worked for several clients while being assigned to the law firm, and appeared to have had access to secret and confidential information of other clients of that law firm, the law-temp will be treated as "associated" with the law firm for purposes of the imputation rule, unless the law firm is able to demonstrate, "through accurate records or otherwise," that the law-temp "had access to information relating to the representation only of certain other clients."

D. Paralegals and Legal Secretaries

Both the case law and Comment 4 to Rule 1.10, *do* allow screening of *non*-lawyers, such as paralegals or secretaries, who move from one law firm to another. Non-lawyers, unlike lawyers, may not fully appreciate or remember the significance of knowledge that they may have picked up in the prior law firm. Thus, a law firm will not be disqualified if the new law firm carefully screens the non-lawyer who had been exposed to relevant secrets while working in the prior law firm. This rule should apply to third year law students or law school graduates who are not yet admitted to practice.

E. The "of Counsel" Relationship

Sometimes a lawyer not in a law firm will work on a brief with that law firm and then be designated "of counsel" on that brief. When this term, "of counsel," is used in a circumstance to signify only that there is a relationship for a particular case, most (but not all) jurisdictions rule that the designation does not require any imputed disqualification under Rule 1.10. ABA Formal Opinion 90–357 (May 10, 1990).

In other circumstances, a law firm will use the "of counsel" designation—or similar ones, such as "special counsel," "tax counsel," "senior counsel," etc.—in its general announcements, letterheads, office signs, and so forth. The person so designated is neither a "partner" (with the shared liability and managerial responsibility that is implied by the term "partner" or "principal"), nor is the person an "associate" (a salaried non-partner). The "of counsel" may be a lawyer who is retired from the firm but still works on occasion on a particular project, or a retired judge who has associated with the firm and may work part time, or occasionally a probationary partner-to-be. The designation that a lawyer is "of counsel" to a firm typically describes a lawyer having a relationship with the firm, but who does not share directly in the firm's profits.

In legal circles, the use of the "of counsel" appellation in such circumstances implies to the world that there is some sort of on-going, general relationship. Consequently, this type of "of counsel" lawyer is treated as "associated" for purposes of imputed disqualifications. If one lawyer is "of counsel" to two different law firms, that lawyer and both law firms are treated as one firm for purposes of imputed disqualification.

Some courts have rejected the argument that the mere title "of counsel" should demand imputed disqualification; the issue is what the relationship is in fact. *Hempstead Video, Inc. v. Incorporated Village of Valley Stream* (2d Cir.2005) argued that a per se approach ignores the variation in relationships included under the "of counsel" label. The court adopted a functional approach that examines "the substance of the relationship under review and the procedures in place" to guard against possible conflicts. The closer and broader the relationship between the firm and the "of counsel," the more likely it is that the court will impute the attorney's conflicts to the entire firm. The lawyer in question assumed the title "of counsel" and began to share a limited number of clients with a law firm. However, in all other respects, the first lawyer continued to operate a separate firm in the same manner he had before acquiring the new title. The court held that this relationship did not require disqualification of the law firm in that case.

4. Rule 1.10(b): Imputed Disqualification When a Lawyer Leaves the Firm

A basic principle of the Model Rules is that *imputed knowledge is not re-imputed to another lawyer*. In other words, the general rule is that the actual knowledge of one lawyer is imputed to all the lawyers in his firm. However, if one of those other lawyers—the one with imputed knowledge but no actual knowledge—leaves the law firm, he does not carry with him the imputed knowledge, only his actual knowledge, so no one in his new firm would share his imputed knowledge.

Assume, for example, that Lawyer *#1* represents Client *P* in a *P v. D*. In that situation, the conflicts rules provide that no lawyer at the firm where Lawyer *#1* works is allowed to represent *D*, because all of Lawyer *#1*'s knowledge about Client *P* is imputed to every other lawyer in the same firm. Such a representation would breach Lawyer *#1*'s duty to *P*. Similarly, no member of *#1*'s firm could represent *D* because of the firm's duty of loyalty to *P*.

Assume now that Lawyer *#2,* a partner or associate in Lawyer *#1*'s firm, leaves that firm and joins another firm to represent *D*. Lawyer *#2*'s representation of *D* against *P* does not breach *P*'s expectation of loyalty from Lawyer *#1* or Lawyer *#1*'s firm. Neither Lawyer *#1* nor any lawyer in Lawyer *#1*'s law firm is adverse to *P*. If the duty of loyalty would prevent Lawyer *#2* [who is now in a different law firm] from litigating against *P*, then no lawyer could ever represent a client against a former client, yet we know otherwise from Rule 1.9.

On the other hand, if Lawyer *#2* had personally acquired any confidential knowledge about *P* that would be helpful to *D*, then Lawyer *#2*'s representation of *D* would be improper because it would violate Lawyer *#2*'s duty under Rule 1.6 to safeguard client information. Lawyer #2 would be personally disqualified in that case, and that disqualification would be imputed to his new law firm.

Rule 1.10(b) governs the extent to which Firm *#1* is still disqualified from handling a matter when Lawyer Alpha (the cause of the initial disqualification) has left Firm *#1*. Rule 1.10(b) states that, once Lawyer Alpha (by hypothesis, the only personally disqualified lawyer) leaves Firm *#1,* Firm *#1* may then represent clients materially adverse to Firm *#1*'s former clients who had been represented by Alpha when she was with Firm *#1*. This rule applies *unless both* the following two conditions exist: the matter involved is the same as (or substantially related to) the matter in which Alpha (the formerly associated lawyer) had represented the former client *and* at least one of the lawyers still with Firm *#1* has knowledge of the former client's material secrets or confidences.

Assume that Alpha was the only lawyer in Firm *#1* who handled any of a client's ("Client *#1*") affairs; when Alpha left Firm *#1* she took with her both her Client *#1*, and all confidential information relating to Client *#1*. If those are the facts, then there is no need to preclude Firm *#1* from taking matters adverse to that Client *#1* (the law firm's *former* client). Firm *#1* would not be breaching any loyalty it owes to Client *#1* (Lawyer Alpha's Client), because Client *#1* is no longer a present client of Firm *#1* but a former one. And Firm *#1* would not be violating any obligations it has to keep secret any confidential information relating to the firm's former client, because the only person who has that information is Lawyer Alpha, and she is no longer with the law firm.

The application of Rule 1.10 and similar rules therefore often turns on the question whether a lawyer had acquired material client information protected as client confidences or secrets. Rule 1.0, Comment 6 advises that, "in the absence of information to the contrary, it should be inferred that such a lawyer in fact is privy to information about the clients actually served but not those of other clients. In such an inquiry, the burden of proof should rest upon the firm whose disqualification is sought."

The law firm thus has the burden of demonstrating that it is *not* the depository of material protected client information. It is often difficult to prove a negative, but that does not mean that the firm cannot meet this burden. The lawyers can simply testify that they were not privy to the information. The party seeking disqualification may not be comforted by this testimony, for he may suspect that the lawyers are not being entirely candid to avoid a conflict.

5.   Sanctions

If an attorney is involved in a conflict of interest, he or she is subject to several sanctions. FIRST, the lawyer may be subject to **professional discipline**. The decision of a court to refuse to disqualify a lawyer does not preclude discipline, because the court may have only concluded that the conflict of interest did not affect or taint the fact-finding process. The ethical violation remains.

In practice, discipline is not the most frequently used sanction, because private parties seek, and the courts often impose, other remedies, discussed below. These remedies potentially apply to disqualifications under Rules 1.7, 1.8, 1.9, 1.10, 1.11, and Rule 1.12.

SECOND, if an attorney violates one of the disciplinable rules relating to conflicts of interest, and if that violation causes damage to the client, the lawyer may also be liable for **damages for the tort of malpractice**.

THIRD, attorneys involved in conflicts may also be subject to **fee forfeiture**. Judge Learned Hand noted in *Silbiger v. Prudence Bonds Corp.* (2d Cir. 1950): "[B]y the beginning of the Seventeenth Century it had become a common-place that an attorney must not represent opposed interests; and the usual consequence has been that he is disbarred from receiving any fee from either, no matter how successful his labors."

FOURTH, **disqualification** is a common remedy for conflicts of interest that occur in the course of litigation. The court may disqualify the attorney from further representation in that litigation, *if* the conflict is such that it may taint the fact-finding process. The Model Rules, once the state court adopts them as law, are like the Rules of Civil Procedure or the Rules of Evidence. They govern the lawyers appearing before the court, which should not allow a lawyer to appear before it and represent a client in defiance of the court's own rules when that appearance will taint the trial.

For procedural reasons, federal district judges today have broad discretion to disqualify, or not to disqualify as they see fit. While the U.S. Supreme Court is properly concerned about conflicts among the circuits, and will typically grant review to resolve such a conflict, a conflict among district courts in attorney disqualification cases is now standard operating procedure, ever since the U.S. Supreme Court ruled that a trial court's order *denying* disqualification motions is not immediately appealable. *Firestone Tire & Rubber Co. v. Risjord* (S.Ct.1981) (under 28 U.S.C.A. § 1291). Later the Court also concluded that order *granting* disqualification motion is not immediately appealable. *Richardson–Merrell, Inc. v. Koller* (S.Ct.1985). Hence, the federal appellate courts rarely rule on the trial judge's decision to disqualify or to refuse to disqualify. In contrast, some state courts allow such motions on appeal. And, some federal courts are more generous than others in allowing *mandamus* to be used as a way of reviewing the issue on appeal.

This relative dearth of appellate court precedent is significant, because it gives greater prerogative and freedom to a judge faced with a motion to disqualify a law firm. In the meantime, law firms and their clients are subjected to expensive litigation, with little hope for appeal as of right. Lawyers who are very ethical do not want to go near the line that separates ethical behavior from unethical behavior. Disqualified lawyers lose their clients for that particular case, and—depending on the client's reactions—perhaps for others as well. In addition, ethical lawyers are reluctant to risk soiling their reputation by being disqualified.

The vague conflicts test and the non-appealability of the courts' orders involving disqualification are two factors that serve to give a competitive advantage to the less ethical lawyer, one who is willing to play the lower-court lottery. The risk of being disqualified is tempered by the reality that the lawyer who turns down business because of possible disqualification will lose the client for sure, while the lawyer who takes the doubtful case might, after all, not be disqualified.

Vague rules mean that some judges do not disqualify when they should, which gives a competitive advantage to lawyers who are willing to go to the edge of the ethical line (and occasionally cross it). We live in a world where law firms anxious to avoid conflicts of interest find they are handicapped and penalized compared to ethically-challenged firms.

RULE 1.11: SPECIAL CONFLICTS OF INTEREST FOR FORMER AND CURRENT GOVERNMENT OFFICERS AND EMPLOYEES

1. Introduction to the Ethics Rules Governing "The Revolving Door" Between the Lawyer Moving Between Government Service and Private Practice

Model Rule 1.10 is the basic rule dealing with imputing the conflicts of one lawyer in a law firm to other lawyers in the same firm. Before the 2002 revisions, this Rule defined "firm" as denoting lawyers in a "private firm." Rule 1.10, former Comment 1. The 2002 revisions struck the word "private." However, Rule 1.10(d) now provides explicitly that the "disqualification of lawyers associated in a firm with former or current government lawyers is governed by Rule 1.11."

Model Rule 1.11 deals with what is often called the "revolving door" of lawyers who move between private practice and government service. The goal of the ethics rules in this area is to limit potential abuses—*e.g.*, the risk of improper use of confidential government information or the risk that the government lawyer might use that position to benefit a future private employer—without unduly restricting the ability of the government to attract lawyers.

Rule 1.11 is nuanced and does not simply forbid the revolving door because there are public benefits, within limits, to having this door revolve. For one thing, if lawyers who worked for government could not leave for private practice, then the decision to enter government service would be irreversible, which would greatly hinder government recruitment. Rule 1.11, Comment 4. In addition, when government lawyers leave government for the private sector, they take with them their expertise and mindset, which should help enforcement efforts. Thus, the lawyer who formerly worked for the SEC thoroughly understands the need to prevent securities fraud when she drafts offering memoranda in the private sector. And the lawyers who enter government service from the private sector should carry with them an understanding of how that sector works, which should aid the government lawyers in doing their job to police the private sector.

There was no general provision of the former Model Code dealing with this issue. Instead, case law and ethics opinions derived rules from more general provisions in the Model Code. Rule 1.11 both builds on, and helps codify the prior law. Also, it adds several additional, distinct requirements.

2. The Government Lawyer Moving Into Private Practice

A. General

In analyzing the revolving door between government work and private employment, let us distinguish the situation where the lawyer remains in private practice and simply has, as one of her clients, a government agency. ABA Formal Opinion 342 (Nov. 24, 1975) explains that "private employment" means work "as a private practitioner." If a lawyer remains in private practice and accepts, as one of her clients, a government agency, that lawyer is accepting *private* employment from the government agency. In this case, the lawyer in private practice would have various clients, including the government agency.

Sometimes the private lawyer represents the government agency on a contingent fee arrangement, like those who represented various state governments suing tobacco companies. The lawyer remains in private practice while representing various private clients, including one or more governments or governmental agencies. For another example, see *General Motors Corp. v. City of New York* (2d Cir. 1974), where the private lawyer accepted an antitrust contingent fee case from New York City.

Even if the government pays the lawyer's entire salary, a lawyer may be in private practice. For example, public defenders do not work on behalf of the government when they represent criminal defendants. The defendant whom the public defender represents is the client; the government is merely paying for the services. See Rules 1.8(f) and 5.4(c), governing third-party payers.

A lawyer may be a full time employee of a government agency who then shifts jobs and works for a different agency. Assume that another government agency recruits a lawyer to change jobs. It "may be appropriate to treat that second agency as another client for purposes of this Rule," thus treating the shift in jobs as if the lawyer moved to the private sector. Rule 1.11, Comment 5. A typical example would be when the lawyer moves from a federal government agency to a state government agency. Rule 1.11, Comment 5.

However, the new agency does not have to screen the lawyer because, as Rule 1.11(d), Comment 5 advises, the lawyer is a salaried, full time employee, so there is less of a risk that she will abuse her government office for private gain merely because she moves from one salaried government position to another salaried government position. In contrast, Rule 1.11(b) requires the private law firm to screen.

Next, let us consider the meaning of the term *matter*. Rule 1.11(e) defines "matter." This term generally refers to "a discrete and distinct transaction or set of transactions between identifiable parties" ABA Formal Opinion 342 (Nov. 24, 1975). If two situations involve the same parties and the same facts, they very likely will be considered the "same matter."

For instance, Lawyer A might represent Government in a suit against Widget, Inc. for a strip-mining violation. Then Lawyer A leaves Government and represents Widget, Inc. in its defense of this suit. Or, Lawyer A, who used to represent the Government against Widget, now represents a class action plaintiff suing Widget for pollution damage growing out of the same facts. These law suits involve the same "matter" because they involve litigation and specific parties.

By contrast, consider the case where Lawyer B is counsel to a congressional committee. Lawyer B helps the committee draft a new law governing the coal industry and establishing requirements for returning land back to its natural form after strip mining. He then leaves the congressional committee and begins work for Coal Co., Inc. on cases involving the issue of strip-mining. The two situations are not the same "matter" because there is no discrete transaction between identifiable parties in a particular situation. Drafting a law for the government, or drafting general agency regulations, or engaging in policy making does not disqualify a lawyer from later private employment involving the same area of law—even if that later employment entails contesting the government's current interpretation of that law. Similarly, Rule 1.11 does not disqualify a lawyer who worked for a government claims administration agency from later representing private parties who have claims before the agency, except in connection with a *particular* claim that the lawyer personally and substantially handled while she was a government lawyer.

In deciding whether two particular matters are the same, "the lawyer should consider the extent to which the matters involve the same basic facts, the same or related parties, and the time elapsed." Rule 1.11, Comment 10.

A government lawyer does not participate *personally and substantially* in a matter if he only gives perfunctory approval or disapproval. "Personal" and "substantial" in Rule 1.11 are narrower concepts than "represented," in Rule 1.9. Consequently, Rule 1.9(a) and Rule 1.9(c) more readily disqualify a private lawyer moving from one private firm to another private firm than Rule 1.11 will disqualify a private lawyer moving from the government to a private law firm. For example, if a government lawyer merely enters an appearance on behalf of the government, he has "represented" the government, but he was not participating "personally and substantially" for purposes of Rule 1.11.

The term, *public officer or employee*, in Rule 1.11(a), encompasses every capacity in which the government employs the lawyer. It is not necessary that the government employ the government official in his capacity as a lawyer. The lawyer might be a policy adviser to the President, or the administrative head of an agency. Model Rule 1.11 still governs.

B. Imputation, Waiver, and Screening of Conflicts

Model Rule 1.11 and ABA Formal Opinion 342 (Nov. 24, 1975) both conclude that there is no pressing need to always impute a former government lawyer's disqualification. An inflexible rule would restrict government recruitment and limit a client's choice of lawyers. If a lawyer participated in a matter "personally and substantially" as a public officer or employee, that lawyer is *personally* disqualified from representing another client in connection with that matter, unless the government agency gives its "informed consent," "confirmed in writing." Rule 1.11(a)(2).

However, Rule 1.11(b) makes clear that this lawyer's personal disqualification is *not* imputed to the former government lawyer's new law firm, if *and only if* the disqualified lawyer [1] is "timely screened" from any participation in the matter; [2] is apportioned no part of the fee from this particular matter, and [3] gives prompt, written notice to the agency so that it can assure itself that the lawyer has complied with Rule 1.11. In that way, the government agency can assure itself that the screen is effective and opaque.

What is a "screen"? Rule 1.0(k) defines "screening" as the "isolation of a lawyer from any participation in a matter through the timely imposition of procedures within a firm that are reasonably adequate under the circumstances to protect information that the isolated lawyer is obligated to protect under these Rules or other law."

In order for the screen to be effective, i.e., opaque and not translucent, the screened lawyer must not communicate with any other lawyers in the firm with respect to the matter. And the firm must inform the other lawyers so that they know that they may not communicate with the personally disqualified lawyer with respect to the matter that is the subject of the screen. The prudent firm will confirm all of this in writing and give written instructions to those involved. With the advent of computers it is easy to deny the screened lawyer access to any screened material by use of computer passwords. The firm should also periodically remind the screened lawyer and all other firm personnel because memories may be short and the firm will be hiring new lawyers from time to time.

Rule 1.11(b)(2) requires the lawyer to notify the relevant agency of the conflict and the screen, the Rule does not impose any requirement that notice be given to any adverse *private party* to enable it to ascertain that there has been compliance with this Rule.

The screened lawyer must be "apportioned no part of the fee" from the disqualifying matter. This provision is much less restrictive than it first appears, because it does not prohibit the screened lawyer from receiving a salary or partnership share established by prior independent agreement. The phrase "apportioned no part of the fee" means only that the "lawyer may not receive compensation directly relating the lawyer's compensation to the fee in the matter in which the lawyer is disqualified." Rule 1.11, Comment 6. The lawyer can continue to receive her basic partnership draw (*e.g.* .5% of all partnership profits) even though those profits will be comprised of receipts from all cases at the firm, including the case from which she was screened. The law firm is *not* required to offer the personally disqualified governmental lawyer .5% of net profits (i.e., all partnership profits *minus* any profits from the particular case in which the lawyer had been screened). However, the law firm may not single out this one case and offer the disqualified lawyer a percentage of that case.

C.   Confidential Governmental Information

Rule 1.11(c) articulates a special rule concerning confidential government information. "Confidential government information" is defined as information obtained pursuant to government authority and not legally available to the public at the time the Rule is applied. If the former government lawyer opposes an adverse third party after leaving government service, Rule 1.11(c) serves to protect that third party by not allowing the former government lawyer to use against that person confidential government information about that person that the lawyer learned during government service.

Thus, a former government lawyer may represent a private party challenging generally applicable agency regulations that the former government lawyer personally helped draft, because drafting those regulations is not a "matter" under Rule 1.11. However, that former government lawyer is still subject to Rule 1.9, and therefore forbidden from using nonpublic confidential information relating to her earlier representation of the government. If her representation of her private client would require her to use this nonpublic government information, she would not be able to represent her private client because of Rule 1.9(c) and Rule 1.11(c), but her firm could take the case as long as it screened her.

D. Negotiating for Private Employment

The lawyer in government service (other than a law clerk) must not negotiate for private employment with a party who is involved in a matter in which the government lawyer is then participating personally and substantially, under Rule 1.11 (d)(ii). This common-sense rule protects the government against indirect corruption and against the moral hazard of an attorney who engages in a half-hearted effort against an adversary of government, all the while bargaining for employment with that adversary.

E. Judicial Law Clerks

Law clerks seeking private post-clerkship employment are treated differently than other former government lawyers. A special provision allows the law clerk to negotiate for employment with a party or lawyer even though the law clerk is personally and substantially involved in the "matter" (i.e., even though the clerk is working on the case being heard by the clerk's judge), but the law clerk must first notify the judge. Rules 1.1(d)(2)(ii); 1.12(b). Many judges have multiple clerks, and the judge may decide to assign the case to another clerk, but the judge need not do so. After all, law clerks are not as powerful as some people may think, or the law clerk may wish. The judge, not the clerk, decides the case.

3. The Private Lawyer Moving Into Government Practice

Just as government lawyers move to private practice, a lawyer in private practice may move to government service. Rule 1.11(d) is the basic rule governing this situation.

The fundamental principle is that a lawyer now working for the government may not participate in a matter unless Rules 1.7 and 1.9 permit. In addition, she may not participate in a matter if, while in private practice, she had "personally and substantially" participated in that matter, unless the appropriate government agency gives its informed written consent to the representation.

The rationale for this rule is easy to understand. If the lawyer had participated "personally and substantially" while in private practice, she is likely to have learned confidential information from the private client, and as we already know she may not use that information to the detriment of the former client. She also should not switch sides in that same matter by now working for the government in a position adverse to her former private client. Moreover, she should not use her position while in public service to give special, inappropriate benefits to her former private client, perhaps by working less diligently for the government on this particular matter.

In the case of the private lawyer moving into government service, the benefits related to *imputed* disqualification are not considered significant enough to justify the burdens associated with it. Consequently, the disqualification imposed on the former private practitioner now in government service is not imputed to any other lawyers within the government. To impute disqualification would place a tremendous cost on the government. If the disqualification were imputed to all the other lawyers in the particular agency or department, like the Department of Justice, it would often be hard for the government to hire a lawyer from private practice because so many other government lawyers would then be disqualified by imputation.

Also, the reward structure in the government is different than the reward structure of private firms, where the disqualification of a lawyer moving from one firm to another is automatically imputed. For example, consider the case of the government lawyer formerly in private practice who knows confidences and secrets of her former client. This lawyer, now working for the government, obviously cannot ethically reveal her former client's secrets to her new colleagues because of Rule 1.6. But her knowledge of these secrets is not imputed to her new colleagues because there is less financial incentive for her to breach the screen that walls her off on this matter from her colleagues. A salaried government lawyer does not have the financial interest in the success of the government's representation that is inherent in private practice.

In criminal cases, which represent a substantial portion of the workload of some government lawyers, the ethical duty of a government lawyer is different than that of a private lawyer. It is often said that the duty of the prosecutor is to seek justice, not merely to convict. The sovereign wins whenever justice is done. The prosecutor in the Perry Mason series should have felt good that he never convicted an innocent defendant whenever Perry Mason was counsel for the defense.

Unlike Rule 1.11(b), Rule 1.11(d) does not require a formal screen. But, screened or not, this new government lawyer must not "participate" in the particular matter, because the government official cannot use the confidential information she acquired while in private practice. See Rule 1.11(d)(1), which specifically incorporates Rules 1.7 and 1.9.

Rule 1.11(d)(2)(i) states that a lawyer may participate in a matter *even though* she had participated in it "personally and substantially while in private practice or nongovernmental employment" *if* the appropriate government agency gives its written consent. This provision does not authorize government agencies to exploit a tremendous advantage by allowing the new government lawyer to tell the other government lawyers the secrets of the first lawyer's former client because Rule 1.11(d)(1) explicitly imposes and incorporates the requirements of Rule 1.9, governing the duties owed to former clients. Rule 1.9 prohibits the lawyer from using the information against the former client unless the former client gives his consent or unless the information has become generally known.

In short, the government lawyer cannot participate personally unless the government consents—to fulfill the requirement of Rule 1.11(d)(2)(ii)—*and* the former client consents—to fulfill the requirement of Rule 1.9(a), (b), and (c).

RULE 1.12: FORMER JUDGE, ARBITRATOR, MEDIATOR OR OTHER THIRD PARTY NEUTRAL

1. Former Judges and Other Third–Party Neutrals

The ABA Model Code of Judicial Conduct applies to sitting judges. For the restrictions on *former* judges, one turns primarily to ABA Model Rule 1.12. A former judge or other third-party may not accept private employment in a matter if she acted in a judicial capacity on the merits of that matter unless all parties agree in writing.

On the other hand, a *partisan* arbitrator—*i.e.,* the partisan member of a multimember arbitration panel—is not disqualified from later representing *that same party* to the arbitration because that type of arbitrator did not serve, in that matter, as an impartial decision-maker. Rule 1.12 governs third-party *neutrals*, and the *partisan* arbitrator is not neutral.

The general rule requiring disqualification of former adjudicative officers is for the protection of the parties. Consequently, they may knowingly waive this protection.

Similarly, the disqualification of a former judge is *not* imputed to any other lawyer in the former judge's new law firm *if* two conditions exist: first, the former judge is screened from the disqualifying matter and apportioned no part of the fee from it; second, the law firm promptly gives written notice to the appropriate tribunal so that it can determine that the screening is adequate. This screening and notice provision parallels the rule concerning former government lawyers.

Rule 1.12(a) applies to lawyers who are also acting as judges in a particular matter, such as special masters, part-time judges, hearing officers or any other "adjudicative officer." Comment 1. This Rule also includes mediators or any other "third-party neutral." Comment 3. If the Rule had treated such adjudicative officers or third-party neutrals as a lawyer for a party, then Rule 1.10 would impute the adjudicative officer's disqualification (or the third-party neutral's disqualification) to all the members of the law firm. However, because Rule 1.12(b) applies, that adjudicative officer's work (or the third-party neutral's work on a matter) only disqualifies her but does not disqualify the firm if the law firm institutes a timely screen and otherwise complies with Rule 1.12(c). Comments 3, 4.

2. Law Clerks

If a judge's *law clerk* "personally and substantially" participated with the judge on the case, then that law clerk is also disqualified from later representing anyone in the same matter. Rule 1.12(a).

The judge's law clerk may, as we have seen, negotiate for employment with a party or attorney involved in a matter—even though the clerk is participating personally and substantially on that matter—so long as the clerk notifies the judge beforehand. Law clerks seeking private employment are treated differently than other former government lawyers. Rule 1.12(b).

RULE 1.13: THE ORGANIZATION AS A CLIENT

1. Introduction

A lawyer may represent an entity such as a corporation, an unincorporated association, a partnership, a union or a government agency. In such cases, EC 5–18 of the former Model Code of Professional Responsibility provided that the lawyer owes his or her allegiance to the incorporeal entity and not to any "stockholder, director, officer, employee, representative, or other person connected with the entity." Unfortunately, the Model Code did not offer further direction in applying this entity theory. ABA Model Rule 1.13 goes beyond the Model Code by elaborating on the entity theory and offering more concrete guidance.

The lawyer may well represent an incorporeal "entity," but of course this entity can only act through people, *i.e.*, through officers and other duly authorized agents. If a competitor sues a corporate client alleging an antitrust violation, it is easy to conclude that the corporate lawyer does not represent a shareholder of the corporation. Rather, the lawyer represents the corporation as an entity. But what of other, more difficult cases—where, say, shareholders of the corporation sue "derivatively," alleging that the directors have poorly performed their legal obligations? What a corporation asks the lawyer to defend it from a hostile takeover, which may arguably be in the best interests of shareholders? What are the ethical obligations of a corporate lawyer who discovers that one of the officers of the corporation is violating a law (*e.g.*, engaging in price-fixing)? This violation, which is imputed to the entity through *respondeat superior*, in a sense, "benefits" shareholders but *only if* it is not detected.

Rule 1.13 sets up what is basically an "exhaustion of internal remedies" requirement. It provides guidance as to when a lawyer must climb up the corporate ladder (or the chain of command of any other legal entity) in order to adequately advise the entity and determine what it really "wants" to do. Once the lawyer determines what the entity really wants to do, other Rules determine the manner in which the lawyer will proceed. In other words, Rule 1.13 is in addition to and does not replace Rules 1.6 (Confidentiality of Information); 1.7, 1.8, 1.9, 1.10, 1.11 (Conflicts of Interest); 1.16 (Withdrawal); 3.3 (Candor Towards the Tribunal); and 4.1 (Truthfulness to Others).

Rule 1.13(b) provides that if the lawyer for the entity learns that an agent of the entity is acting (or refusing to act) in a matter that is "related to the representation," *and that is:*

[1] a violation of a legal obligation to the organization, *or* [2] a violation of law that reasonably might be imputed to the organization, *and* [3] is likely to result in substantial injury to the organization,

then the lawyer shall proceed as is reasonably necessary in the best interest of the organization. (emphasis added).

Before determining what is in the "best interest" of the entity, it is useful to point out two significant ambiguities in this subsection.

First, it is unclear whether the requirement of "substantial injury to the organization" means substantial "if discovered."

Assume, for example, that a corporate lawyer discovers that a corporate officer is engaging in price-fixing on behalf of the corporation. Assume that if the agent's criminal actions are discovered, the violation of law will be imputed to the corporation and will result in substantial treble damages. On the other hand, if the violation is never discovered, the corporation will reap higher profits from price-fixing.

It is unclear how Rule 1.13(b) is intended to apply in this situation. It makes more sense to interpret this Rule to mean that the subsection applies if the cost of the behavior to the company is "substantial" *assuming* the crime is discovered. An alternative interpretation—which the sentence structure does not grammatically disallow—would reward constituents of the entity if they were successful in hiding illegal activity, and encourage lawyers to be ignorant, to "see no evil." That approach, however, is contrary to the premise of Rule 1.13 and to the lawyer's basic role as a vital component in furthering respect for the Rule of Law. If, for example, the entity really "wants" to commit a crime (*e.g.*, price-fixing) then the attorney may resign pursuant to Rule 1.13(d) or take other action pursuant to other applicable rules. The lawyer should not, ostrich-like, stick his head in the sand.

A second interpretive question surrounds the meaning of the term "substantial". If a violation of law imputed to the organization is a crime, but the criminal penalties are relatively minor, is the violation "substantial" simply because it is a crime? If all criminal violations are "substantial," the lawyer would have no choice but to demand reconsideration of the choice of a corporate employee to engage in speeding while on corporate business, or to take this decision to a higher authority within the organization. If the highest authority refuses to comply with the law, the lawyer would have to consider withdrawal under Rule 1.13(c). In contrast, if a penalty is minor and therefore insubstantial, then the decision to speed may be a judgment call to be left in the hands of those empowered to make such judgments for the organization.

Some violations, though technically "criminal," may result in very minor penalties that reflect society's toleration. A hardware store may violate a Sunday closing law (a so-called blue law), but the jurisdiction might provide that the criminal fine is only $20 per violation, and each day that the store is open is counted as only one violation. In that circumstance, whether the law calls this penalty a civil charge or a criminal fine, its imposition would result in no substantial injury to the entity. By contrast, if an officer of a corporation engages in price-fixing on behalf of the corporation and if the price-fixing is discovered, the violation of law will be imputed to the corporation and likely result in substantial treble damages. Or, assume that the entity is developing a product that officers know does not comply with certain federal safety guidelines. While the criminal penalties are minor (assuming the violation is discovered), the risk of class action tort suits and punitive damages may be substantial (assuming that the violation is discovered).

While Rule 1.13(b) does not clearly explain how it should apply in this situation, it makes more sense to limit the Rule to "substantial", i.e., significant and potentially damaging, violations, whether the violation is civil or criminal.

Rule 1.13 obligates the attorney to find out what the entity really wants. If the entity "wants" to engage in a crime, then the attorney may resign or take other action pursuant to other applicable rules. Similarly, if the entity really "wants" to engage in a course of conduct that, while legal, is "likely to result in substantial [tort] injury to the organization, the lawyer may [but is not required to] resign in accordance with Rule 1.16."

Once the lawyer meets the requirements of Rule 1.13(b), he should proceed in the "best interest" of the entity. The lawyer must weigh the seriousness and consequences of the violation, the scope and nature of the lawyer's representation, the entity's responsibility, the apparent motivation of the person involved, the organization's policies concerning such matters, and anything else deemed relevant.

Depending on how the lawyer weighs such considerations, the lawyer may decide to (1) ask that the matter be reconsidered; (2) advise that a separate legal opinion be sought to present to the organization's appropriate authority; or (3) refer the matter to a higher authority. If the highest authority of the organization (*e.g.*, the board of directors if the entity is a corporation) engages in action (or inaction) that is "clearly a violation of law *and* is likely to result in substantial injury to the organization" then the lawyer may resign, following the requirements of Rule 1.16.

2. Actual or Apparent Representation of the Organization and One or More of Its Constituents

Occasionally the lawyer representing the organization also will have a relationship with the entity's employees, who may believe that the lawyer also represents their interests. The lawyer should clarify his role and must explain the identity of the client if it is apparent that the organization's interests are adverse to those people with whom the lawyer is dealing. The lawyer may represent both the organization and one or more of its constituents if the normal requirements of knowing consent are met, and the potential conflict can be waived. The organization's consent should be given by an "appropriate" person representing the organization "other than the individual who is to be represented, or [it may be given] by the shareholders." Rule 1.13(e). One might have to turn to other bodies of law, such as corporate law, to determine who that official is: the President, the Chair of the Board of Directors or perhaps the entire Board.

Substantive law in some states treat partnerships as "aggregates" of individuals, while other states consider partnerships as "entities." The ethical rules do not rely on partnership law distinctions. Whether a partnership is an entity or an aggregate for purposes of partnership law, all partnerships are "entities" for purposes of the law of legal ethics. If the rule were otherwise, and the default rule were that a lawyer for a partnership treats the partnership as an aggregate for ethics purposes and thus represents each of the members of a partnership, then that lawyer would be in a conflict whenever a partner of the partnership sued the partnership, because the lawyer for the partnership would automatically be treated as representing the partnership and each of its members, including the partner who is suing the partnership.

Consequently, Rule 1.13 explicitly provides that it applies to unincorporated associations. A partnership, after all, has its own legal rights and obligations. It can enter into contracts and sue in its

own name. It may have objectives that are different
than those of some of its members. The lawyer is
the agent of the partnership and may even represent the partnership in a dispute with one or more
of the individual partners. In general, the lawyer
representing a partnership represents the entity
rather than the individual partners *unless the specific circumstances dictate otherwise.*

In determining whether there is an attorney-
client relationship between the partnership lawyer
and one or more individual partners, one relevant
factor is whether the lawyer led that partner to
believe that the lawyer was working for him.
Whether the individual partner retained his own
lawyer on the matter, and whether there was evidence the individual partner relied on the lawyer as
his or her separate counsel, are also relevant.

3. Representing Trade Associations

The ethics rules also treat trade associations as
"entities." A lawyer who represents a trade association (*e.g.*, the Tobacco Growers' Association, the
American Bar Association, the National Rifle Association), normally represents the "entity," and not
each, any or every individual member of the trade
association. A lawyer, for example, can ethically
represent the American Bar Association while simultaneously representing an automobile accident
victim suing an ABA member following a car wreck.

There may be special circumstances where the
facts indicate that this normal rule does not apply.
Consider *Westinghouse Electric Corp. v. Kerr–*

McGee Corp. (7th Cir.1978). The Chicago office of the law firm of Kirkland & Ellis filed an antitrust action on behalf of its client, Westinghouse, against various corporations alleging price-fixing violations in the uranium industry. Meanwhile, a trade association, the American Petroleum Institute ("AmPI"), hired Kirkland's Washington office to oppose legislative proposals introduced in Congress that would require energy companies to divest uranium companies they owned. As luck would have it, on the very same day that Kirkland's Chicago office (representing Westinghouse) filed this antitrust suit against several corporations, Kirkland's D.C. office released a report that argued that there already was sufficient competition in the oil-uranium industry. Kirkland did not sue AmPI, but several corporations that it did sue on behalf of Westinghouse were members of AmPI.

In connection with the AmPI representation, individual members of AmPI had given confidential information on their uranium assets to Kirkland & Ellis' Washington office, in order to aid that law firm in opposing the threatened legislation. The lawyers for AmPI had promised AmPI members that they would treat this information as confidential, and would not release it either to the general public or to the other members of AmPI. In this case, each of the individual members of AmPI "entertained a reasonable belief that it was submitting confidential information regarding its involvement in the uranium industry to a law firm" that AmPI members thought "was acting in the undivided interest of each company.'' Yet, this information was now in the hands of a law firm that was suing several trade association members from whom the association had obtained the information *after giving a promise of confidentiality*.

The court disqualified Kirkland & Ellis, but not use the rationale that lawyers for a trade association automatically must treat as clients each of the trade association's members. Rather, in this case, the law firm must treat these trade association members as if they were clients because the law firm used its representation of the trade association to acquire information under a promise of confidentiality; this information was relevant to the law suit, and the firm must keep its promise. The court, in effect, concluded that the law firm must be disqualified because it may not use information relating to the representation to disadvantage one from whom it had acquired that information under a promise of confidentiality.

The court never ruled that the law firm had breached its duty to keep information confidential. But, if the law firm has this information, it is disqualified because of the normal rule that does not allow a law firm to sue a former client if it acquired confidential information that is relevant to the present suit. Kerr–McGee was not a former or present client, but it was treated as if it were protected by that principle because of the promise of confidentiality on which it reasonably relied.

4. Derivative Suits

In a derivative suit, shareholders take action (usually, sue a corporate insider) on behalf of the corporation, which is unwilling to take action itself. In such cases the corporation may be aligned as a defendant while other defendants may include corporate officers or directors. May the corporate counsel also defend these other corporate constituents against the claims of the corporate shareholders, or does the lawyer's representation of both the corporation and corporate officers and directors constitute an improper conflict of interests with the corporation? For example, if the shareholder/plaintiffs are successful, the officers and directors may have to pay a money judgment to the corporation. The corporate-defendant then is like a reluctant plaintiff; it benefits from the lawsuit brought against it and the other defendants.

Many derivative actions are a normal incident of an organization's affairs, to be defended by the organization's lawyer like any other suit. However, Rule 1.13, Comment 14 advises that "if the claim involves serious charges of wrongdoing by those in control of the organization, a conflict may arise between the lawyer's duty to the organization and the lawyer's relationship with the board. In those circumstances, Rule 1.7 governs who should represent the directors and the organization."

For example, in *Musheno v. Gensemer* (M.D.Pa. 1995), the plaintiff shareholders moved to disqualify a law firm from continuing its dual representation of the corporation and its board of directors. Relying on Model Rules 1.7 & 1.13, the court disqualified the law firm that represented the board from also representing the corporation. The plaintiffs had alleged that the directors committed fraud by concealing the fact that they exceeded the legal lending limit, and engaged in self-dealing and willful misconduct that was contrary to the corporation's interests and favorable to their own. Also, the court found no evidence that the plaintiffs' claims were "patently frivolous." Thus, the corporation must retain separate, independent counsel.

Contrast *Bell Atlantic Corp. v. Bolger* (3d Cir. 1993). The court agreed that it would have "no hesitation in holding that—except in patently frivolous cases—allegations of directors' fraud, intentional misconduct, or self-dealing require separate counsel." But the court did not require separate counsel: Plaintiffs did not allege self-dealing, stealing, fraud, intentional misconduct, conflicts of interest, or usurpation of corporate opportunities by defendant directors. Moreover, "Bell Atlantic's board charged a special committee along with independent counsel to investigate the shareholder plaintiffs' demands. The special committee and independent counsel found prosecution of these demands not in Bell Atlantic's interest." Moreover, "independent counsel, after undertaking an exhaustive investigation, determined the corporation's interests were more in line with those of the defendants than plaintiffs."

5.   Corporate Family Issues

A.   The Entity Theory

Should separate corporations that are affiliated with each other (as parent/subsidiary, or as sister subsidiaries of a common parent company) be considered the same company for purposes of determining whether the lawyer representing one corporation has a conflict of interest if she takes a case adverse to another? In the typical situation, Corporation *X*, a client of Lawyer, asks her to file suit against Corporation *A*. Corporation *A* is not a client of Lawyer, but Corporation *B* is, and Corporation *A* is a subsidiary of Corporation *B*, or Corporation *B* owns a major stake in Corporation *A*, or both Corporation *A* and Corporation *B* are subsidiaries of Corporation *C*.

May Lawyer sue Corporation *A* while simultaneously representing its parent or sister corporation, Corporation *B*, on an unrelated matter? Lawyer, of course, may not represent a client in one matter while suing it in another, even though the two matters are unrelated. Should the parent and subsidiary (Corporations *A* and *B*) be treated as one client, or does the Law Firm represent only "the entity," that is, Corporation *B*?

Some cases have assumed, without extensive analysis, that representing a corporation in one matter while undertaking a representation directly adverse to an affiliate of that corporation, such as a parent corporation, subsidiary, or sister corporation, is an improper conflict of interest. However, that assumption does not follow at all from the entity theory of representation, which states that the lawyer for an entity, such as a corporation, represents that entity and *not* its shareholders (in our example, the shareholder is the parent company B, an existing client of the lawyer).

The law in this area is not entirely clear. When confronted with corporate family issues and the possibility of conflicts, the lawyer should evaluate how separate the corporate entities really are. Are corporate formalities really observed? To what extent are the two entities run separately? What is the nature of the dispute that the client, Corporation X has with the prospective defendant, Corporation A? For example, does Corporation X's lawsuit allege fraud or criminal conduct by Corporation A? Was this conduct in fact undertaken by Corporation B's officers?

Are the personnel with whom the lawyer must deal the same people? Is one corporation the "alter ego" of the other? It would be difficult for the lawyer, on day one, to call the general counsel of Corporation B, loyally advise the General Counsel about the firm's latest strategies on behalf of Subsidiary, and then, on day two, call the same General Counsel and engage in tough negotiations on behalf of another client suing the Subsidiary in a RICO action.

Did the lawyer learn from the Corporation B confidential information that is now material in the suit against subsidiary Corporation A?

The case where one corporation is the subsidiary of one or more other corporations is merely a situation where the shareholder of the corporation happens to be another corporation. But the client should normally be thought to be the entity, not the shareholders, even if the shareholders are corporations. Thus, Rule 1.13, Comment 10 warns that "the organization's interest may be or become adverse to those of one or more of its constituents." In such cases, the lawyer should advise the constituent that the lawyer cannot represent such constituent. The lawyer, however, can continue to represent the corporation. Rule 1.13 does not accept the view that a law firm is in a *per se* conflict whenever it advances a position that is adverse to a constituent element (a corporate affiliate) of one of its clients.

The leading ABA ethics opinion on this issue is ABA Formal Opinion 95–390 (Jan. 25, 1995). Over several dissents, it concluded that the Model Rules do not prohibit a law firm from representing a party adverse to a corporation merely because the law firm represents, in an unrelated matter, another corporation that is affiliated (*e.g.*, as parent, subsidiary, sister corporation) with the adverse corporation. Because there is no conflict, the lawyer need not secure any consent from the subsidiary, sister corporation or parent.

However, there may be circumstances in a particular case where it is reasonable to treat the corporate family as a client, either generally, or for purposes of client conflicts. One example would be where the lawyer works for the corporate parent on a stock issue intended to benefit all subsidiaries and collects confidential information from all of them. Another situation may be where the lawyer's relationship with the corporate affiliate leads that affiliate to reasonably believe that it is a client of the lawyer, such as when an officer or general counsel of the parent hired the lawyer for a subsidiary and this lawyer reports directly to an officer or general counsel of the parent. The relationship between the corporate client and the affiliate may be such that the lawyer must regard the affiliate as its client, where one corporation is the alter ego of the other.

B. Situations Where the Courts May "Pierce the Corporate Veil" for Conflicts Purposes

The distinct legal identity of corporations is a basic principle of corporate law. The reason why corporations create corporate families is because the law confers various substantive benefits on the corporate form. Courts occasionally pierce the corporate veil, but they do not do so casually. Corporate law normally treats each corporation as a separate "person." Courts in general disregard the corporate form only when necessary to avoid misuse of the law of incorporation, such as when a subsidiary is undercapitalized.

In ethics as in corporate law, if one is to pierce the corporate veil for the purpose of deciding a disqualification issue, one should determine when public policy demands a piercing. A similar analysis should apply to disqualification issues. Model Rule 1.7 invites such an analysis. See, Rotunda, *Conflicts*

Problems When Representing Members of Corporate Families, 72 Notre Dame L. Rev. 655 (1997).

Rule 1.7(a)(1) disqualifies a lawyer who represents one client "directly adverse to another client," unless the lawyer reasonably believes that her representation will not be adversely affected and secures the consent of both clients. Model Rule 1.7(a)(2) similarly disqualifies if the attorney's representation of the plaintiff against one corporation might be compromised or, in the words of that rule, "materially limited" by her obligations to another person (*e.g., a sister corporation*), unless first, each client consents, and second, the lawyer reasonably believes that her representation will not be "adversely affected." Rule 1.7(b).

Consider *Gould, Inc. v. Mitsui Mining & Smelting Co.* (N.D.Ohio 1990). In that case, Law Firm represented plaintiff Gould suing various defendants, including Pechiney, alleging unfair competition. Pechiney moved to disqualify Law Firm because Law Firm also represented (in unrelated patent matters) IG Technologies, a wholly-owned subsidiary of Pechiney. The court noted that Law Firm "has made no effort to obtain the consent of Gould or Pechiney, nor did it ever attempt to notify them of this conflict of interest." Still, the court refused disqualification as a remedy because—

"*First*, there has been no demonstration that Pechiney has been prejudiced in any way by [the Law Firm's] representation of Gould. *Confidential Pechiney information has not passed to Gould* as a result of [the Law Firm's] representation of IGT, which is unrelated to the instant case. *Second*, disqualifying [the Law Firm] from representing Gould would not only cost Gould a great deal of time and money, in retaining new counsel, it would significantly delay the progress of this case.... *Finally*, the conflict was created by Pechiney's acquisition of IGT several years after the instant case was commenced, not by any affirmative act of [the Law Firm]. In short, *the integrity of the judicial process in this case has not been threatened by the conflict.*''(emphasis added).

A threat to the integrity of the judicial process *would* occur, for example, if the lawyer, as part of her representation of Corporation 1, learned secrets about another member of the corporate family (e.g., Corporation 2) and then represented a third party and used that confidential information against Corporation 2. In that case, the representation would taint the judicial process because the lawyer learned relevant confidences that would be used to her advantage without the consent of Corporation 2 or Corporation 1.

Another example is when the lawyer suing the corporation affiliated with a current client is asking for declaratory or injunctive relief that would impose restrictions on the current client itself. For example, *Hilton v. Barnett Banks, Inc.* (M.D.Fla. 1994). The law firm for Hilton sued Barnett Banks while representing a subsidiary of Barnett Banks. Hilton's law firm did not name its client-affiliate as a party, but it did ask for injunctive relief against "all affiliates" of Barnett Banks. Hence, the court treated the affiliate as a *de facto* party and disqualified the law firm. The affiliated client was not (or soon would not be) a mere bystander to this particular lawsuit.

Law firms and corporate clients can avoid problems by clarifying, in the initial retention agreement, the extent to which the client consents to adverse representation against an affiliate of the corporate client. The initial engagement letter could state that some or all members of the corporate family should be treated as a single entity, or as separate entities. If a law firm's decision to represent a particular corporation means it must forego the opportunity to represent a whole host of other clients, the corporate client can easily inform that law firm, which should know that it is making a decision with significant opportunity costs. Clients, as well, should think through whether it is worthwhile to impose this opportunity cost on the law firm.

The ethics issues involved in the corporate family situation are somewhat analogous to the case where a lawyer, in a private law firm, represents—as one of its clients—the government or a government agency. To that issue we now turn.

C. Representing Government Entities While Simultaneously Representing Private Parties

Sometimes governments hire private law firms to represent them. That law firm may also be simultaneously representing private clients, some of whom may develop interests adverse to the government. That can create a conflict. There may be a statute or regulation that controls this situation, and, if so, one must first turn to it. The statute may provide that the government automatically waives certain conflicts. Of course, the lawyer still must obtain informed consent from the private client.

Assuming that there is no relevant statute that mandates a different result or procedure, and that Rule 1.11 does not command a different result, then one must turn to the other ethics rules. If there is a simultaneous representation of adverse interests, then Rule 1.7 applies, and the law firm is in a conflict. But who is the governmental client? Is it the *entire* "government" as an entity, or is it just a certain agency or a particular department?

Rule 1.13, Comment 9 essentially punts on this issue, and moves on: "Defining precisely the identity of the client and prescribing the resulting obligations of such lawyers may be more difficult in the government context and is a matter beyond the scope of these Rules. See Scope [18]. Although in some circumstances the client may be a specific agency, it may also be a branch of government, such as the executive branch, or the government as a whole."

The ABA Committee on Ethics, in Formal Opinion 97–405 (April 19, 1997), proposed a functional analysis to decide these issues. In order for the lawyer to determine if the client is the government as a whole or a smaller entity, such as a particular agency or department, the lawyer should look at the retention agreement, if there is one, because it may answer the question. Of course, this agreement with the government as to the scope of employment and the definition of the government "client" is not allowed to frustrate the reasonable expectations of the private client, who expects a conflict-free representation. Lawyers and the government client cannot prevent the private client from asserting a conflict by the simple expedient of agreeing to an unusually narrow and artificial definition of the "government client." On the other hand, the agreement should prevent the government client from later arguing that the definition of the government "client" should be retroactively enlarged.

If there is no express agreement, then the ABA Formal Opinion advises that one should look at the reasonable expectations of the government client, such as how the government entity is funded, how it is legally defined, and whether it has independent legal authority on the matter for which it hired the lawyer. This recommendation makes sense. One can think of many cases where it would be unnatural to treat the government client as the government as a whole. One obvious example is the case where one branch of "the government as a whole" has a dispute with another branch of "the government," as when Congress and the President dispute the constitutionality of a legislative veto. Each branch will have its own counsel, neither of whom will be representing the "government as a whole."

If we assume that the lawyer represents a private client who is adverse to one government agency, while that same lawyer represents a different government agency who is not adverse to the private client, then the lawyer is not representing one client adversely to a present client, in violation of Rule 1.7(a)(1). However, the lawyer may still have a conflict under Rule 1.7(a)(2). The lawyer must decide if her representation of her client will be adversely affected—or "materially limited" in the words of Rule 1.7(a)(2)—because of the relationship between the government entities. A key issue is whether the lawyer will be pulling her punches on behalf of the private client because of her desire to continue to represent the particular government agency.

RULE 1.14: CLIENT WITH DIMINISHED CAPACITY

A client's youthful or advanced age may impair his ability to render a considered judgment, or the client may suffer from a mental disability, so that he does not appreciate the full significance of a problem. In such cases the lawyer should endeavor, insofar as possible, to maintain a normal client-lawyer relationship. Even if the client is disabled, she might still be capable of understanding the matter, and the lawyer should therefore consult with her to the extent possible under the circumstances.

Rule 1.14 does not give the lawyer carte blanche to impose on the client the lawyer's personal view of what is in the client's best interest. Rather, Rule 1.14 authorizes the lawyer to engage in a limited intervention when the client's mental incapacity is such that she cannot adequately protect her own interests.

The client, though legally competent, may not fully appreciate the significance of the lawyer-client relationship. Even if the client has the legal capacity to discharge the lawyer, the lawyer should make a "special effort" to educate the client and explain the consequences and significance of the discharge. Rule 1.16, Comment 6.

ABA Formal Opinion 96–404 (Aug. 2, 1996) deals with the problems of clients who have become legally incompetent to handle their own affairs. In such cases, a lawyer should take the "least restrictive action under the circumstances;" the lawyer should not seek the appointment of a guardian "if other, less drastic, solutions are available." Further, if a guardian is needed for some purposes, something less than a general guardianship should be sought if possible. While the lawyer may file a petition for guardianship, it must be because the lawyer concludes it is necessary, not simply because someone else (such as a family member) requests it. Finally, if the lawyer is asked to recommend a guardian, the lawyer must disclose to the court the lawyer's expectation of future employment by the guardian. The lawyer must also disclose if the client expressed a different preference for a guardian.

Rule 1.14, Comment 5 advises that the lawyer, to protect the client, should take protective measures such as consulting with family members, using voluntary surrogate decision-making tools such as durable powers of attorney, turning to professional services, adult-protective agencies or others who have the ability to protect the client, and so forth. "In taking any protective action, the lawyer should be guided by such factors as the wishes and values of the client to the extent known, the client's best interests and the goals of intruding into the client's decision-making autonomy to the least extent feasible, maximizing client capacities and respecting the client's family and social connections."

RULE 1.15: SAFEKEEPING PROPERTY

1. The General Rule

Lawyers must be careful not to commingle a client's funds with their own funds. Lawyers, after all, hold client property as fiduciaries. This basic principle has led to various subsidiary rules.

Rule 1.15 requires the lawyer to keep separate, identifiable accounts of client funds. The law firm may not commingle the firm's (or lawyer's) own funds with these client funds. For example, a law firm must not pay its debts by drawing a check on a client's fiduciary account. The firm first should withdraw from that account any amount to which it is entitled. The firm then should place that amount in the firm's own account and draw a check on its own account. Nor may the lawyer borrow client funds, even temporarily.

The trust fund rule prohibits commingling client funds with the lawyer's funds. In addition to money and other such property, the lawyer must take reasonable steps to safeguard documents that the lawyer possesses that relate to her representation of a client or former client. However, the lawyer may deposit his own funds in the trust account "for the sole purpose of paying bank service charges on that

266

account,'' and then he may deposit only as much money as is needed. Rule 1.15(b).

The old Model Code *exempted* from the trust fund requirement any client funds paid as *advances for costs and expenses*. There is no policy justification offered to support this exception, and thus the Rules do not continue it. Such funds are now subject to the trust fund requirement.

The lawyer must also safeguard the client's property. For example, the client's securities should be kept in a safe or safe deposit box, unless circumstances dictate a different form of safekeeping. The lawyer must keep all property that belongs to clients or third persons separate from the lawyer's business and personal property, and should identify tangible property as belonging to the client.

When the lawyer administers estate monies or acts in a similar fiduciary capacity, separate trust accounts may be warranted. The trust fund bank account should be maintained in the state where the law office is, unless the client consents to a different place. Assume that Client gives Lawyer bearer bonds for safe-keeping while Client is in Europe on an extended vacation. Lawyer then places these bonds in the office safe, but does not identify them as belonging to Client. In this situation, Lawyer is subject to discipline because of sloppy record keeping.

Rule 1.15(c) requires the lawyer to ''deposit into a client trust account legal fees and expenses that have been paid in advance, to be withdrawn by the lawyer only as fees are earned or expenses incurred." This provision responds to the sad fact that the single largest class of claims made on client protection funds is for taking unearned fees.

Based on a study of existing court rules, the ABA has codified a Model Rule on Financial Recordkeeping. That Model Rule—*not* part of the ABA Model Rules on Professional Conduct—makes clear, for example, that only a lawyer admitted to practice in the relevant jurisdiction (and therefore subject to discipline in that jurisdiction) may be an authorized signatory on the account, and that withdrawals must be made only by bank transfer or by a check payable to a named payee, not "to cash."

2. Disputes Regarding Trust Fund Property

Occasionally the client and lawyer may have a dispute regarding trust fund property. For example, assume that the lawyer, who deposits a settlement check for $90,000 in the client account, would like to withdraw the agreed upon fee of one-third (plus an amount to cover disbursements). But the client may claim that less money is due the lawyer, perhaps because of a dispute regarding whether one-third was reasonable under the circumstances, or because of a disagreement over disbursements. The lawyer may *not* withdraw the disputed portion of the money until the dispute is resolved. On the other hand, the lawyer must promptly distribute the undisputed portion to the client and withdraw for himself the undisputed portion of the funds from the trust fund account when they are due. The lawyer may not coerce the client to give up his claim by refusing to deliver to the client the money that is undisputedly the client's.

While we normally think of trust fund disputes involving only the lawyer and the client, at least two other kinds of disputes are in fact possible: client-creditor disputes and lawyer-client's creditor disputes. Rule 1.15(e) tries to take all three kinds of disputes into account by providing that when the lawyer possesses property that two or more persons claim, the lawyer must keep the property separate until the dispute is resolved. However, the "lawyer shall promptly distribute all portions of the property as to which the interests are not in dispute."

3.   Audits of Trust Fund Accounts

The Model Rules do not require bar authorities to engage in any systematic auditing of client trust funds. However, the ABA's Model Rules for Lawyer Disciplinary Enforcement give Bar disciplinary Counsel ready access to records of the location and number of client trust fund accounts held by all of the lawyers in the state. The ABA also recommends that Bar Counsel should to verify the accuracy of these accounts *if* there is "probable cause" that the lawyer has maintained the funds properly or has mishandled them. The ABA justified this limitation on Bar Counsel in order to preserve client confidences. However, clients would be more protected if the Bar Counsel had power to examine trust fund accounts without having to cross the hurdle of probable cause.

The ABA has proposed random audits of lawyers' trust fund accounts, and approved a Model Rule for Random Audit of Lawyer Trust Accounts. Empirical studies have shown that random audits are a proven deterrent to the misuse of money and property in the practice of law and that examination of trust accounts by court-designated auditors provide practitioners with expert and practical assistance in maintaining necessary records and books of account. The burden of this proposed rule would be minimal, because all audits would be random and would not be imposed on any law firm more than once every three years. But, one cannot effectuate a complete audit if one cannot verify the accuracy of the trust fund account, and the Model Rules do not require any systematic audit of these funds.

Some states require spot checks, and Canadian provinces such as Québec require annual accounting certificates of trust fund accounts. Some commentators have proposed that all attorneys be bonded, or that at least lawyers who have been suspended or disbarred and are seeking reentry to the profession be bonded.

4. Interest Earned on Client Trust Funds

Under common law rules, interest earned on client trust accounts does not belong to the lawyer. If funds are invested, the interest earned on the client's property belongs to the client, not to the lawyer. The principal, not the agent, owns the fruits of the principal's capital. Ethics rules reflect this common law principle.

The Model Rules do not specifically deal with the question of the investment of client trust accounts. Normally a lawyer is under no duty to invest client funds because he is usually keeping these funds in his capacity as one who merely safeguards them, not as one who makes investment decisions. However, in some cases the large amount of money and length of time involved may require the lawyer to secure investment instructions from the client.

Historically, client funds held for a short time were kept in non-interest-bearing bank accounts. The administrative difficulty of apportioning to each of the clients their share of interest in a multi-client account with other clients' funds played a part in the proliferation of non-interest bearing lawyer trust accounts. However, thanks to, apportionment of interest is easy.

In recent years, the organized bar has attempted to capture the interest generated by pooling small amounts of funds into much larger state-wide trust funds totaling in the millions. The bar has created an exception to basic common law rules in order to collect the interest from the pool of trust fund accounts and use this otherwise untapped resource to fund law-related activities that bar authorities consider worthwhile, such as "public service" advocacy and legal services for the indigent. These programs are typically called IOLTA ("Interest on Lawyer Trust Account") plans.

The ABA Ethics Committee has concluded that ethics rules do not stand in the way of such programs. Even without prior client consent or notice, the "interest earned on bank accounts in which are deposited client's funds, nominal in amount or to be held for short periods of time, under state-authorized programs providing for the interest to be paid to tax-exempt organizations," is not treated as funds of the client within the meaning of the ethics rules. ABA Formal Opinion 348 (July 23, 1982).

The Supreme Court first raised questions about the constitutionality of taking interest earned from pooled income fund accounts in *Phillips v. Washington Legal Foundation* (S.Ct.1998). The question before *Phillips* was narrow. The Court assumed that a lawyer was required to put funds into an IOLTA account only if the interest generated on the funds would be insufficient to offset bank service charges and other charges. The issue was whether the interest was nevertheless "property" of the lawyer or client in such a case so that the Takings Clause could apply.

Chief Justice Rehnquist, speaking for the Court (5 to 4), held that the interest on a client's funds in a lawyer's hands is property of the client even if bank charges would mean the client could never spend it. For example, rental income is the property of the owner of a building even if collecting the rent costs more than the tenant owes.

Because factual questions had not been decided below, the Court left for another day whether IOLTA programs constituted an unconstitutional taking of the clients' property and what, if any, compensation might be due. That day came in *Brown v. Legal Foundation of Washington* (S.Ct. 2003), when a differently constituted 5 to 4 majority held that, since banking regulations prohibit interest-bearing client accounts outside IOLTA plans, clients lose nothing from these ''takings.'' Thus, the Court held that no compensation is due.

RULE 1.16: DECLINING OR TERMINATING REPRESENTATION

1. Accepting a Case

The American lawyer, unlike the American taxi-cab driver, is not bound to respond to the first hail and the law does not normally obligate him to accept any individual client. However, if the court appoints a lawyer to a case, it is unethical to reject that appointment for the wrong reason, for example, because the client or the cause is unpopular.

While ethics rules do not require a lawyer to take a case (except when appointed), they sometimes require a lawyer to decline a case. For example, a lawyer may not accept a case if doing so will violate a rule of professional responsibility or other law, or if the lawyer cannot perform reasonably prompt and competent service.

2. Terminating Representation

A. General Principles

The rules regarding withdrawal are more complex than the rules regarding accepting a case. One must keep in mind several overriding principles.

First, if a matter is before a tribunal, the lawyer must follow that tribunal's rules, which typically require securing the tribunal's permission before withdrawing. That tribunal may simply refuse to allow the lawyer to withdraw. For example, in *Haines v. Liggett Group, Inc.* (D.N.J.1993), plaintiff's lawyer moved to withdraw from tobacco litigation on the grounds that the firm could no longer absorb the high cost of financing the litigation. The judge, relying on Rule 1.16(c), noted that financial loss is an inherent risk in contingent fee litigation, and concluded that the law firm could not walk away from its contract just because the case would not generate the return initially expected.

If the tribunal does not grant permission to withdraw, the lawyer must continue his representation even if he would otherwise have a right, or even a duty, to withdraw. If the tribunal asks the lawyer why he is seeking withdrawal, the lawyer's duty to keep client confidences may prevent the lawyer from responding in detail. However, the confidentiality rules do not prevent the attorney from filing a "notice of the fact of withdrawal" and withdrawing or disaffirming any opinion, document, affirmation, or the like. Rule 1.2, Comment 10; Rule 4.1, Comment 3. If the client tries to discharge the lawyer during trial but the tribunal does not permit the lawyer to withdraw, the lawyer must comply with the orders of the tribunal.

Second, the client always has a right to discharge a lawyer at any time, with or without cause, subject to court order and to liability for payment of the lawyer's services. If a client fires her lawyer, the lawyer must withdraw.

Agency law recognizes the concept of a "power coupled with an interest," such as a lender's power to sell the house when the mortgagor defaults. Principals cannot fire agents who have a "power coupled with an interest." But lawyers are not agents with a power coupled with an interest. No lawyer can continue to represent a client who does not wish to be represented. Even a lawyer's contingent fee arrangement cannot be used to prevent the client from discharging the lawyer. If the client discharges the lawyer, he shall withdraw. Rule 1.16(a)(3).

Third, when terminating representation the lawyer must make reasonable efforts to protect the client's interests, such as giving reasonable notice to the client and surrendering any papers and property to which the client is entitled. This duty exists whether the client fires the lawyer or the lawyer withdraws from representing the client. Rule 1.16(d).

The client who discharges the lawyer is still liable for fees earned, or for other contractual or quasi-contractual damages. And the lawyer must return any fee advanced but not yet earned.

B. Wrongful Discharge

Can the lawyer sue the client for the tort of wrongful discharge? We know that landlords can dismiss at will those tenants who are tenants at will, but the law might still impose a damages remedy if the landlord dismisses the tenant for the wrong reason, such as retaliation for reporting a housing code violation, or retaliation for refusing to engage in racial discrimination. On the other hand, a landlord is not a client, and being a tenant is not a profession.

What if a client decides to fire her lawyer because the lawyer has hired an associate who is a member of ''the wrong race'', or because the lawyer has converted to a different religious faith than that of the client. While the lawyer has no right to enjoin the client from terminating the representation, is the client liable for damages, for wrongful discharge? The wrongfully terminated lawyer would not be suing for injunctive relief; he is not asking for his job back. He wants damages for wrongful discharge.

In-house counsel have occasionally brought wrongful discharge suits after being fired by their corporate client, and lawyers have also sued their law firm employers for wrongful discharge. The typical defendants in these suits are either law firms (which do not have a client relationship with the lawyers that they employ) or corporations (which hire in-house counsel, so the corporations *are* both clients and employers). For suits against an employer who is not a client (e.g., the law firm) the tort of wrongful discharge is almost surely available. E.g., *Wieder v. Skala* (N.Y.1992), held that a law firm is liable for firing an associate alleging that he was fired for complying with his obligation to inform the Bar of a colleague's unethical behavior. When a lawyer sues her client for wrongful discharge, some courts grant the suit if "public policy" has been violated (if, say, sex or race discrimination is involved, or if a lawyer is fired for doing his duty under ethics rules). A few courts emphasize the uniqueness of the lawyer-client relationship, and argue that the lawyer alone must bear the cost of her ethical duties, and that the client is always free to fire a lawyer without legal penalties other than those provided in the retainer contract.

This argument, if one accepts it, does not apply in the case of lawyers suing their own law firms, which do not have the rights of clients. Nor would that argument apply to any lawyer-employers (e.g., a lawyer employed as inside legal counsel by a corporation or government agency). The Restatement of the Law Governing Lawyers, Third, § 32, comment *b* (ALI 2000) advises that, at least with respect to lawyer-employees, "the client's right to discharge the lawyer does not abridge the lawyer's entitlement to salary and benefits already earned. A lawyer-employee also has the same rights as other employees under applicable law to recover for bad-faith discharge, for example if the client discharged the lawyer for refusing to perform an unlawful act." The power that a client-employer "possesses over a lawyer-employee is substantial, compared to that of a client over an independent lawyer. Giving an employed lawyer a remedy for wrongful discharge does not significantly impair the client's choice of counsel." The client can fire the lawyer wrongfully, but the client may have to pay damages.

C. Mandatory and Permissive Withdrawal

The Model Rules—like their predecessor, the Model Code—divide withdrawal into two basic types: mandatory and permissive. Both forms of withdrawal are subject to the overriding principles discussed above.

The lawyer *must* withdraw from a case: if (1) continued employment would result in violating the disciplinary rules or other law; or if (2) the lawyer's physical or mental condition results in a material adverse impact on the client; or if (3) the client discharges the attorney.

The Model Rules *allow* the lawyer to withdraw for no reason, if "withdrawal can be accomplished without *material adverse* effect on the interests of the client." Rule 1.16(b)(1) (emphasis added). The Restatement of the Law Governing Lawyers rejects that view, for the uncomplicated reason that it appears to violate the lawyer's fiduciary obligation to her client. The Restatement proposes a more vague proportionality test. In light of the fiduciary nature of the lawyer-client relationship, the Restatement argues that a lawyer may not withdraw if there is "a significant disproportion between the detrimental effects that would be imposed on the client by the contemplated withdrawal as against detrimental effects that would be imposed on the lawyer or others continuing the representation." Restatement of the Law Governing Lawyers, Third, § 32(4) & Comment *h(i)* (Official Draft, 2000).

The Reporter's Note to this section candidly acknowledges that states have "widely adopted" the proposition that lawyers can permissively withdraw so long as there is no material adverse effect on the client. Nonetheless lawyers are fiduciaries and some courts may find the Restatement persuasive authority to change the rule.

The Model Rules also *permit* withdrawal (even if it causes material adverse impact to the client) if the client: (1) persists in using the lawyer's services in an action that the lawyer reasonably believes is a crime or fraud; (2) has used the lawyer to perpetrate a crime or fraud; (3) insists on conduct the lawyer believes is repugnant or with which the lawyer has a fundamental disagreement (even though it is not illegal); (4) fails substantially to fulfill an obligation to the lawyer (for example, nonpayment of fees), and the client has been warned; or (5) has made representation unreasonably difficult. The Rules add a catch-all provision: the lawyer may withdraw when "other good cause" exists. This catch-all is not limited to cases where the *tribunal* finds good cause.

RULE 1.17: SALE OF LAW PRACTICE

1. The General Rule on Selling a Practice

The former Model Code prohibited a lawyer from "selling" her law practice because "clients are not merchandise." However, this Code did not concern itself with division of fees among lawyers within the same firm. Thus, a firm could always add another lawyer as a partner in the firm, and have that new partner purchase equity in the firm. This equity typically included not only the cost of physical assets like law books and desks, but also "good will," that is, the expectation of continued business from the existing clientele.

In effect, this arrangement allowed lawyers to sell a law practice by accepting new members into the partnership. Thus, under the Model Code there was a disparity of treatment between lawyers practicing in a partnership compared to sole practitioners: solos were forbidden from selling "good will," but law firms were not. Because of this difference in treatment, efforts were made to change the rules regarding sale of a law practice.

Spurred by the California State Bar, the ABA adopted a new rule allowing for the sale of a law practice by a living lawyer, or by the estate of a deceased lawyer. In February, 1990, it added Rule 1.17. In 2002, the ABA added another provision, allowing a lawyer to sell *part* of a practice (''an area of law practice'') without leaving the practice of law entirely.

Rule 1.17 imposes various restrictions. First, the seller must cease to engage in the practice of law, or an area of practice, in the jurisdiction (or a particular geographic area). The state court adopting Rule 1.17 should choose one of these alternatives. This Rule does not consider a seller to be returning to private practice if he becomes in-house counsel, or works for the government, or a legal services entity.

Second, the seller must sell the entire practice, or the entire area of practice, to one or more lawyers or law firms. The objection that the Rules use to justify this restriction is that the piecemeal sale of a practice would not protect clients whose matters have turned out to be less lucrative and who might find it difficult to secure other counsel if the sale could be limited to substantial fee-generating matters. Rule 1.17, Comment 6. Rule 1.17 is drafted to force the purchaser to subsidize those clients with less lucrative cases, including clients with lawsuits that the purchaser candidly calculates should not have been brought to begin with. The purchaser cannot avoid accepting the clients with the less lucrative cases by trying to raise their fees, because Rule 1.17(d) prohibits raising any fees because of the sale.

Third, the sale of a law practice raises questions of client confidentiality, for the purchaser is not the lawyer whom the clients retained. Consequently, the seller must give each of the seller's clients written notice of the proposed sale, the terms of any proposed fee changes, the right to retain other counsel, and the right to take possession of his file. These clients are given a reasonable chance to consent or withhold consent *before* the confidences are revealed. Because not all clients may respond to mailed notices, if a client does not object or does not respond within 90 days, the Rule presumes that the client consents. Rule 1.17(c)(3).

If the purchaser cannot send a notice to the client (perhaps he has moved without leaving a forwarding address), he must secure a court order authorizing the transfer. The court can determine if there have been reasonable efforts to find the client and whether it serves the legitimate interests of absent clients to have the purchaser represent them. To protect the client's confidentiality, the seller may disclose to the court *in camera* information about the proposed representation only to the extent necessary to obtain this order.

Recall that, if a lawyer divides fees with another lawyer in a different law firm, each lawyer must assume joint responsibility for the representation, pursuant to Rule 1.5(e)(1). Rule 1.17 does not refer to that section. In fact, Comment 15 to Rule 1.17 specifically provides that Rule 1.17 does *not* apply to the transfer of legal representation unrelated to the sale of a practice.

However, the responsibilities assumed under Rule 1.17 should be no less than those assumed pursuant to Rule 1.5(e)(1). Comment 11 to Rule 1.17 does note that the seller has the obligation to exercise competence in identifying a qualified purchaser. While the seller cannot exercise continuing supervision (he has, after all, left the practice), it is reasonable to argue that he shares malpractice liability (as if they were partners) with the person he chooses to buy his practice. Such a rule would assure that the seller picks carefully, and it is no more onerous than the burden placed by Rule 1.5(e)(1). But that is not the burden that Rule 1.17 accepts.

2. The Death of an Attorney

If a law firm has more than one attorney, the death of one of them does not end the law practice, because there is a least one other attorney to carry on the work. However, in the case of sole practitioners who die without having sold their practice, what happens to the files of their clients? Along with Rule 1.17, allowing a lawyer to sell her law practice to another lawyer, the ABA in 1990 added Rule 5.4(a)(2), which provides that if a lawyer (e.g., Lawyer *A*) purchases the law practice of "a deceased, disabled, or disappeared lawyer," (e.g., Lawyer *B*), then Lawyer *A* may agree to pay the purchase price to the estate or other representative of Lawyer *B*.

The ABA recommends that solo practitioners have a plan to provide for the protection of their clients' interests in the event of their death, if only in order to assure that client matters (*e.g.*, document filings, statutes of limitations) are not neglected. The plan should designate another lawyer who would make reasonable efforts to notify the clients of the sole practitioner's death, review the files, and determine which need immediate attention. Because the designated lawyer does not represent these clients, she should only review as much as needed to identify the clients and determine which files need immediate attention.

RULE 1.18: DUTIES TO PROSPECTIVE CLIENTS

The 2002 revisions added a new rule, Rule 1.18, to deal with the lawyer's duties to prospective clients. The Rule mainly codifies present law (which courts implied from other ethics rules), except for a new subsection Rule 1.18(d) discussed below.

Rule 1.18(a) defines a "prospective client" as one with whom the lawyer discusses the possibility of creating an attorney-client relationship.

It may turn out that the lawyer, after hearing the problem or doing a conflicts check, decides not to take the matter, or the client may decide not to hire this particular lawyer after all. In that case, the general rule is that the lawyer may neither use nor reveal the prospective client's secret information. The lawyer treats the confidentiality rights of the prospective client as if he were a former client. Rule 1.18(b). This duty to not use or reveal information "exists regardless of how brief the initial conference may be." Rule 1.18, Comment 3.

For example, *Barton v. U.S. District Court for the Central District of California* (9th Cir.2005) held that a law firm's questionnaires regarding antidepressant drugs that prospective clients completed and submitted to the law firm on the internet were submitted in the course of a prospective attorney-client relationship. The disclaimer at bottom of the law firm's online questionnaire stated that it did not constitute a request for legal advice and that the sender did not form an attorney-client relationship by submitting the questionnaire.

The form stated that its purpose is to "gather information about potential class members," which "suggests that the firm is indeed trolling for clients." *Barton* concluded that the information from the prospective clients is protected confidential information. The "vagueness and ambiguity of the law firm's prose does not amount to a waiver of confidentiality by the client." The confidentiality rules protect a person "who consults a lawyer for the purposes of 'retaining the lawyer.'" The questionnaire did "not disclaim the purpose of 'securing legal service,'" because, "[m]ore important than what the law firm intended is what the clients thought."

Rule 1.18(c), like Rule 1.9, prohibits representation adverse to the prospective client in the same or a substantially related matter. However, unlike Rule 1.9, the Rule only bars representation if the lawyer received information from the prospective client that could be "significantly harmful to that person in the matter, except as provided in paragraph (d)."

The rationale behind the differing treatment between prospective and former clients is that, prior to the prospective client's decision to engage the lawyer, there is a period in which it is in the interest of the prospective client to share enough information with the lawyer to determine whether there is a conflict of interest or simple incompatibility. The lawyer may learn very early in the consultation, for example, that the party adverse to the prospective client is a client of the lawyer's firm. If the discussion stops before "significantly harmful" information is shared, the drafters of Rule 1.18 concluded that the law firm's regular client should not be denied its chosen counsel if a substantially related matter arises. Hence, the lawyer should conduct these initial interviews carefully. If the lawyer elicits substantially harmful information, he will be unable to continue to represent the adverse party unless the lawyer complies with Rule 1.18(d).

Rule 1.18 and particularly Rule 1.18(d) are derived from the Restatement of the Law Governing Lawyers, Third, § 15 (Official Draft 2000), "A Lawyer's Duties to a Prospective Client." Rule 1.18(d) provides that if a prospective client has given the lawyer disqualifying information, the lawyer can still represent a client adverse to this prospective client under two conditions.

First, representation is proper if both the affected client and the prospective client have given informed consent in writing. Rule 1.18(d)(1). This provision is not controversial.

Second, even if the prospective client objects, a lawyer can continue to represent an adverse client

if the lawyer receiving the disqualifying information took reasonable measures to avoid exposure to more information than was necessary to determine whether to represent the prospective client; **and** if the law firm screens that the lawyer from participation in the matter and from fees from the case. The lawyer must give prompt written notice to the prospective client. Rule 1.18(d)(ii). See Restatement, § 15(2), and Rule 1.0(k) (requirements for screening procedures).

INA Underwriters Insurance Co. v. Rubin (E.D.Pa.1983), is a case that would probably be decided under Rule 1.18 today. The court held that it would not disqualify a law firm whose lawyer held only a preliminary discussion with the prospective client and the lawyer was screened. The court noted: "Legal scholars and the American Bar Association have suggested the use in certain cases of a 'Chinese Wall,' a mechanism that would screen secret documents and firm members possessing knowledge of secrets and confidences in order to avoid disqualification of the entire firm."

RULE 2.1: THE LAWYER AS ADVISOR

The lawyer's role in giving advice often depends on whether the lawyer is acting as an advocate or as a consultant. If the attorney is acting primarily as advocate, he may urge upon the courts any nonfrivolous interpretation of the law that favors the client. In contrast, when the client consults the attorney in order to seek advice on how to proceed in a matter, the attorney should give the client his or her good faith opinion on how the courts will likely rule, and the full effects of such a decision. The lawyer's efforts to comfort the client cannot limit her duty to give an honest assessment of unpleasant facts.

Rule 2.1 imposes a duty on the lawyer to exercise *independent* judgment and to render *candid* advice. *In re DeFrancesch* (La.2004)(per curiam) held holding that a lawyer failed to act as an independent advisor to his client, a violation of Rule 2.1, when he solicited a client to have sex with him. This conduct would also violate Rule 1.8(j), which regulates a lawyer's sexual relations with a client.

In offering legal advice, the lawyer need not limit her comments to purely technical legal considerations but may refer to economic, political, social and moral considerations. The lawyer may offer her judgment as to what effects are morally just as well as legally permissible. The lawyer who couches her advice too narrowly ill-serves her client. However, the client, not the lawyer, ultimately must make the final decision whether to accept the lawyer's nonlegal advice. Rule 2.1, Comments 2 & 3.

The lawyer, advising a client with respect to a *tax return*, is acting both as an advisor and as a potential advocate. The general rule is that the lawyer may advise her client on taking a position on a tax return—

> "even where the lawyer believes the position *probably will not prevail*, there is no 'substantial authority' in support of the position, and there will be no disclosure of the position in the [tax] return. However, [the lawyer must believe in good faith that the position] is warranted in existing law or can be supported by a good faith argument for an extension, modification *or* reversal of existing law. This requires that there is *some realistic possibility of success* if the matter is litigated." ABA Formal Opinion 85–352 (July 7, 1985), at 4 (emphasis added).

In this situation, the lawyer also must advise the client of the risks of taking this position on the tax return, including adverse legal consequences or penalties that the Internal Revenue Service might impose.

Sometimes the client asks the lawyer to evaluate a matter for the benefit of a third person, such as when she writes an opinion concluding that it is legal to sell certain securities registered for sale under the securities laws. If the lawyer reasonably knows that the client will use that opinion to justify its action to third parties, the lawyer is then an *evaluator*, governed by Rule 2.3, discussed below. However, if the client asks for *confidential* advice, then the lawyer is an *advisor*, governed by Rule 2.1.

The lawyer's role as evaluator for the benefit of a third party also should be distinguished from the lawyer's role as *investigator* solely for the benefit of her client. A prospective purchaser may retain a lawyer to do a title search on property that the purchaser is planning to purchase. The lawyer's client is the purchaser, not the seller, and the lawyer's duty of loyalty is only to this client. If the seller hires the lawyer to do a title search to persuade the purchaser that the title is good, then the seller is hiring the lawyer as an evaluator and Rule 2.3 governs that situation.

Some law firms have found investigation so lucrative that they now have special teams to conduct them. Some courts are more likely to dismiss shareholder suits against officials if a law firm finds the officials to be without blame after an investigation and evaluation, and companies often believe that they can avoid more extensive government inquiries by showing that they are willing to clean their own house by hiring a lawyer-investigator. In addition, these independent investigations may generate good will with the general public. The companies treat these investigations as secret, though they may loudly trumpet the conclusions. These investigations may turn into "evaluations" for the benefit of third parties, when the companies and the lawyers whom they hire seek to have third parties rely on these evaluations.

In some cases, lawyers have liabilities towards nonclients. For example, assume that the seller of real estate retains a lawyer to conduct a title search and furnish an opinion that the seller's title is good. The seller plans to show this opinion to the purchaser. In this case, the seller retains the lawyer to evaluate the property for the benefit of the purchaser, a nonclient. The lawyer's duty of loyalty is to the client (the seller), but the lawyer also has assumed legal obligations to the third party (the purchaser), whom he knows will rely on his evaluation. Negligence in the preparation of this document could expose the lawyer to tort liability to this third party. See *Greycas, Inc. v. Proud* (7th Cir.1987). Similarly, a lawyer who drafts a tax shelter opinion knowing that it will be shown to and relied on by investors may be liable to those investors.

RULE 2.2: INTERMEDIARY

Before the 2002 ABA Model Rule revisions, Rule 2.2 dealt with the lawyer as intermediary. That concept is now treated in the Comments 28–33 to Rule 1.7. The drafters of the 2002 revisions concluded that old Rule 2.2 caused confusion and is not needed given the expansion of the Comments in Rule 1.7. These Comments prefer the term ''common representation'' instead of ''intermediation.''

Now, let us turn to Rule 2.3.

RULE 2.3: EVALUATION FOR USE BY THIRD PERSONS

Sometimes clients hire a lawyer to evaluate a matter for the benefit of third parties. Model Rule 2.3 governs this situation. Lawyers have assumed this special role with greater frequency in recent times.

The lawyer is an evaluator when she issues a legal opinion concerning the title of property rendered at the request of a vendor for the information of a prospective purchaser. Or she may write an opinion concerning the legality of the securities registered for sale under the securities laws because a government agency may require this legal evaluation. Or, a government agency may ask its lawyer to furnish an opinion on the legality of contemplated action, so that the agency can make the opinion public and use it to justify its action. In all these cases, the lawyer is an evaluator. See, e.g., ABA Formal Opinion 335 (1974). Often the client specifically requests the evaluation although his authorization may be implied. Rule 2.3, Comment 1.

One should distinguish an evaluation for the benefit of a third party from an investigation for the benefit of a client. There is an important difference between a lawyer's opinion that is expected to be made *public* and shown to third parties, versus a lawyer's opinion that is expected to *remain private* and shown only to the client. If, for example, the governmental agency discussed in the prior paragraph asks for confidential advice, then the lawyer is acting as an advisor, and therefore Rule 2.1 applies.

Consider the case where a prospective buyer of an apartment building hires a lawyer to complete a title search on this property. The lawyer's client is the buyer, not the seller, and the lawyer's duty of loyalty is only to his client. In contrast, if the seller retains a lawyer to furnish a title opinion that the seller plans to show to the buyer to bolster his claim that the title is a good one, then the client is retaining the lawyer to *evaluate* the property for the benefit of a nonclient. The lawyer's duty of loyalty is to the client, but the lawyer may also have assumed legal obligations to the third parties who rely on the evaluation.

To protect clients, and to take into account the needs of third parties, Rule 2.3 places several important restrictions on the evaluations. The lawyer must reasonably believe that conducting an evaluation is compatible with other aspects of the lawyer's relationship with the client. For example, if the lawyer had been an advocate defending the client on charges of fraud, it would usually not be compatible for the lawyer to conduct an evaluation of the same or related transaction. The client should also knowingly consent to this arrangement.

In order for the consent to be an informed consent, the client should know that the lawyer will not act as a typical partisan advocate because of "the lawyer's responsibilities to third persons and the duty to disseminate the findings." Rule 2.3, Comment 3. If it is reasonably likely that the lawyer's evaluation will affect the client's interests materially and adversely, then she must first obtain the client's consent after she has adequately informed the client of the important possible effects on the client's interests. Rule 2.3, Comment 5.

The client may place limits on the scope of an evaluation, e.g., by excluding certain issues, or imposing time constraints. Or, some persons may simply refuse to cooperate with the lawyer's evaluation; Rule 2.3 does not arm the lawyer with a subpoena power. The lawyer's evaluation should disclose in the evaluation all material limits.

To the extent an evaluation is shown to third parties, there can be no client confidences. But otherwise, all information relating to the evaluation is confidential because of the client-lawyer relationship. Rule 1.6 continues to protect information related to the evaluation except to the extent that the evaluation authorizes disclosure.

RULE 2.4: LAWYER SERVING AS THIRD–PARTY NEUTRAL

Rule 2.4 governs the situation where the lawyer acts as a neutral third-party (a mediator, arbitrator, conciliator or evaluator) who assists non-clients in resolving a dispute or another matter without representing any of these parties as their attorney. Alternative dispute resolution (ADR) has become a substantial part of the civil justice system. The 2002 revisions to the Model Rules added this new provision.

A prior version of the Model Rules had a provision, called Rule 2.2, which had envisaged the possibility of *intermediation*, where the lawyer represented *every one* of a set of persons with conflicting interests. Rule 1.7 now governs all situations where lawyers represent multiple parties. In contract, under Rule 2.4, the lawyer represents *none* of the parties when serving as a third-party neutral. When a lawyer serves as a third-party neutral in this way, the parties themselves may or may not be separately represented.

Lawyers are not the only third-party neutrals, and one need not normally be a lawyer to serve in this capacity, though in some court-connected contexts only lawyers can serve in this role. Even when the context does not require a lawyer, it is common for lawyers to serve in the role of third-party neutral. Unlike lay people, lawyers should be concerned about some unique ethical problems arising from the possible confusion others may have about the nature of the lawyer's role. Rule 2.4 deals with this issue.

These persons, especially if not personally represented, may mistakenly believe that the third-party neutral is acting as their lawyer. Thus, Rule 2.4(b) requires a lawyer-neutral to inform these nonclients that she is not representing any of them. The lawyer must explain to the nonclients, in a way that they can understand, the ramifications of this lack of representation—e.g., that attorney-client privilege will not apply, etc.

What happens if one of the parties to the joint proceedings subsequently asks the lawyer who served as a third-party neutral to be her attorney? It is necessary to refer to Rule 1.12, which governs that situation to determine the extent and consequences of any conflict of interest for the third-party neutrals.

Lawyer-neutrals may also be subject to various codes of ethics, depending on their precise role. The ABA and the American Arbitration Association jointly prepared the *Code of Ethics for Arbitration in Commercial Disputes*. The ABA, the AAA, and the Society of Professionals in Dispute Resolution prepared the *Model Standards for Mediators*. In any case, lawyers remain governed by their jurisdiction's version of the Rules of Professional Responsibility when they are engaged as third-party neutrals.

Counsel may represent one or more of the persons involved in alternative dispute resolution. The Model Rules will govern these counsel. If the ADR takes place before a tribunal, Rule 3.3 will govern the counsel's duty of candor. Otherwise, the counsel's duty of candor to the other parties and to the third-party neutral is governed by Rule 4.1, dealing with truthfulness in statements to others. See Rule 2.4, Comment 5.

RULE 3.1: MERITORIOUS CLAIMS AND CONTENTIONS

1. Meritorious v. Frivolous Claims

When the client consults the lawyer as an advisor contemplating litigation, the lawyer should provide the client her good faith opinion on how the courts will likely rule, and the implications of this outcome. The lawyer's natural inclination to comfort and to side with the client cannot limit her duty to give an honest assessment of unpleasant facts.

In contrast, in her role as an advocate, the lawyer may urge upon the courts any non-frivolous interpretation of the law that favors the client. The ethics rules prohibit lawyers from asserting *frivolous* positions, claims, defenses, or motions. Lawyers may not make frivolous discovery requests nor fail to make a reasonably diligent effort to comply with discovery requests.

The mere fact that a legal argument is ''creative'' or contrary to existing law does not make that position frivolous. Existing law is replete with ambiguities and, even if clear, is always subject to change if the lawyer makes a convincing argument. A permissible, non-frivolous position includes any good faith argument for extension, modification, or even *reversal* of existing law.

A claim does not become frivolous merely because the lawyer believes that her client will not prevail. Whether the case is civil or criminal, the lawyer need not fully substantiate all the facts before making a claim. The lawyer may expect to develop vital evidence through discovery. Discovery, after all, normally comes *after* the complaint is filed, not before. On the other hand, if the pleading or oral representation when made "is *without any* reasonable basis *and* is designed merely to embarrass or [for other] ill-conceived or improper motives, such a pleading or oral representation would clearly be subject to disciplinary action." *State v. Anonymous (1974–5)* (Conn.Super.1974) (emphasis added).

Lawyers should not file claims without any basis in law or in fact. Rule 3.1 responds to a common complaint of the public, *i.e.*, that lawyers file too many frivolous lawsuits. While lawyers should not file "frivolous" lawsuits, Rule 3.1 does allow them to file "creative" law suits.

A claim is "not frivolous" if it consists of a "*good faith* argument" for a modification of the law. Rule 3.1 If the lawyer can make such an argument, it matters not that the chances of success are slim. What is required is that lawyers inform themselves about the facts of their clients' cases and about the applicable law, before making their claims.

Before the 2002 revisions, the Rule 3.1, Comment 2 specified that a lawyer's action is frivolous if the client "desires to have the action taken primarily for the purpose of harassing or maliciously injuring a person.'' The 2002 revisions removed that language. If the plaintiff has a good legal case, it is irrelevant that the plaintiff may file suit primarily for the purpose of causing ''pain'' to the defendant. It is not necessary for plaintiffs to love or even respect the people they sue.

The duty to refrain from asserting frivolous claims includes the duty to refrain from pursuing dilatory tactics, which are not even permissible in criminal defense. However, the duty to avoid frivolous claims does not preclude the attorney from forcing the state to meet its burden of proof in a criminal case. See Rule 3.1, Comment 3. The government, in every criminal case, has the constitutional duty to prove every element of the charge if the defendant pleads not guilty. The government cannot constitutionally shift that burden to the defendant. The defense lawyer is acting properly in requiring the state to prove all elements of the crime, even if she offers no legal or factual defenses to the charges. A plea of ''not guilty'' is *never* frivolous, nor is it fraud on the court—a defendant is not under oath when making his plea. Rather, a plea of ''not guilty'' really means ''I concede nothing, which is my right.''

The choice to plead ''guilty'' or ''not guilty'' belongs to the defendant, not to his lawyer. The criminal defendant also has the right to decide whether to appeal a guilty verdict, although he should exercise this right after ''full consultation'' with counsel.

In a criminal appeal, the appellate defense counsel "should not seek to withdraw from a case solely on the basis of his or her determination that the appeal lacks merit." If the appellate lawyer can find no non-frivolous ground for the convicted client's appeal, the U.S. Supreme Court has ruled that the lawyer instead must file what is called an *Anders* brief—named after *Anders* brief—named after *Anders v. California* (S.Ct.1967). In that brief, the appellate defense lawyer explains why there are no non-frivolous grounds for the appeal.

A client, on the other hand, has no constitutional right to force appointed counsel to press all non-frivolous issues that the client wants advanced. Defense counsel, as a matter of competent professional judgment, may decide not to present every conceivable argument, but rather to focus on a few arguments and winnow out weaker ones. *Jones v. Barnes* (S.Ct.1983).

It is rare that a court will sanction a criminal defense lawyer for taking a frivolous position, but it can happen. In one criminal case, the defense lawyer filed a petition for rehearing on the grounds that federal tax statutes did not apply to resident U.S. citizens. The court fined the lawyer $2,500 for this frivolous legal argument. *In re Becraft* (9th Cir.1989).

2. Nondisciplinary Sanctions for Frivolous Advocacy

Rule 11 of the Federal Rules of Civil Procedure was amended in 1983 to provide that an individual lawyer must sign every pleading, motion, or other paper. This signature certifies that she has read the paper, that to the best of her knowledge, ''formed after reasonable inquiry,'' it is well grounded in fact and warranted by existing law or good faith argument to extend, modify, or reverse existing law, and that it is not filed for any improper purpose. For violations of Rule 11 the court may sanction the party *or the lawyer*. The purpose of this amendment was to arm federal courts with the means to deter and punish what many judges saw as an increase in dilatory practices and frivolous motions. Many states have enacted their own versions of Rule 11.

Rule 11 has spawned a great deal of satellite litigation over its scope, meaning, procedures, and application. Opponents claim that it has chilled lawyers' enthusiasm to pursue novel legal theories, and that it is biased against plaintiffs, particularly against plaintiffs in civil rights suits. Since adoption of Rule 11 in 1983 there have been thousands of decisions dealing with its sanctions; in one case, sanctioned lawyers spent $100,000 to reverse a $3,000 sanction to vindicate their reputations. In many circuits, a small number of judges are responsible for a disproportionate number of Rule 11 sanctions.

The Advisory Committee on the Federal Rules of Civil Procedure responded to trial lawyers' criticisms, and a revised Rule 11 went into effect in 1993. The Advisory Committee Notes to the 1993 amendments explained that the new Rule 11 was drafted to place ''greater constraints on the imposition of sanctions" and to "reduce the number of motions for sanctions presented to the court." Rule 11 as modified provides a safe harbor for the subject of the Rule 11 sanctions if the lawyer withdraws or timely corrects a challenged paper, claim, defense, etc. Moreover, the judge's sanctions must be limited to "what is sufficient to deter repetition" of the conduct.

Rule 11 as modified offers a greater range of choices in sanctioning violations of the Rule. Sanctions may include "directives of a non-monetary nature," or an order to pay a penalty to the court, or an order to pay the complaining party "*some* or all of the reasonable attorneys' fees and other expenses incurred as a direct result of the violation."

Other rules and statutes, as well as the judiciary's inherent powers over attorneys, give judges tools to control the proceedings before them. For example, 28 U.S.C. § 1927 prohibits a lawyer from multiplying proceedings "unreasonably and vexatiously." A lawyer may violate this section without filing any written motion.

Rule 38, Federal Rules of Appellate Procedure, confers on federal appellate courts power similar to that which Rule 11 confers on district courts. Appellate courts can award "just damages and single or double costs" for an appeal judged to be "frivolous." In addition, state and federal courts have the "inherent power" to control the proceedings and lawyers before them, including holding lawyers in contempt.

In some circumstances common law torts provide another remedy for those injured by the lawyer's conduct. Common tort remedies, depending of course on each state's law, include "abuse of process," *Board of Education v. Farmingdale Classroom Teachers Association* (N.Y.1975) (cause of action against attorney who subpoenaed 87 teachers to appear and testify on the very same day as a means of forcing the Board of Education to hire substitute teachers); malicious prosecution; defamation, *Green Acres Trust v. London* (Ariz.1984) (cause of action against attorney for his statements in a press conference, a forum in which the statements were not privileged); unlawful imprisonment; and tortious interference with contract, *Duggin v. Adams* (Va.1987) (lawyer advised client to breach a sales contract so that he, the lawyer, could purchase the property himself).

RULE 3.2: EXPEDITING LITIGATION

The former Model Code imposed ethical restraints on dilatory practices in litigation. The Model Rules maintain those restrictions but in a more affirmative manner, by requiring the lawyer to make "reasonable efforts to expedite litigation," but those efforts must be "consistent with the interests of the client."

If it is in the client's best interest to expedite litigation, it is easy to comply with Rule 3.2. However, sometimes prompt litigation is not in the client's best interest. Some well-known lawyers have boasted about their ability to delay a case for years.

May a lawyer file a non-frivolous motion that is likely to fail when the real purpose of the motion is to take advantage of the delay that it causes? The test that Model Rule 3.2 proposes appears, at first, to bar this practice:

> "The question is whether a competent lawyer acting in good faith would regard the course of action as having some substantial purpose *other than delay*. Realizing financial or other benefit *from otherwise improper* delay in litigation is not a legitimate interest of the client." Rule 3.2, Comment 1.

The first sentence quoted above may mean that, in determining whether to take a position in litigation, or file a motion, and so forth, a lawyer may not consider the benefits of delay that flow from the action. But it is not clear that the Rule adopts this view unequivocally, for the second sentence points in the opposite direction. It announces that when the lawyer considers the legitimate interests of the client, he may not consider the benefits of delay *if* the delay is "otherwise improper." If the motion, filing, or other action is non-frivolous, then it is not otherwise improper.

Cases in which judges have relied on Rule 3.2 to sanction lawyers tend not to be cases where the lawyer has filed a non-frivolous motion or taken other non-frivolous action that results in and is motivated by the desire for delay. Instead, lawyers are more likely sanctioned under 3.2 for misconduct that involved doing nothing after taking fees from their clients. *E.g., Carter v. The Mississippi Bar* (Miss.1995).

RULE 3.3: CANDOR TOWARD THE TRIBUNAL

1. Introduction

Rule 3.3, "Candor Toward the Tribunal," brings together several different rules that focus on the litigator's duty of candor. When lawyers deal with a tribunal, in some very important respects they must do more than merely tell the truth. Instead, the litigator must be "candid," *i.e.*, frank, without guile, straightforward. While lawyers have the duty not to lie to their opponents [Rule 8.4], the title of Rule 3.3 advises that lawyers have a higher duty to judges, the affirmative duty to be candid.

Note that Rule 3.3 applies to a "tribunal." It is not limited to a *court*. Thus, an arbitrator in a private arbitration is a "tribunal" for purposes of Rule 3.3. See Rule 1.0(m), defining "tribunal." This interpretation advances the disclosure obligations of Rule 3.3, because arbitrators have the power to issue subpoenas, compel the production of relevant documentary evidence, administer oaths, find the law and facts of the case, and, in general, exercise the powers of a court in the management and conduct of the hearing.

Rule 3.3 does not apply in mediation because a mediator is not a "tribunal" as defined in Model Rule 1.0(m). See also, Rule 2.4, Comment 5. Rule 3.3 does apply, however, to statements made to a tribunal if the tribunal itself is participating in settlement negotiations, including court-sponsored mediation in which a judge participates. ABA Formal Opinion 06–439 (April 12, 2006).

2. Making False Statements of Fact or Law: Rule 3.3(a)(1)

Rule 8.4, discussed below, adopts the general principle that a lawyer may not make misrepresentations or engage in any dishonest, fraudulent or deceitful conduct. A specific corollary of this principle is that a lawyer may not make a false statement of fact to a tribunal or offer evidence he knows to be false.

In addition, the lawyer must correct a false statement of law or fact that the lawyer made previously (even if the lawyer did not know that at the time) to the tribunal. Rule 3.3(a)(1). For example, a lawyer who discovers that her client has violated a court order prohibiting the transfer of assets must reveal that fact to the court if necessary to avoid "or correct" an affirmative misrepresentation that the lawyer had made to the court. ABA Formal Opinion 98–412 (September 9, 1998).

It is not always necessary, and it is sometimes not even permissible, to volunteer adverse *facts* when appearing before a tribunal. However, in some circumstances, the failure to make a disclosure is the equivalent of an affirmative misrepresentation. Consider *In re Jeffers* (Cal.Bar Ct.1994), where the State Bar Court of California concluded that a lawyer had "intentionally" misled a trial judge as to his client's death. The lawyer was not "directly asked" if his client was dead, and "his answers to the judge's questions may have been facially truthful" but that did not save him. This lawyer failed to inform the court of his client's death, and represented to the court, during settlement discussions, that he could not communicate with client because the client's "brain was not functioning." It wasn't functioning because the client was dead.

The court placed the respondent on probation for two years and required him to take and pass the professional responsibility examination. Rule 3.3(a)(1) provides explicitly that the lawyer shall not knowingly "make a false statement of fact or law" and shall not knowingly "fail to correct a false statement of material fact or law previously made to the tribunal by the lawyer." The lawyer misled the court. A half-truth is a full lie.

Even if a lawyer did not know a statement of fact or law was false when he made it, he must correct the statement when he discovers its falsity. Rule 3.3(a)(1). This duty applies "even if compliance requires disclosure of information otherwise protected" by the confidentiality requirements of Rule 1.6. This duty continues "to the conclusion of the proceeding." Rule 3.3(c).

3. Disclosure of Adverse Legal Authority: Rule 3.3(a)(2)

A lawyer is subject to discipline if he knowingly makes a false statement of law to a tribunal. A lawyer also must affirmatively disclose to a tribunal any legal authority in the controlling jurisdiction that he knows is directly adverse to his client's position and that opposing counsel has not disclosed.

This rule does not require a lawyer to make a disinterested exposition of the law. The interested party hires his lawyer, after all, to present that party's interests. But the advocate may not fail to disclose pertinent, adverse legal authority in the controlling jurisdiction. After disclosing these decisions he may seek to distinguish them, or challenge their soundness.

Note that the rule does not speak of "controlling authorities." It is broader and refers to "legal authority in the controlling jurisdiction." ABA Formal Opinion 280 (June 18, 1949) speaks to this issue and rejects the narrow view that the lawyer must only cite decisions that are decisive of the pending case. Rather, the disclosure rule applies to—

"a decision directly adverse to any proposition of law on which the lawyer expressly relies, which would reasonably be considered important by the judge sitting on the case.... The test in every case should be: Is the decision which opposing counsel has overlooked one which the court should clearly consider in deciding the case? Would a reasonable judge properly feel that a lawyer who advanced, as the law, a proposition adverse to the undisclosed decision, was lacking in candor and fairness to him? Might the judge consider himself misled by an implied representation that the lawyer knew of no adverse authority?"

Rule 3.3(c) makes clear that the lawyer's duty to disclose adverse legal authority extends until the proceedings are concluded "even if compliance requires disclosure of information otherwise protected by Rule 1.6."

4. Offering Evidence that the Lawyer Knows or Comes to Know is False: Rule 3.3(a)(3)

Is there a constitutional right to commit perjury? Some commentators have argued that the accused has a constitutional right to testify, and to testify falsely, without his or her lawyer revealing the client's perjury. E.g., Monroe Freedman, Understanding Lawyer's Ethics (1990). Comment 7 to Rule 3.3 acknowledges that some jurisdictions may hold this position. This Comment states that if a jurisdiction requires that the lawyer present the accused as a witness if the accused wishes to testify, "even if counsel knows the testimony or statement will be false," then the lawyer must follow the constitutional requirement of that jurisdiction. But it is trivial for the Model Rule to state that the lawyer must obey the law. The Model Rules do not grant such right, nor do states that follow the Model Rules, nor does the U.S. Constitution.

This federal constitutional issue came up in the Supreme Court decision in *Nix v. Whiteside* (S.Ct. 1986). The Supreme Court, with no dissent, held that there is no violation of the Sixth Amendment right to effective assistance of counsel when the lawyer refuses to cooperate with the defendant in presenting perjured testimony at the trial.

The criminal defendant Whiteside, in order to buttress his self-defense claim to a murder charge, in Iowa state court, wanted to testify that he had seen something "metallic" in the victim's hand. However, until a week before trial, Whiteside had consistently told his lawyer that he had not actually seen the victim with a gun. When his lawyer asked him about the intended change in testimony, Whiteside said: "If I don't say I saw a gun I'm dead." His lawyer responded that if Whiteside insisted on committing perjury, then "it would be my duty to advise the Court of what he [Whiteside] was doing and that I felt he was committing perjury; also, that I probably would be allowed to impeach that particular testimony." The lawyer also said that he would seek to withdraw from further representation.

At trial, Whiteside testified that he knew that the victim had a gun, but he admitted that he had not actually seen a gun in the victim's hand. Whiteside appealed his conviction claiming ineffective assistance of counsel because his lawyer's admonition against his proposed perjury had prevented him from giving false testimony. The Eighth Circuit granted habeas relief to Whiteside but the Supreme Court reversed, relying in part on Model Rule 3.3 (as well as Iowa state law) and holding that the lawyer acted properly and there is no constitutional right to commit perjury.

One year after *Nix*, the ABA Ethics Committee issued ABA Formal Opinion 87–353 (April 20, 1987), elaborating on Rule 3.3 and advising that the disclosure obligation is "limited" to the case where "the lawyer *knows* that the client has committed perjury, ordinarily based on admissions the client has made to the lawyer. The lawyer's suspicions are not enough."

This Opinion also advised that, if she cannot dissuade her client from testifying perjuriously, and cannot withdraw from representation, then the lawyer should either not call the client as a witness (if "the only testimony the client would offer is false"), or should question the client only on those matters that would not produce perjury. If the client does testify falsely, the lawyer cannot sit idly. She *must disclose* the false testimony. It is irrelevant whether the lawyer or the opposing lawyer asked the question that elicited the false reply.

The lawyer's "reasonable belief" does not preclude him from using testimony, but later on, the fact-finder who seeks to determine if the lawyer "knew" of the falsity can make that finding by inferring from the circumstances, so that "the lawyer cannot ignore an obvious falsehood." Rule 3.3 Comment 8.

ABA Formal Opinion 87–353 makes clear that the lawyer cannot avoid the responsibility that Rule 3.3 imposes by having the client testify in narrative form, without questioning. The Model Rules decisively reject the narrative approach outlined in the 1979 version of the ABA *Proposed Defense Function Standards*. Indeed, the present ABA Defense Standards, written in 1992, explicitly reject the narrative approach. Of course, if the lawyer is in a jurisdiction that rejects the ABA solution and require the narrative approach, then the lawyer should comply with that law. Rule 3.3, Comment 7.

What of pre-trial discovery? If a lawyer discovers that her client has lied in a deposition, the lawyer must use all reasonable means to remedy the fraud. The lawyer should first remonstrate with the client to rectify his testimony. If that fails, the lawyer must take other measures, including revealing the perjury to the judge.

An interesting example of a lawyer informing the court of false deposition statements by his client (who, in this case, was also a lawyer) is found in *Jones v. Clinton* (E.D.Ark.1999) (internal citation omitted). In the course of Judge Wright's opinion, she noted:

"Indeed, even though the President's testimony at his civil deposition was entirely consistent with Ms. Lewinsky's affidavit denying 'sexual relations' between herself and the President, the President's *attorney later notified this Court pursuant to his professional responsibility* that portions of Ms. Lewinsky's affidavit were reported to be 'misleading and not true' and that this Court should not rely on Ms. Lewinsky's affidavit or remarks of counsel characterizing that affidavit. The President's testimony at his deposition that Ms. Lewinsky's denial in her affidavit of a 'sexual relationship' between them was 'absolutely true' likewise was 'misleading and not true.' "

This deposition grew out of the litigation in *Clinton v. Jones* (S.Ct.1997), the decision denying the President immunity (permanent or temporary) from the civil suit for sexual assault filed by Ms. Paula Jones. On President Clinton's last day in office, January 19, 2001, he accepted a five-year suspension from the Arkansas Bar, ending disbarment proceedings following his false testimony. He has since been indefinitely disbarred from the bar of Supreme Court of the United States.

The Clinton scenario is one where the opposing party's attorney asks a question during cross examination, to which the lawyer's client responds with an answer the lawyer thought at the time to be accurate. However, the lawyer later learns that the client lied in the deposition. Hence Rule 3.3 applies. It is not necessary that the testimony be given before the judge. In the typical discovery situation, the judge will not have read the deposition and therefore will not be aware of specific testimony. Nonetheless, Rule 3.3 requires the lawyer to take reasonable remedial measures to rectify the false testimony or evidence, including telling the judge if necessary.

5. Remedies: Withdrawal from the Case and Protection of a Client's Secrets: Rule 3.3(b)

In many cases, a lawyer's withdrawal from the case, even a "noisy withdrawal," will not be entirely effective to undo the fraud's impact on the case. For example, the opposing party might drop the case or settle it, in reliance on the false deposition, in spite of a noisy withdrawal. Consequently, "[d]irect disclosure under Rule 3.3, to the opposing party or, if need be to the court, may prove to be the only reasonable remedial measure in the client fraud situations most likely to be encountered in pretrial proceedings." ABA Formal Opinion 93–376 (August 6, 1993).

What of cases where withdrawal will be effective to fulfill the lawyer's obligations, but the very fact that the lawyer has withdrawn will undermine the client's confidences or secrets? The client may even specifically instruct the lawyer not to broadcast the fact of his withdrawal. The client, in short, would like the lawyer to tiptoe away *quietly* and not announce his withdrawal. The Model Rules make clear that the lawyer cannot respect the client's interest in keeping secret his lawyer's withdrawal. The Rules advise, generally, that if the lawyer offered material evidence and later learns of its falsity, she "must take reasonable remedial measures." Rule 3.3(b). This duty applies "even if compliance requires disclosure of information otherwise protected'' by the confidentiality requirements of Rule 1.6. Rule 3.3(c).

Before making this dramatic disclosure to the court, there are other options the lawyer should pursue. First, of course, the lawyer should seek to persuade the client to correct the falsehood. The lawyer should ''remonstrate with the client confidentially,'' and explain to him the lawyer's disclosure obligations under Rule 3.3(c). If the client is still adamant, the lawyer should seek to withdraw if that will ''undo the effect of the false evidence.'' Comment 10.

However, in many cases it will not be enough for the lawyer to wash his hands of the situation. In some cases, withdrawal will not be possible because the court will not allow it. In the middle of a trial or on the eve of a trial, for example, the court is unlikely to allow the lawyer to withdraw. Even if the court allows withdrawal, the lawyer must disclose the perjury or fraud to the judge if withdrawal does not ''undo the effect of the false evidence . . . .'' Comment 10. In those circumstances, the lawyer must disclose the relevant information to the court. The court then decides what to do next: (1) make a statement to the trier of fact; (2) order a mistrial; (3) or perhaps nothing.

If the lawyer discloses client perjury to the court, and the client disputes the charge, then the lawyer obviously cannot represent the client in resolution of this factual issue because the lawyer will be a

witness and have a view of the facts that is contrary
to the client's. The judge may declare a mistrial.

6.   Time Limits on the Lawyer's Duty to Disclose: Rule 3.3(c)

The duties that Rule 3.3(a) and Rule 3.3(b) impose continue until the conclusion of the proceedings. Rule 3.3(c) does not specifically define when
the proceedings have concluded, but Comment 13
offers some explanation.

When proceedings are concluded should depend
on the nature of the case.

- In a criminal case, a verdict of acquittal concludes the proceedings, given that the double
  jeopardy clause prevents the state from retry-
  ing the defendant. But if the defendant is convicted, the case is not yet concluded, because
  the defendant may wish to appeal to secure a
  new trial or an outright reversal; the defendant
  should not be able to benefit from his earlier
  perjury. Accordingly, the proceeding should not
  be treated as "concluded" until at least the
  time for direct appeal has passed.

- In a civil case, the proceedings should not be
  treated as concluded until the time for appeal
  has passed. If the civil case has just concluded
  with a jury verdict in defendant's favor, and
  the defense lawyer then learned that she won
  the case with her client's perjury, the proceedings have not yet concluded, because post trial

motions are still in order and the time for appeal has not yet passed.

Rule 3.3(c) makes clear that, if necessary, the civil lawyer will have to reveal the fact that his client committed perjury in order to comply with the candor requirements of Rule 3.3(a) & (b).

The remedial requirement of Rule 3.3(c) applies to all of Rule 3.3 (a) & (b).

7. *Ex Parte* Proceedings: Rule 3.3(d)

The Model Rules place upon the lawyer a special affirmative duty in *ex parte* proceedings (where the tribunal hears only one side) to disclose all material facts (whether or not thought to be adverse) so that the tribunal can make an informed decision. In an *ex parte* proceeding, one cannot rely on the adversary system to uncover the truth, so Rule 3.3(d) imposes this broader duty to disclose.

Often lawyers act as advisors, not as litigators, as when advising a client that it is lawful to claim a particular tax deduction. The Rules do not treat the Internal Revenue Service like a court, nor do they treat the tax return like a request for an *ex parte* order. The lawyer, advising a client with respect to a tax return, is acting both as an advisor and, potentially as an advocate if the matter is later litigated. The Rules treat the I.R.S. like an opponent, not like a judge.

The general rule is that the lawyer may advise her client on taking a position on a tax return—

"even where the lawyer believes the position *probably will not prevail*, there is no 'substantial authority' in support of the position, and there will be no disclosure of the position in the [tax] return. However, the position to be asserted must be one which the lawyer in good faith believes is warranted in existing law or can be supported by a good faith argument for an extension, modification *or reversal* of existing law. This requires that there is *some realistic possibility of success* if the matter is litigated." ABA Formal Opinion 85–352 at 4 (July 7, 1985).

The prudent lawyer also must advise the client of the risks of taking this position on the tax return, including any adverse legal consequences or possible penalties that the Internal Revenue Service might impose, if the client takes the position on the tax return that the lawyer has offered.

RULE 3.4: FAIRNESS TO THE OPPOSING PARTY AND COUNSEL

1. Distinction Between the Lawyer's Duties of Candor to the Court and the Duty of Fairness to Opposing Counsel

The ethics rules impose on lawyers affirmative obligations of *candor* to a *tribunal*, e.g., to disclose material adverse legal authority. However, with respect to *opposing parties or third parties*, the lawyer's duty is, in general, more limited. Subject to various exceptions, the fundamental principle is that lawyers may not knowingly misrepresent either a material fact or law to opposing parties or other persons. This principle applies whether the lawyer is involved in litigation or negotiation.

The Rules frequently repeat the principle that a lawyer may neither make *any misrepresentation* nor engage in any dishonest, fraudulent or deceitful conduct. Rule 4.1(a) states that, in the course of representing a client, the lawyer "shall not knowingly ... make a false statement of material fact or law to a third person." Rule 8.4(c) provides that a lawyer engages in "professional misconduct" when he or she engages in conduct "involving dishonesty,

fraud, deceit or misrepresentation." And then there
is Rule 3.4, the subject of this section.

Consider this situation. Plaintiff's lawyer (*"P–L"*)
plans to file a claim against defendant. Both *P–L*
and plaintiff know that the statute of limitations
has run, but they hope that defendant and her
counsel (*"D–L"*) will not plead the statute. During
the course of negotiations, *P–L* discovers that both
defendant and her counsel, *D–L*, are unaware of the
limitations defense. *P–L* is careful not to make any
affirmative misrepresentation about the facts showing that the claim is time-barred. *P–L* is acting
properly. The lawyer for one party normally has no
duty to volunteer the existence of adverse facts or
law to the other party. ABA Formal Opinion 94–387
(Sept. 26, 1994). *P–L* may take advantage of *D–L*'s
mistake.

On the other hand, even though *P–L* does not
have to volunteer to her opponent a statutory defense, the lawyer cannot keep the *judge* in the dark.
The Rules impose an affirmative duty of candor to
the judge, as seen in the discussion of Rule 3.3(a).
The lawyer may neither explicitly misrepresent the
state of the law nor mislead the court, by, for
example, by purporting to list all the relevant statutes of limitations but omitting the one that is
adverse and on point. The lawyer must disclose this
legal authority in open court, not in an *ex parte*
communication to the judge. That means that the
opponent will, eventually, also know what is going
on, but that is what Rule 3.3 requires. However, as
"long as the lawyer makes no misrepresentations in

pleadings or orally to the court or opposing counsel, she has breached no ethical duty towards either.'' ABA Formal Op. 94–387.

However, if the matter never reaches the judge, *e.g.,* the parties are discussing settlement before a case is even filed, then the lawyer cannot mislead or lie to the opposing lawyer about the existence of the new statute, but is not obliged to reveal the defense *sua sponte* to the adversary because Rule 3.3(a) does not even come into play.

In short, in negotiations (including negotiations prior to litigation), a lawyer may not make a false statement of material fact to the opposing party. However, statements regarding a party's negotiating goals or willingness to compromise, as well as statements that are negotiation ''puffing,'' are not ordinarily considered ''false statements of material fact or law'' within the meaning of the Model Rules, such as Rule 4.1. For example, a buyer of products ''might overstate its confidence in the availability of alternate sources of supply to reduce the appearance of dependence upon the supplier with which it is negotiating.''

But, the lawyer may not make false statements of law or fact. Thus, a lawyer may not ''declare that documentary evidence will be submitted at trial in support of a defense when the lawyer knows that such documents do not exist or will be inadmissible.'' Similarly, ''neither a prosecutor nor a criminal defense lawyer can tell the other party during a plea negotiation that they are aware of an eyewit-

ness to the alleged crime when that is not the case.''
ABA Formal Opinion 06–439 (April 12, 2006).

2.   Obstructing Access to Evidence

A.   The Lawyer's or Client's Obstruction of Physical Evidence of a Crime

A corollary to the general principle that a lawyer may not engage in deceitful behavior or misrepresent the facts or the law, is Rule 3.4's requirement that a lawyer may not unlawfully obstruct access to, alter, or conceal evidence, or witnesses, or encourage a witness to testify falsely. In addition, Rule 3.3(a)(3) gives the lawyer discretion to refuse to offer evidence (other than the testimony of the defendant in a criminal matter) that he or she ''reasonably believes is false.''

In re Ryder (E.D.Va.1967) (per curiam), involved a criminal defense lawyer who accepted from his client stolen money and a sawed-off shotgun used in an armed bank robbery. The lawyer deposited both in the lawyer's own safe deposit box. This case illustrates what a lawyer may not do in light of Rule 3.3(a), which forbids a lawyer from obstructing another party's access to evidence.

In *Ryder*, the lawyer knew that his client had given him the fruits (stolen money) and the instrumentality (a gun) of a crime. The lawyer intended to keep possession of this evidence until his client's trial unless the government discovered it before then. The court explained that the defense lawyer intended, by his possession, to destroy the chain of evidence linking his client to the contraband and thereby reduce the likelihood that it would be used at trial against his client. The court suspended the lawyer for 18 months, and said that the sanction would have been greater but for the fact that the lawyer intended to return the bank's money after the trial.

In *Morrell v. State* (Alaska 1978), the state supreme court upheld the trial court's admission of incriminating evidence of a kidnapping plan allegedly written by the defendant. A friend of the defendant turned the plan over to defense counsel, who then aided the friend in turning the evidence over to the police. Defense counsel then withdrew from the case. The Alaska Supreme Court held:

> "[A] criminal defense attorney must turn over to the prosecution real evidence that the attorney obtains from his client. Further, if the evidence is obtained from a non-client third party who is not acting for the client, then the privilege to refuse to testify concerning the manner in which the evidence was obtained is inapplicable.... [Defense counsel] would have been obligated to see that the evidence reached the prosecutor in this case *even if he had obtained the evidence from Morrell*. His obligation was even clearer because he acquired the evidence from [a third party], who made the decision to turn the evidence over to [defense counsel] without consulting Morrell and therefore was not acting as Morrell's agent....

"[Defense counsel] could have properly turned the evidence over to the police himself and would have been obliged to do so if [the third party] had refused to accept the return of the evidence. . . .

"[Finally, while] statutes which address the concealing of evidence are generally construed to require an affirmative act of concealment in addition to the failure to disclose information to the authorities, taking possession of evidence from a non-client third party and holding the evidence in a place not accessible to investigating authorities would seem to fall within the statute's ambit. Thus, [the defense lawyer] breached no ethical obligation to his client which may have rendered his legal services to Morrell ineffective." (internal citation and footnotes omitted).

B. Discovery Abuses in Civil Cases

The problem of lawyers and clients destroying or withholding evidence that is subpoenaed is not limited to solo practitioners representing criminal defendants. Renowned law firms and large corporations have violated these principles in civil cases. Sometimes these violations have been thwarted by attorneys who fulfilled their ethical duties, e.g., John J. Fialka, *Lawyer Says He Was Told to Destroy Documents*, WALL STREET JOURNAL, March 26, 1999, at B8, col. 4–6. A lawyer in the Interior Department told Federal Judge Royce C. Lambreth that the department's deputy solicitor "directed" him to "purg[e] from the files" certain documents involving allegations that Indian trust funds had been mishandled. Judge Lambert ordered the Interior Department not to take any retaliatory action against the lawyer.

On other occasions lawyers act unethically in connivance with their clients, with disastrous results for both. See, *e.g.,* Paul M. Barrett, *Libel Verdict Against Dow Jones To Be Thrown Out, Says Judge*, WALL STREET JOURNAL, April 9, 1999, at B19, col. 1–2 reporting a case where the trial judge announced that he threw out a $22.7 million libel verdict against Dow Jones & Co., publisher of the *Wall Street Journal.* Plaintiff sued over a 1993 *Journal* article about a now defunct investment firm, MMAR Group, Inc. The judge said: "From clear and convincing evidence, the Court finds that MMAR obtained its favorable verdict through its own misconceptions and misrepresentations." The judge's opinion explained that MMAR should have, during discovery, surrendered secret tape recordings that would have helped Dow Jones prove the truth of three of the five statements the jury found false and defamatory. A former MMAR employee told Dow Jones lawyers that a MMAR official pressured him to erase certain tapes.

3. Money Payments to Fact and Expert Witnesses

The former Model Code, DR 7–109(C), specifically prohibited a lawyer from paying a witness any money contingent on the outcome of the case. The lawyer could only advance, guarantee, or acquiesce in the non-contingent payment of (1) a witness' *expenses* in attending or testifying; (2) compensation for the witness' *loss of time* because of attending or testifying, and (3) *a reasonable fee for an expert witness*' professional services. Curiously, the Model Rules have no explicit provision against paying contingent fees to witnesses. However, Comment 3 to Rule 3.4 notes that the "common law rule in most jurisdictions is that it is improper to pay an occurrence witness any fee for testifying and that it is improper to pay an expert witness a contingent fee." This prohibition is long-standing. *In re Schapiro* (N.Y.App.Div.1911), disbarring a lawyer who paid a contingent fee to a witness.

Washington, D.C. is an exception to the general rule. It does have an unusual and explicit provision that allows a fee to an expert witness to be contingent on the outcome of the proceeding but not contingent on the amount actually recovered:

> "A fee for the services of a witness who will be proffered as an expert may be made contingent on the outcome of the litigation; provided, however, that the fee, while conditioned on recovery, shall not be a percentage of the recovery."
> Washington, D.C. Rules of Professional Conduct, Rule 3.4, Comment 8.

The Restatement squarely rejects this D.C. Rule: *Restatement of the Law Governing Lawyers*, Third, § 117(2) (Official draft, 2000) (the lawyer may not pay a witness based "on the content of the witness's testimony or the outcome of the litigation").

The general rule is that lawyers can pay expert witnesses for their time, but not for their testimony. In other words, the lawyer can pay an expert witness an hourly fee, which represents a fee for the expert's time to evaluate the case and give her advice and expert opinion. But the lawyer may not make this fee contingent on the outcome of the expert witness's testimony or the outcome of the litigation.

When lawyers deal with *fact* witnesses, the lawyers may only pay these witnesses for the "reasonable *expenses* of the witness incurred and the reasonable value of the witness's time spent in providing evidence." Restatement of the Law Governing Lawyers, Third, § 117 (1) (Official Draft 2000). Lawyers cannot pay fact witnesses money in exchange for their testimony.

The ABA has opined that lawyers may compensate non-expert witnesses for their time spent attending a deposition or trial or meeting with the lawyer preparatory to testimony. However, the lawyer may not condition the payment on the content of the testimony. In addition, any payment must be consistent with other law in the jurisdiction. ABA Formal Opinion 96–401 (Aug. 2, 1996). The Committee referred to Comment 3 and then announced that "compensating a witness for his loss of time" does not "amount to paying him a 'fee for testifying.' " In addition, 18 U.S.C.A § 201(j) provides that payments to lay witnesses for "the reasonable value of time lost in attendance at any such trial, hearing or proceeding" do not violate federal bribery statutes. The lawyer may also compensate the witness "for time spent in reviewing and researching records that are germane to his or her testimony, provided, of course, that such compensation is not barred by local law."

The compensation must be reasonable "to avoid affecting, even unintentionally, the content of a witness's testimony." ABA Formal Opinion 96–401. Thus, *Golden Door Jewelry Creations, Inc. v. Lloyds Underwriters Non–Marine Ass'n* (S.D.Fla.1994) excluded all evidence tainted by a violation of the ethics rules. In that case, the insurer with knowledge of its counsel, paid $120,000 to fact witnesses to testify at depositions. The court found this payment violated the Florida analogue to Model Rule 3.5(a). The court found no violation of the bribery statute (there was no evidence of money offered for "false" testimony) but concluded that there was an ethical violation. Paying money to a witness to "tell the truth" is as "subversive of the proper administration of justice as to pay him to testify to what is not true." The court excluded all evidence tainted by the ethical violation.

Prosecutors offer witnesses other inducements to testify but Rule 3.4 does not forbid that. Sometimes these witnesses are informants who receive money for living expenses from law enforcement authorities; sometimes they are criminal defendants who testify in exchange for immunity from prosecution or for the possibility of a lighter sentence. Courts have permitted these inducements because their purpose is not to change the content of the testimony but simply to get information that, realistically, would not otherwise normally be forthcoming. Indeed, courts are often involved in the decision to grant a favor (immunity, a reduced sentence) in exchange for the witness' cooperation. On the federal level, for example, 18 U.S.C.A., §§ 3553(e) & 994(n), permit federal courts, acting pursuant to Sentencing Guidelines and upon motion of the government, to reduce sentences for individuals who provide "substantial assistance in the investigation or prosecution of another." Federal immunity statutes require courts, upon the request of the government, to confer immunity upon witnesses for their testimony in aid of the prosecution. The Witness Relocation and Protection Act allows the government to bestow various benefits to protect cooperating witnesses.

A federal statute, the anti-gratuity statute, 18 U.S.C.A. § 201(c)(2), makes it a crime for "whomever" to "promise anything of value to any person, for or because of the testimony under oath. . . ." A panel of the Tenth Circuit, in 1998, concluded that this section prevents federal prosecutors from offering leniency to an accomplice in exchange for truthful testimony. The panel reasoned that, when the Government offers a witness statutory immunity, it promises that his immunized testimony cannot be used to prosecute him. Thus, the witness is given something of value (immunity) and the Government receives something of value (testimony) in return.

The *en banc* court reversed this panel. *United States v. Singleton* (10th Cir.1999). The majority ruled that the reference in the statute to "whomever" does not include the United States acting in its sovereign capacity. The Government, in short, did not intend, by one statute, to criminalize that which several other federal statutes specifically authorize.

4. Coaching Witnesses, Preparing Witnesses, and Counseling a Witness to Testify Falsely

Lawyers may interview and prepare witnesses for trial, but lawyers may not suggest that a client or witness testify falsely. If the suggestion is baldly or even impliedly made, the lawyer is violating ethical requirements and may be guilty of suborning perjury.

For trials, attorneys often prepare witnesses by trying to refresh their recollection. For example, lawyers show witnesses documents that they may have seen (or even written themselves) years earlier. But when lawyers put their own words into witnesses' mouths, there is a danger that lawyers are not preserving evidence but simply making it up. Careful trial lawyers must therefore find out if a witness is giving his own testimony or merely repeating what an unethical lawyer told him to say. If a witness' testimony appears to have been memorized or rehearsed or if it appears the witness is testifying using the lawyer's words rather than his own, or has been improperly coached, the careful lawyer should explore such matters on cross-examination.

An example of an attorney crossing ethical lines occurred when an attorney said to a plaintiff, "You will be asked if you ever saw any WARNING labels on containers of asbestos. It is important to maintain that you NEVER saw any labels on asbestos products that said WARNING or DANGER." Quoted in Rotunda & Dzienkowski, *Legal Ethics: The Lawyer's Deskbook on Professional Conduct* § 3.4–3 (ABA Thomson-West 4th ed. 2006). This statement invites or instructs perjury, unless the attorney already knew that the witness never actually saw any warning labels and was just reminding him of that fact.

Courses in legal ethics often refer to Judge John D. Voelker's famous novel, *Anatomy of a Murder.* There, the defense lawyer, in developing a homicide defense of temporary diminished mental capacity, planted words in the defendant's mouth. The defendant supplied the requisite "facts" only after having been told in advance by counsel what types of facts would constitute a successful defense. The lawyer was planting testimony, not discovering it.

There is no scientific study that measures how often attorneys cross the line from ethically preparing witnesses to planting false statements, but there is some empirical evidence that gives cause for concern. Before the Johns–Manville Corporation filed for bankruptcy, workers testified that Johns–Manville manufactured about 70 to 80 percent of the asbestos products in certain workplaces. After Manville filed for bankruptcy and became judgment-proof, workers began to testify that Manville's product share was only 10 to 20 percent. As other companies being sued went bankrupt, testimony changed again. *See* Lester Brickman and Ronald D. Rotunda, *When Witnesses Are Told What to Say*, WASHINGTON POST, January 13, 1998, at A15.

5. Responses to Discovery Requests

Rule 3.1 prohibits frivolous claims, and Rule 3.2 urges lawyers to make "reasonable efforts to expedite litigation." Rule 3.4 builds on these general principles by its more specific command that prohibits lawyers from making frivolous discovery requests. This Rule also covers the failure to make a reasonably diligent effort to comply with legitimate discovery requests.

The mere fact that a legal position is "creative" or contrary to existing law does not make it frivolous. Existing law often has ambiguities and potential for change. Therefore a lawyer, in seeking to subpoena a document that appears to be protected as privileged, may still make a "good faith argument for an extension, modification or reversal of existing law."

6. Disobeying a Tribunal's Orders

In general, the ethics rules mandate that the lawyer obey a judge's orders. The lawyer and client, of course, have the right to claim an evidentiary privilege or to object to a judge's rulings, but Rule 3.4(c) states that they must do so openly, so that the judge can rule on the validity of the claim.

Eyewitness identification is one of the most persuasive types of evidence, but it is often wrong, as shown by overturned jury verdicts based on eyewitness testimony and later contradicted by DNA testing. Some criminal defense counsel have sought to refute eyewitnesses by having someone who is not their client sit at counsel table and pretend to be the accused. Courts have held lawyers in contempt for this tactic, on the grounds that it violates court rules and misleads the court. *See, e.g., United States v. Thoreen* (9th Cir.1981). Hence, the lawyer who wishes to engage in such conduct should tell the judge first.

7. Trial Tactics, Inadmissible Evidence, and Closing Arguments

During the trial the lawyer may not "allude" to any matter not reasonably believed to be relevant or admissible. Nor may he, in closing argument or otherwise, assert his personal opinion or knowledge regarding facts at issue, unless he is actually testifying as a witness. However, the lawyer may argue for any position or conclusion based on his analysis of the evidence. Rule 3.4(e).

Consider two examples that illustrate this principle. First, assume that in closing argument the lawyer states: "How can you believe Witness? I've seen many people testify over the years, and in my experience, Witness is lying. I don't believe him, can you?" The lawyer's action is improper, even if Lawyer really believes that Witness is lying because the lawyer may not assert his personal opinions regarding the facts at issue.

Now, assume that in closing argument the lawyer states: "How can you believe Witness? His testimony contradicts the sworn testimony of three other people who, unlike Witness, have no financial interest in this case." The lawyer's action is proper, whether or not Lawyer personally believes Witness is lying, because Lawyer is just arguing from the evidence in the record.

8. Asking Witnesses Not to Volunteer Information

A lawyer may not obstruct her opponents' ability to collect evidence. However, she may advise *her client* that he should not volunteer information to the opponent. Rule 3.4(f).

If the client does not volunteer information, the opposing lawyer may simply subpoena the client for a deposition. Then, the lawyer will be able to protect the client's interest by reviewing documents before they are turned over to make sure no privileges are waived. During the deposition, the lawyer's participation will similarly serve to protect the client's interest.

There are certain types of non-clients whom lawyers can *request* not to volunteer information. The general rule is that, on behalf of his client, the lawyer may always request an *unrepresented non-client* witness to refrain from voluntarily giving relevant information to another party *if* the witness is the client's *relative, employee, or agent* whose interests will not be adversely affected if this request is honored. The lawyer, of course, cannot *forbid* such witnesses from being interviewed.

Lawyers have no right to request other non-clients—*i.e.,* witnesses with no connection to the client—to refrain from volunteering information to the opposing lawyer. For example, in *North Carolina State Bar v. Graves* (N.C.App.1981), the court disciplined an attorney who had attempted to persuade a witness to refuse to testify or, in the alternative, to plead the Fifth Amendment.

Harlan v. Lewis (8th Cir.1993) ruled that a defense lawyer in a medical malpractice case violated Rule 3.4 by suggesting to a treating physician of the plaintiff that, although the plaintiffs could also sue him for malpractice, that suit would be unsuccessful if the doctor refused to testify in the instant case. The court sanctioned the lawyer $2,500.

RULE 3.5: IMPARTIALITY AND DECORUM OF THE TRIBUNAL

A lawyer may not attempt to influence a judge, juror, prospective juror, or other official by means prohibited by law or by court order. Rule 3.5 incorporates by reference this other law, then imposes the additional threat of legal discipline.

The Model Rules forbid improper *ex parte* communications with jurors or prospective jurors during the proceeding. Similarly, it forbids improper efforts to influence judges, jurors, prospective jurors, or other officials. Deliberate efforts to disrupt a tribunal are of course also sanctionable.

Just as the lawyer-official may not accept anything of value offered to influence her own actions as a public official, neither may a lawyer seek to influence a public official (or juror) improperly.

In 2002, the ABA added Rule 3.5(c), specifying when the lawyer may not contact jurors *after* the conclusion of proceedings. If a juror lets the lawyer know of a desire not to receive his communications, the lawyer must respect this wish, unless he can obtain a court order to the contrary. A court may, in advance, also prohibit contact with jurors after

discharge. No contact may involve "misrepresentation, coercion, duress or harassment."

RULE 3.6: TRIAL PUBLICITY

The tension between a commitment to a robust discussion of public issues in a free press on the one hand, and a commitment to a criminal process in which the conclusions reached in a case will come only from evidence and argument in open court on the other, has been a subject of long standing debate as Chief Justice Burger noted in *Nebraska Press Association v. Stuart* (S.Ct.1976). The problem becomes more acute with the growth of electronic media. The issue is the extent to which the disciplinary rules may insulate a courtroom from the intrusion of outside prejudice caused by publicity surrounding the case. The primary ethics rule is Rule 3.6. Rule 3.6 attempts to balance the right of free speech with the right to a fair trial. After *Gentile v. State Bar of Nevada* (S.Ct.1991), discussed immediately below, the balance now swings closer to First Amendment concerns.

Any limits on a lawyer's right to comment raise serious questions regarding possible unconstitutional restrictions on the lawyer's First Amendment rights. A leading decision is *Gentile v. State Bar of Nevada*, where a fragmented Supreme Court held that a Nevada Supreme Court Rule, almost identical to the then existing version of ABA Model Rule

3.6, governing a lawyer's pretrial statements about a case, incorporated a standard that was "void for vagueness."

Attorney Gentile held a press conference a few hours after Nevada had indicted his client. Gentile made a brief statement, mentioning generally his client's defense, and stating that he thought certain policemen he named had committed the crime for which his client was being charged. He declined to answer reporters' questions seeking more detailed comments. Six months later a jury acquitted Gentile's client of all counts. Then the State Bar of Nevada filed a complaint against Gentile for allegedly violating Nevada's Supreme Court Rule 177, governing pretrial publicity. The Nevada Disciplinary Board recommended a private reprimand for Mr. Gentile and the State Supreme Court agreed. The U.S. Supreme Court reversed.

Justice Kennedy, for the Court, concluded that the existing Rule misled Mr. Gentile to believe that he could make statements on the general nature of his client's defense, even if he knew that these statements would have a substantial likelihood of prejudicing an adjudicative proceeding. The present version of Rule 3.6(b), modified after the *Gentile case*, creates a safe harbor that is no longer void for vagueness. The lawyer may disclose certain specific matters, such as information contained in a public record, the claim, offense, or defense involved, and so forth. See Rule 3.6(b).

Rule 3.6(a) adopts a general test restricting speech if the extrajudicial statement "will have a substantial likelihood of materially prejudicing an adjudicative proceeding in the matter." Whether the case is civil or criminal, with or without a jury, it is important to remember that Rule 3.6(b) creates a safe harbor allowing certain extrajudicial statements including, *e.g.*, information contained in a public record, a request for assistance in obtaining evidence, a warning of the danger concerning an individual if there is reason to believe that there exits the likelihood of substantial harm, the scheduling or results of any steps in litigation, the general nature of the claim, the general scope of an investigation, the identity of the accused, and the identity of the arresting and investigating officers.

Rule 3.6 distinguishes between criminal and civil cases by allowing a bit more speech in criminal cases. Rule 3.6(a)(7) says that, in addition to what Rule 3.6(a)(1)–(6) allow, the lawyer, in a criminal case, may also disclose the identity, residence, occupation, and family status of the accused, whether the accused has been apprehended and a request of information to apprehend him, the fact, time, and place of the arrest, and the identity of the arresting and investigating officers and the length of the investigation.

Rule 3.6(c) adds a new right not found in the Model Code: a lawyer may make an extrajudicial statement that would otherwise be improper, if it is in response to statements by others, when a reasonable lawyer believes that the response is necessary to avoid prejudicing his client. These self-defense-type statements should be limited to information that is necessary to mitigate any undue prejudice created by the statements that others have made. In a sense, the lawyer can fight fire with fire, by using his free speech rights to counteract negative publicity about his client.

Attorney Grievance Commission of Maryland v. Gansler (Md.2003) held that, the safe harbor provisions of Rule 3.6 relating to "public record" should be limited to public government records, *i.e.*, "the records and papers on file with a government entity to which an ordinary citizen would have lawful access." The court then imposed a public reprimand of a state's attorney for, among other things, making a statement at a press conference discussing defendant's confession to murder.

Rule 3.8(f) is also not found in the old Model Code. Rule 3.8, unlike Rule 3.6, only applies to prosecutors as discussed below. Rule 3.8(f) specifically warns prosecutors to refrain from making, or from allowing other law enforcement officers to make, any extrajudicial comments that serve no legitimate law enforcement purpose and have a substantial likelihood of heightening public opprobrium of the accused.

RULE 3.7: LAWYER
AS WITNESS

The Model Rules limit the instances when an advocate may simultaneously act as a witness. The Model Rules treat the case where the advocate is asked to be a witness as an instance of conflict of interests. However, Rule 3.7 does not automatically impute this conflict of interest to other members of the disqualified lawyer's firm. See Rule 3.7(b) & Comment 7.

The reason this conflict is not imputed is apparent once one looks at the reason for its existence. For many years some commentators, as well as the former Model Code, offered various inconsistent rationales for the advocate-witness rule. Lawyers were told that the restrictions on the testifying advocate should exist because, *e.g.*, such an advocate may be "more easily impeachable for interest." At the same time that they were told that the lawyer-witness should be disqualified because "the opposing counsel may be handicapped in challenging the credibility of the lawyer . . . ." Model Code of Professional Responsibility, EC 5–9.

The primary rationale supporting Rule 3.7 is that the fact-finder may be confused if the person actually acting as an advocate before the fact-finder also offers testimony with his or her argument: "The tribunal has proper objection when the trier of fact may be confused or misled by a lawyer serving as both advocate and witness." Rule 3.7, Comment 2.

This is of course what happens when someone represents himself *pro se*. The advocate-witness rule would not prevent a *pro se* litigant from testifying. If a lawyer represents himself *pro se* he still may testify. Rule 3.7 exists so that lawyers, who are officers of the court, may not create unnecessary confusion. Indeed, Rule 3.7(a)(3) allows an exception to the advocate-witness rule when disqualification of the lawyer "would work a substantial hardship on the client."

The advocate-witness rule basically provides that the advocate should withdraw if she is "likely to be a necessary witness" unless the testimony relates to an uncontested issue, or it relates to the nature and value of legal services in that case. Nor should the lawyer accept employment if she likely to be called as witness, unless one of the exceptions is applicable.

The Model Code explicitly imputed the advocate-witness disqualification to all lawyers in the firm. However, in conformity with the rationale of the rule, the Model Rules do not impute the advocate-witness prohibition. Where the witness is a partner of another lawyer who is the advocate, there is no automatic imputation because there is no realistic danger of confusing the fact-finder. The same person will not be testifying and then arguing the significance of that testimony to the jury.

Given this rationale of confusion of the fact-finder—an interest of the judicial system rather than an interest of the client—the Rules do not provide for client waiver of the advocate-witness rule. The party represented by the advocate-witness may seek to "waive" the disqualification because she wants jury confusion. Or the attorney for the other side may avoid pressing for disqualification out of a desire to avoid clashing with opposing counsel. None of these reasons affect the rationale of the Rule and thus none justify waiver. Accordingly, where neither party moves for disqualification, the court should act *sua sponte*.

If the advocate-witness rule requires a lawyer to be disqualified, then the disqualified lawyer may consult with the party's substitute counsel and assist in preparing for trial. The reason offered for the advocate-witness rule (confusion of fact-finder) does not justify prohibiting the disqualified advocate-witness from consulting with the new lawyer (or with other lawyers in his firm, if the other lawyers become the trial counsel). E.g., *MacArthur v. Bank of New York* (S.D.N.Y.1981). For example, the disqualified lawyer will not divulge any forbidden confidences or other improper information to the new lawyer, because the court did not disqualify the lawyer-witness for that reason; nor will the lawyer-witness, who is no longer a lawyer-advocate, be able to confuse the fact-finder.

Many ethical restrictions are enforced primarily in the course of proceedings before disciplinary tribunals. Not so with the advocate-witness rule.

Courts routinely enforce the advocate-witness rule in the course of litigation.

The fact that Rule 3.7 does not provide for imputation does not mean that another rule might apply. If Rule 1.7 or Rule 1.9 applies, then those other rules impute the disqualification. See Rule 3.7, Comment 7.

RULE 3.8: SPECIAL RESPONSIBILITIES OF A PROSECUTOR

1. Introduction

It is often said that the duty of the public prosecutor is to seek justice, not merely to convict. From this principle the law has imposed limitations that modify the duty of zealous behavior of government attorneys when they are acting as prosecutors in criminal cases. Sometimes, courts state that government lawyers, *even in civil cases*, are under a higher standard than their civil counterparts. However, if one actually looks at the case results, as opposed to the dicta, one finds that, outside of the area of criminal prosecution, this does not appear to be the case. ABF Formal Opinion 94–387 (Sept. 26, 1994) at Part III. This section lists the principal differences discussed in Rule 3.8.

2. Criminal Cases

Ordinarily a lawyer may bring any nonfrivolous action. The criminal prosecutor's obligations are stricter: a prosecutor may not institute charges—even if they are not frivolous—if he knows that they are not supported by *probable* cause. Rule 3.8(a).

Civil litigants have, in general, no ethical duty to volunteer adverse information to their opponents in litigation. In contrast, criminal prosecutors must volunteer adverse information. The prosecutor must inform the accused of the existence of evidence that tends to negate the guilt of the accused or mitigate the punishment. Moreover, the prosecutor should not intentionally fail to follow certain leads because he believes the information secured might damage his case. Prosecutors must turn over not only exculpatory evidence but also evidence that can be used to impeach government witnesses. Similarly, the prosecutor must also inform the sentencing tribunal of all mitigating information not covered by a protective order or otherwise privileged.

The prosecutor should give the accused a reasonable opportunity to obtain counsel, and should not urge an unrepresented accused to waive important pretrial rights, such as the right to a preliminary hearing.

In recent years, the Government has appeared to increase its subpoenas of criminal defense lawyers to testify before the grand jury. The Government often seeks information on the amount of the fee paid to the attorney, whether this fee was paid in cash, and whether the client or a third party paid the fee. The answers to these questions are relevant in light of various federal laws such as the Racketeer Influenced and Corrupt Organizations Act [18 U.S.C.A. §§ 1961–68] and the Continuing Criminal Enterprise Statute [21 U.S.C.A. §§ 848–53]. The fee may be subject to forfeiture if the client acquired it through certain criminal activity or it is evidence of a criminal enterprise.

Attorneys who are witnesses to criminal acts have no privilege to refuse to testify about those acts, even if the perpetrator is their client. An interesting case on this issue is *In re January 1976 Grand Jury* (7th Cir.1976). The lawyer refused to comply with a grand jury's *subpoena duces tecum* to turn over money that the lawyer received from clients suspected of bank robbery. The Seventh Circuit affirmed the contempt order, and Judge Tone, concurring, offered a perceptive analysis of this question:

"We must assume for purposes of this appeal that shortly after robbing a savings and loan association, the robbers delivered money stolen in the robbery to appellant. If that occurred, the money was delivered either for safekeeping, with or without appellant's knowledge that it was stolen, or as an attorney's fee.

"If it was the latter, the robbers voluntarily relinquished the money and with it any arguable claim that might have arisen from their possession or constructive possession.... [P]ayment of a fee is not a privileged communication. The money itself is non-testimonial and no plausible argument is left for resisting the subpoena.

"If the money was not given as a fee but for safekeeping, the delivery of the money was an act in furtherance of the crime, regardless of whether appellant knew it was stolen. The delivery of the money was not assertive conduct and therefore was not a privileged communication, and, as we just observed, the money itself is non-testimonial. The attorney is simply a witness to a criminal act. The fact that he is also a participant in the act, presumably without knowledge of its criminal quality, is irrelevant since he is not asserting his own privilege against self-incrimination. There is no authority or reason, based on any constitutional provision or the attorney-client privilege, for shielding from judicial inquiry either the fruits of the robbery or the fact of the later criminal act of turning over the money to appellant. Accordingly, it is immaterial that in responding to the subpoena appellant will be making an assertion about who turned over the money and when."

A lawyer, like any other witness who is called to testify before a grand jury, can always raise any applicable privilege, such as the attorney-client evidentiary privilege. In the context of government subpoenas, the lawyer has a special ethical obligation to seek to limit the subpoena or court order (such as a search warrant) on any legitimate available grounds so as to protect documents that are deemed to be confidential under Rule 1.6. Notwithstanding this fact, attorneys have typically argued that they should not be subpoenaed unless there is first an adversary hearing before a judge, who can determine if the information is privileged, if the evidence is "essential," and if there is "no other feasible alternative" to secure it. After most courts rejected this position, the ABA in February, 1990 added what is now Rule 3.8(e). Comment 4 explains that the purpose of Rule 3.8(e) is to "limit the issuance of lawyer subpoenas in grand jury and other criminal proceedings to those situations in which there is a genuine need to intrude into the client-lawyer relationship." Rule 3.8(e) does not require the prosecutor to seek the judge's permission to subpoena a lawyer before a grand jury.

Some commentators questioned whether it is proper for the ABA, via ethics rules, to try to change substantive law or the rules of procedure or evidence. The ABA has, in effect, sought to impose a special, additional requirement on federal and state prosecutors if they wish to subpoena a lawyer in a criminal proceeding. This rule does not apply to lawyers subpoenaing other lawyers in civil proceedings, nor does it impose any requirement on prosecutors who subpoena other individuals who may have a confidential relationship with the accused, such as a spouse, priest, accountant, medical doctors, and so forth. And, this new restriction applies even though the substantive law gives witnesses other remedies if they believe they should not be subpoenaed. (For example, they can move to quash the subpoena.)

If the ABA had proposed a statutory change, it would not go into effect until a legislature adopted the proposal. And if a state court adopted such a rule of procedure or evidence, it would not bind federal prosecutors in federal court. But if a state court adopts a provision from the ABA Model Rules, this state rule of ethics will bind all lawyers who are members of the bar of that state. Federal prosecutors, because they are members of at least one state bar, will normally be subject both to federal law and also to the ethics rules of the state where they practice. The full effect of new Rule 3.8(e) remains to be seen.

United States v. Klubock (1st Cir.1987) (en banc), a divided federal appellate court approved a federal rule similar to Rule 3.8(e). Other federal courts have invalidated, on supremacy clause grounds, similar state rules to the extent that the state seeks to apply this disciplinary rule to federal prosecutors. Critics of Rule 3.8(e) are concerned that it distorts evidentiary privileges, imposes the organized bar's view of subpoena law on criminal prosecutors, disrupts existing subpoena practice, and compromises the authority and investigative function of the modern grand jury. Proponents believe that the rule does not hamstring prosecutors and protects the client-lawyer relationship.

The 2002 revisions added Rule 3.8(f), which warns prosecutors to take reasonable steps to prevent other law enforcement personnel from making any extrajudicial comments that serve no legitimate law enforcement purpose and have a substantial likelihood of heightening public opprobrium of the accused. This rule serves to reemphasize the general concerns involving pretrial and trial publicity found in Rule 3.6.

RULE 3.9: ADVOCATE IN NONADJUDICATIVE PROCEEDINGS

A lawyer appearing before a tribunal may not mislead the tribunal regarding the fact that the lawyer appears in a representative capacity. This point is understood in any normal court proceeding, because lawyers have to file as counsel of record. Many nonadjudicative proceedings are a different matter, because there often is no formal procedure requiring the lawyer to "enter an appearance" as counsel of record. For example, lawyers may give testimony before a legislative hearing or appear before an administrator and may never be asked if the attorney is there on behalf of a client or on her own behalf. Rule 3.9 corrects that anomaly by requiring the lawyer to disclose if she is representing another party or representing her own interests in nonadjudicative proceedings.

The identity of the lawyer's client is rarely privileged. Even when it is, the lawyer may not mislead the tribunal regarding the fact that the lawyer appears in a representative capacity. It is not misleading for a lawyer to disclose that she appears on behalf of another, whose name is privileged. Court rules allow a Jane Doe or John Doe litigant in certain circumstances. But, it is misleading for the lawyer to pretend that she appears pro se when in fact she does not. In judicial as well as nonadjudicative proceedings (such as those involving lobbying), the government has a legitimate interest in knowing whom the lawyer represents.

Rule 3.9, Comment 3 explains that Rule 3.9 applies when the lawyer is presenting evidence or an argument in connection with a meeting or official hearing of a government agency or legislative body. It does not apply where one represents a client "in a negotiation or other bilateral transaction with a governmental agency or in connection with an application for a license or other privilege...." In those cases, the lawyer is governed by Rule 4.1 through 4.4, the rules that govern transactions where the lawyer is dealing with nonclients on behalf of clients.

Even in the situation where the lawyer represents the client in *litigation* before an agency, Rule 3.9 does not impose on a lawyer all of the ethical requirements that are thrust on lawyers who represent clients in litigation in court. Rule 3.9 provides that the lawyer must conform to Rule 3.3(a) through 3.3(c), as well as Rule 3.4(a) through 3.4(c). Notably, Rule 3.9 does not incorporate Rule 3.3(d), which governs *ex parte* proceedings, because those proceedings involve applications for a type of relief—a temporary restraining order, a default judgment—that are simply inapplicable to the nonadjudicative proceedings governed by Rule 3.9. Similarly, Rule 3.9 does not incorporate the portions of Rule 3.4 governing, for example, a lawyer's obligations regarding discovery, or the limitations on a lawyer asserting personal knowledge, because they are often inapplicable before municipal councils, legislatures, and agencies acting in a rule-making capacity. Of course, if the agency has particular rules of procedure, the lawyer must follow them.

Rule 3.9 incorporates Rule 3.5, requiring a lawyer to deal with the tribunal with impartiality and not to seek to influence it corruptly or engage in *ex parte* communications unless other law permits those communications. But Rule 3.9 does not incorporate the restriction in Rule 3.1 that prohibits making frivolous arguments because, in politics, it is standard operating procedure to design arguments that appeal to emotion and may not follow the rigorous rules of Euclidian logic. So Rule 3.9 deliberately omits any citation to Rule 3.1.

RULE 4.1: TRUTHFULNESS IN STATEMENTS TO OTHERS

Rule 4.1 governs the lawyer's obligations to *persons* other than the lawyer's own client. If the failure to disclose a material fact involves a *tribunal*, then the broader obligations of Rule 3.3 apply—the basic Rule governing the lawyer's duty of candor to a tribunal.

At first, the disclosure obligations that Rule 4.1 imposes may appear to be broad. Rule 4.1(a) appears to forbid making any false statements of law or fact to anyone, and Rule 4.1(b) appears to create affirmative duties when it provides that lawyers may not "fail to disclose a material fact to a third person...." But Comment 2 takes away some of the sweep of Rule 4.1. Let us turn to the Comment and Rule 4.1(a).

Rule 4.1 applies to negotiations and mediations. Typically, in mediation, all participants in the mediation hear whatever a party communicates to the mediator or its counsel. "In contrast, the mediator in a caucused mediation meets privately with the parties, either individually or in aligned groups. These caucuses are confidential, and the flow of information among the parties and their counsel is controlled by the mediator subject to the agreement of the respective parties." Rule 4.1 also applies to "caucused mediation." ABA Formal Opinion 06–439 (April 12, 2006).

Rule 4.1(a) states that a lawyer, while representing her client, "shall not knowingly ... make a false statement of material fact or law to a third person," such as the opposing lawyer in the course of litigation. However, immediately following that statement, Comment 2 looks in a different direction. It advises: "Under generally accepted conventions in negotiation, certain types of statements ordinarily are not taken as statements of material fact. Estimates of price or value placed on the subject of a transaction and a party's intentions as to an acceptable settlement of a claim are ordinarily in this category, and so is the existence of an undisclosed principal except where nondisclosure of the principal would constitute fraud."

So, one cannot "lie," but one can make statements regarding the party's intention as to an acceptable settlement, such as: "My client will never accept a penny less than $285,000," even when the lawyer knows that statement is simply not true. This "false" statement is not a "lie" because the official Comment says so; it announces: "a party's intentions as to an acceptable settlement of a claim" are not considered a material fact.

ABA Formal Opinion 93–370 (Feb. 5, 1993) explains that a "deliberate misrepresentation or lie *to a judge* in pretrial negotiations would be improper under Rule 4.1.'' (emphasis added). So it appears that one could not falsely tell a judge, in a settlement conference, that ''My client will never accept a penny less than $285,000,'' even though one could make that same false statement to the opposing party when the judge is not there.

Contrast, ABA Formal Opinion 06–439 (April 12, 2006). It says that in negotiation, a ''plaintiff might insist that it will not agree to resolve a dispute for less than $200, when, in reality, it is willing to accept as little as $150 to put an end to the matter.'' Such comments do not violate Rule 4.1(a) because they are really ''posturing'' or ''puffing.'' Parties to a negotiation ordinarily would not justifiably rely on them. They ''must be distinguished from false statements of material fact.'' An example of a material misstatement of fact [which Rule 4.1(a) forbids] is if a lawyer representing an employer in labor negotiations stated to union lawyers that a proposed employee benefit ''will cost the company an additional $100 per employee, when the lawyer knows that it actually will cost only $20 per employee.''

In general, there is not duty to volunteer adverse facts. Formal Opinion 94–387 (1994) explained that a lawyer representing a client in negotiation has no obligation to inform the other party that the statute of limitations has run on the client's claim, but the lawyer cannot make any affirmative misrepresentations about the facts.

In some circumstances, Rule 4.1(a) has real bite. While Comment 1 to Rule 4.1 advises that, in general, a lawyer has "no affirmative duty to inform an opposing party of relevant facts," it warns: "Misrepresentations can also occur by partially true but misleading statements *or omissions . . . .*" (emphasis added). A half truth is a whole lie.

Virzi v. Grand Trunk Warehouse & Cold Storage Co. (E.D.Mich.1983), is a leading case offering an example of an affirmative obligation to volunteer a fact to opposing counsel. The court held that when the lawyer's client dies in the midst of a settlement of a pending lawsuit, the lawyer has the duty to so inform the opposing counsel and the court. The lawyer not only has a duty of candor to the *court* but also a duty *"to opposing counsel."* In *Virzi* the court set aside the settlement because of the lawyer's failure to volunteer this fact. *Virzi* does not mean that counsel has a general ethical duty to volunteer adverse facts to her opponent. The death of a client is an unusual fact; it means that the lawyer no longer represents that client and—if she continues in the case—will be appearing on behalf of another client, i.e., the estate. The lawyer has to disclose this change in clients.

Rule 4.1(b) provides that a lawyer shall not knowingly "fail to disclose a material fact to a third person when disclosure is necessary to avoid assisting a criminal or fraudulent act by a client, *unless* disclosure is prohibited by Rule 1.6." The "unless" clause places meaningful limitations on the disclosure obligation found in the first part of that Rule, because the "unless" clause incorporates, by reference, the broad rule governing client confidences. Rule 4.1(b) does not require a lawyer to assist a client in a crime or fraud even if failure to assist would amount to a disclosure prohibited by Rule 1.6. These misrepresentations can also occur by failure to act. So, in the situation where the lawyer has an affirmative obligation to do something, but cannot disclose because of Rule 1.6, the only alternative must be that he or she must withdraw. The lawyer may also file a notice of withdrawal, as provided for in Rule 4.1, Comment 3.

RULE 4.2: COMMUNICATION WITH A PERSON REPRESENTED BY COUNSEL

1. The General Principle

Rule 4.2 is often called the anti-contact rule because it places important restrictions on lawyers who seek to contact other persons whom the lawyer knows are represented in the matter. If a lawyer for a client (Lawyer #1) knows that another party is represented by his own attorney (Lawyer #2), then Lawyer #1 may not communicate with the party represented by Lawyer #2 in that matter unless Lawyer #2 consents. The obvious reason for this requirement is to prevent lawyers from over-reaching the person contacted.

This Rule has a long lineage. The original ABA Canons of Professional Ethics included a no-contact rule. The ABA Model Code adopted this requirement, as did the Restatement of the Law Governing Lawyers. The same no-contact rule applies to nonparties who happen to be represented by counsel for that particular matter. This extension of the requirement to all ''persons'' is quite consistent with the rationale of preventing counsel from over-reaching by counsel.

2. Securing Consent from the Person's Lawyer: The Rule, and Sanctions for its Breach

If Alpha is represented by counsel, then the lawyer [Lawyer #1] who wants to talk to Alpha, a represented person, has to go through Alpha's lawyer [Lawyer #2]. Lawyer #2 may allow Lawyer #1 to speak to Alpha alone, or Lawyer #2 may insist on being there in person, or Lawyer #2 may refuse to give Lawyer #1 permission to talk to Alpha, in which case Lawyer #2 may only talk to Alpha pursuant to subpoena and deposition. This requirement of securing the lawyer's consent clearly covers any person, whether or not a party to a formal proceeding, who is represented by counsel concerning the matter in question.

Of course, Lawyer #1 will not know that she must ask Lawyer #2 for consent to contact a person unless Lawyer #1 first "knows" that Lawyer #2 represents this person in the matter. In typical litigation, counsel for plaintiffs and defendants will normally know that the other party is represented. All counsel file appearances in court. However, in some cases—particularly in cases where a witness is separately represented, or where litigation has not yet begun—the lawyer may not "know" that a particular person is already represented by a lawyer for the matter in question.

"Know" means "really know;" that is, to have "actual knowledge of the fact in question." Model Rule 1.0(f)). "Know" does not mean "reasonably suspect." The lawyer must have actual knowledge of the representation though such knowledge may be inferred from the circumstances. Willful blindness offers the lawyer no defense. Rule 4.2, Comment 8.

The Rule applies even where the represented opposing party is the one who initiates communication with the other party's attorney. Rule 4.3, Comment 3; *Pleasant Management, LLC v. Carrasco* (R.I.2005). If the opposing party tells a lawyer that he is not represented by counsel, the lawyer is no longer bound by Rule 4.2. If the lawyer does not know that the person is represented, then Rule 4.3 applies. See Rule 4.3, Comment 9. Rule 4.3 governs the lawyer's dealings with unrepresented persons.

Other law may preempt the no-contact Rule 4.2. This "other law" can include a statute or a regulation, a constitutional provision, or a judicial precedent. Rule 4.2, Comment 5 acknowledges that a communication "authorized by law" includes "investigative activities of lawyers representing governmental entities, directly or through investigative agents, prior to the commencement of criminal or civil enforcement proceedings." However, the Comment asserts that the mere fact that a government lawyer communicating with the accused does not violate any state or federal constitutional right "is insufficient to establish that the communication is permissible under this Rule."

Court orders frequently allow otherwise prohibited contacts, and the 2002 revisions to Model Rule

4.2 made that clear. For example, in a class action, defense attorneys may secure a court order allowing communication with members of the plaintiff class in appropriate circumstances. Constitutional law may authorize a party or lawyer in a controversy with a government agency to speak directly to government officials about the matter.

For instance, assume that an Indian tribe is suing the U.S. Government complaining about the Federal Government's interpretation of a treaty. The Indian Chief should have the same right as any other individual to complain to the Government (the House of Representatives, the Senate, the Attorney General, the President) that the Executive Branch should change its interpretation of the treaty. The trial lawyer handling the case may not like it that the lawyers for the tribe are going over his head, but the President of the United States does not need the permission of the government trial lawyer before he directly speaks with these lawyers. Rule 4.2, Comment 5. "Insofar as a party's right to speak with government officials about a controversy is concerned, Rule 4.2 has been uniformly interpreted to be inapplicable." *Camden v. Maryland* (D.Md. 1996).

The purpose of this contact must be "to petition" the government. Its purpose should not include the objective of trying to gain useful admissions against interest, or confessions from a low-level government employee who is in no position to resolve any controversies.

If a plaintiff is suing both the government official in her personal capacity and the government, the government official may be separately represented in a particular matter. In that case, the petition clause does not create an exception to Rule 4.2 as to this separately-represented official: in other words, the lawyer for the plaintiff may not talk to the represented official, who is separately represented, although the right to petition still applies to the government.

A lawyer who violates Rule 4.2 is obviously subject to discipline. In addition, a court may void agreements reached with represented parties in violation of the rule. Courts have elected to exclude from use at trial the evidence and information obtained during an improper ex parte communication until the excluded evidence is later obtained through properly conducted discovery. Some courts have elected to disqualify the party's counsel who improperly engaged in ex parte communications with the represented party. E.g., *Cagguila v. Wyeth Laboratories, Inc.* (E.D.Pa.1989).

3. Criminal Prosecutions

Rule 4.2 is intended to govern not only civil but also criminal cases. The applicability of the Rule in that situation has spawned a great deal of controversy. First, it has long been quite clear that Rule 4.2 is inapplicable to grand jury proceedings. Prosecutors routinely question witnesses in grand jury proceedings, without their counsel's presence. Grand jury rules do not even allow a lawyers to accompany her client-witness in the grand jury room. The witness may plead the Fifth Amendment, or leave the grand jury room between questions to consult with her lawyer, but the lawyer has no right to be present during her client's examination.

Prosecutors have tools of criminal investigation that go beyond the grand jury, and the exercise of these other tools has provoked controversy with the defense bar. Often, the prosecutor may wish to secure evidence from a suspect covertly (by wiring an undercover agent or informant) without seeking permission from the suspect's counsel. Defense attorneys in some criminal cases have argued that such investigative techniques violate various ethics rules, and that courts should enforce these rules by suppressing any evidence acquired by their violation. The U.S. Attorney General has disagreed and argued that prosecutors are authorized ''by law'' to make such contacts directly or through agents.

Attorney General Janet Reno, continuing a policy of her predecessor, Richard Thornburg, emphasized that the Department of Justice ''has long maintained, and continues to maintain, that it has authority to exempt its attorneys from the application of Model Rule 4.2 and their state counterparts.'' 59 FED. REGISTER 39910, 39911 (Aug. 4, 1994). Attorney General Reno enacted detailed regulations outlining when federal prosecutors could initiate direct contact. State supreme courts and state disciplinary authorities do not take kindly to claims that the U.S. Attorney General has the power to exempt federal prosecutors from state rules of ethics.

The Attorney General's effort to override the ethics rules has, thus far, not succeeded. The leading case is the New Mexico State Supreme Court decision, *In re Howes* (N.M.1997) (per curiam). When a murder suspect (represented by counsel) *initiated* a conversation with an Assistant U.S. Attorney ("AUSA"), and the AUSA responded by talking with the suspect without the suspect's lawyer being present or consenting to the contact, the New Mexico Supreme Court assumed disciplinary jurisdiction over the AUSA who was practicing in Washington, D.C. at the time but was admitted in New Mexico. Both the DOJ and the AUSA filed unsuccessful federal suits challenging New Mexico's state court jurisdiction. Rule 4.2, Comment 3 now makes clear that it applies even though the represented person "initiates or consents to the communication."

In 1998, Congress enacted a law that provides that U.S. government lawyers are subject to state laws, state rules, and federal court rules governing lawyers in each state "to the same extent and in the same manner as other attorneys in that State." 28 U.S.C.A. § 530B. The statute requires the Attorney General to make and amend Department of Justice rules to "assure compliance with this section." 28 CFR § 77.1.

4.   Some Limitations on the Coverage of Rule 4.2

The requirements of Rule 4.2 are inapplicable if the communication does not concern the subject of representation but rather another, separate matter. For example, if a person files for personal bankruptcy and hires a lawyer to represent him in that matter, that does not mean that this person is "represented" by counsel in a hit and run accident.

Nor does the Rule prohibit lawyers from advising principals to speak directly with their counterparts. The Rule governs lawyers, not their clients, so parties to a matter may communicate directly with each other.

However, Rule 4.2, when read in connection with Rule 8.4(a)—a lawyer may not violate a Rule "through the acts of another"—suggests that a lawyer is precluded from "using an intermediary to carry a message from the lawyer to the opposing party. . . ." Consequently, the 2002 revisions added new language in Rule 4.2, Comment 4, that makes clear that parties "to a matter may communicate directly with each other, and a lawyer is not prohibited from advising a client concerning a communication that the client is legally entitled to make."

Consider the situation where a lawyer representing a party believes that the opposing lawyer is not communicating a reasonable settlement offer to the opposing party. If Lawyer *A* (on behalf of Client *A*) makes a settlement offer to the opposing party's lawyer (Lawyer *B*), but Lawyer *A* believes that Lawyer *B* will not communicate that offer to Client *B*, even then Lawyer *A* may not communicate directly with Client *B* to determine whether the offer has been communicated. But Lawyer *A* may recommend to Client *A* that Client *A* may or should communicate directly with Client *B* about the offer. Sometimes, such direct encounters may lead to a fruitful settlement. And, in some cases, such direct encounters may be quite natural: if General Motors sues General Electric, the two CEOs may find it quite natural to meet face to face and talk.

5. Employees and Agents of Organizations and Other Parties

A corporation or other entity only speaks through flesh and blood agents. Consequently, the restrictions of Rule 4.2 apply to these flesh and blood agents when they are, in effect, alter egos of the entity. The general rule is that if a corporation or other entity is represented by counsel, then alter egos of that organization are also treated as persons represented by that counsel for purposes of the rule restricting communications to persons represented by counsel.

The ABA Model Rule adopts the alter ego test, elaborates on it, and appears to expand it as well in Comment 7:

> ''In the case of a represented organization, this Rule [4.2] prohibits communications with a constituent of the organization who supervises, directs or regularly consults with the organization's lawyer concerning the matter or has authority to obligate the organization with respect to the matter or whose act or omission in connection with the matter may be imputed to

the organization for purposes of civil or criminal liability.''

Rule 4.2 does not require the lawyer to secure consent of the organization's lawyer for communication with a *former* constituent of the organization. Rule 4.2, Comment 7. When the lawyer does talk to the former constituent, he must not use methods of obtaining evidence that violate the legal rights of the organization.

For example, the adverse lawyer should not solicit information if she knows or should reasonably know that this information is privileged. If the adverse lawyer violates this rule, she may find that the court will disqualify her and strike the testimony of the witness who should not have spoken on such matters. This, in fact, is the rule that courts are adopting. See, e.g., *Zachair, Ltd. v. Driggs* (D.Md. 1997).

The purpose of the anti-contact rule is to prevent imprudent settlements and serious admissions by a momentarily uncounselled, but represented, party, and also to facilitate the corporation lawyer's ability to maintain an effective lawyer-client relationship with members of management. Thus, in the case of corporate and similar entities, the anti-contact rule should only prohibit contact with those officials who have the legal power to bind the corporation in the matter or who are responsible for implementing the advice of the corporation's lawyer, or any member of the organization whose own interests are directly at stake in a representation. The trend in the case law favors this view. E.g., *Niesig v. Team I* (N.Y. 1990).

Rule 4.2 generally does not prohibit a lawyer who represents an organization in a matter from communicating with the organization's inside counsel about the subject of the representation, even though outside counsel represents the organization in the matter. There is no ethical rule that requires the lawyer to obtain first the prior consent of the organization's outside counsel. The rationale is easy to understand. When "the constituent of an organization is a lawyer employee of that organization who is acting as a lawyer for that organization," then the protections that Rule 4.2 provides are not needed. ABA Formal Opinion 06–443 (August 5, 2006).

There are a few exceptions to this general principle. If an inside counsel has her own independent counsel in the matter (and is not using the organization's counsel), then Rule 4.2 would apply. If the inside counsel is in fact a party in the matter (whether she uses or own counsel or uses the organization's counsel), then Rule 4.2 applies. The inside lawyer may be a part of a constituent group of the organization, see Rule 4.2 Comment 7, "for example, when the lawyer participated in giving business advice or in making decisions which gave rise to the issues which are in dispute." ABA Formal Opinion 06–443. If the outside counsel asks the adverse lawyer not to communicate with inside counsel, that would be "a rare case," and in that instance, "con-

tact by the adverse counsel *might* violate Rule 4.4.''
Id. (emphasis added).

If an employee's only relation to a case is as a
holder of factual information, the employee-witness
should be freely accessible to either lawyer.

The lawyer for the client-employer can instruct
the client's employees that they should not volunteer information to the other side and should only
speak through deposition, Rule 3.4(f), but the lawyer for the client-employer should not be able to
prohibit the other party's lawyer from speaking
with these witnesses if the witnesses wanted to
speak to the other party's lawyer.

RULE 4.3: DEALING WITH UNREPRESENTED PERSON

Rule 4.3 restricts the lawyer's communications with unrepresented persons. If a person is not represented by counsel, the lawyer for the represented person may neither state nor imply that the lawyer is disinterested. If the unrepresented person does not understand the lawyer's role, the lawyer should correct the misunderstanding. If the lawyer thinks that the unrepresented person has an interest adverse to his client, he should not give any legal advice to this unrepresented person, other than the advice to seek counsel.

Rule 4.3 does not prohibit a lawyer from negotiating the terms of a transaction or settling a dispute with an unrepresented person (let us call him Alpha), if the lawyer has explained that he represents an adverse party, not Alpha. The lawyer may explain to Alpha the terms on which the lawyer's client will settle the matter, or prepare documents that require the person's signature and explain the lawyer's own view of the meaning of the document or the lawyer's view of the underlying legal obligations. Rule 4.3, Comment 2.

In other words, the lawyer can tell Alpha, "You must sign on the dotted line here, and initial over there, to make this contract effective." The lawyer may be giving legal advice ("sign here, if you want to sign the contract"), but that does not violate Rule 4.3 if there is no reasonable possibility that Alpha's interests on that particular issue (where to sign) will conflict with the lawyer's client.

RULE 4.4: RESPECT FOR RIGHTS OF THIRD PERSONS

A lawyer's duty to represent a client competently and effectively does not allow a lawyer to harass another person, to violate another's legal rights, or to use means that serve no substantial purpose but to "embarrass, delay, or burden a third person. Does a lawyer violate this rule if she secretly tapes a conversation with someone? Does she violate the rule if she threatens criminal prosecution in order to gain an advantage for her client?

In 1974, shortly after the Senate Watergate Committee discovered that President Nixon (who was a lawyer) had created an elaborate taping system and had been secretly taping many Oval Office conversations, the ABA Ethics Committee issued ABA Formal Opinion 337 concluding that it was unethical for a lawyer to engage in secret tape recordings, even if the recordings were not a violation of criminal law. Ominously, the Opinion issued a caveat: "the mere fact that secret recordation in a particular instance is not illegal will not necessarily render the conduct of a public law enforcement officer in making such a recording ethical."

In 2001, the ABA reversed itself and officially withdrew Formal Opinion 337. Now ABA Formal

Opinion 01–422 (June 24, 2001) concluded that it is not inherently "misleading" for a lawyer to tape record a conversation.

There are several reasons for this about-face. First, the Model Rules, like the former Model Code, have no specific provision prohibiting lawyers from engaging in surreptitious tape recordings of their conversations with witnesses, opposing parties, or clients if these recordings are otherwise legal. In addition, most state ethics opinions rejected the ABA's opinion and allow such secret tape recordings. Also, federal law and many states do not make it illegal to make a secret tape recording if one party consents to the taping (but the other party remains unaware).

The Restatement of the Law Governing Lawyers, Third, also rejected ABA Formal Opinion 337. The Restatement allows lawyers to make secret recordings of conversations with another person, without that person's consent to being recorded, *if* that recording does not violate the law of the relevant jurisdiction and is in response to a compelling need to collect reliable evidence. Restatement of the Law Governing Lawyers § 106 (Official Draft, 2000), at Comment *b*.

The ABA Model Rules do not prohibit a lawyer in a civil case from threatening the opposing party with criminal prosecution if that threat does not violate any other law (such as the state law of extortion), if the criminal matter is related to the civil claim, if the lawyer reasonably believes that the civil claim and the possible criminal charge are warranted, and if the lawyer does not attempt to exert "improper influence" over the criminal process. Thus, ABA Formal Opinion 92–363 (July 6, 1992) concluded that a lawyer may agree (and have her client agree) to refrain from pursuing criminal charges in return for satisfaction of the civil claim, assuming that other law does not prevent this agreement.

For example, assume that a lawyer threatens his client's adversary (the client's husband in divorce proceedings) with informing the police that the husband had embezzled money, unless the husband agrees to share that money with her client. That lawyer would be committing the crime of theft by extortion. See the American Law Institute's *Model Penal Code* § 223.4 (1962). On the other hand, assume that the lawyer tells the opposing litigant, "You took my client's car without authorization. Unless you return it promptly, she will file charges with the police." That would not violate the ethics rules unless some other law in the jurisdiction makes that statement a crime.

ABA Formal Opinion 94–383 (July 5, 1994) dealt with the case where a lawyer threatens to file a disciplinary complaint against an opposing lawyer in order to gain advantage in a civil case (or the lawyer agrees not to report the lawyer if a satisfactory settlement is made). The Opinion this fact situation argued that presents a disciplinary violation.

Sometimes a lawyer mistakenly sends documents to his opponent, such as faxing a document to the wrong phone number. Or, a lawyer may send a document electronically to the opponent without realizing that it contains metadata that the other side would find very useful (such as computer-embedded information indicating prior drafts of the document that show the other side's bottom line in settlement negotiations).

If the material is sent inadvertently, the receiving lawyer "shall promptly notify the sender." Rule 4.4(b). This duty to notify, however, "does not require" the receiving lawyer to refrain "from reviewing the materials or abiding by instructions of the sender." ABA Formal Opinion 06–440 (May 13, 2006). Presumably, the sending lawyer will seek court protection, but the court may rule that the mistake has caused the loss of the attorney client privilege.

The lawyer may also receive confidential information *advertently*, as when a whistle-blower sends it. There "is no Model Rule that addresses the duty of a recipient of advertently transmitted information." ABA Formal Opinion 06–442 (August 5, 2006), note 7. Rule 4.4(b) does *not* require the receiving lawyer to notify the other side that he has received the material. ABA Formal Opinion 06–440 (May 13, 2006).

For further discussion of the issues of metadata and inadvertently or advertently sending confidential information, see the discussion in Rule 1.6, which governs client information and the lawyer's duty to safeguard it.

RULE 5.1:
RESPONSIBILITIES OF PARTNERS, MANAGERS, AND SUPERVISORY LAWYERS

Part 5 of the Model Rules has a specific section dealing with "Law Firms and Associations." Rule 5.1 focuses on the responsibilities of partners, managers, and supervisory lawyers in a law firm or other association of lawyers.

The partners in a law firm have the duty to make reasonable efforts to assure that all of the lawyers in the firm comply with the ethics rules. This duty similarly applies to other lawyers with general supervisory powers, such as the head of a corporate law department, the head of a government agency, or the shareholders of a professional legal corporation. The Rules do not specify the appropriate procedural safeguards. Rather, the Rules provide that the question whether the supervisory lawyers have instituted reasonable measures depends on all the facts and the measures may vary depending on the size of the firm.

Even if a lawyer is not a partner or other general supervisor, he or she may have direct supervisory authority over another lawyer. For example, a senior associate may have some authority over a junior associate. Such a supervisor has the same responsibility as a partner or manager to assure compliance with the ethical rules by those lawyers under her direct supervisory authority. While the partner's or general manager's responsibilities relate to *all* lawyers in the firm, the supervisory lawyer's responsibilities relate only to those lawyers under her direct supervisory authority.

As a general principle, a lawyer may not knowingly assist another to violate the ethics rules or to violate those rules through the acts of another. Consequently, a lawyer is responsible for another lawyer's ethics violation if the first lawyer orders the second to engage in misconduct, or knowingly ratifies the second lawyer's misconduct. The supervisory lawyer is also responsible for the other lawyer's ethical misconduct if the supervisory lawyer fails to take reasonable remedial action to avoid or mitigate the misconduct. For example, "if a supervising lawyer knows that a subordinate misrepresented a matter to an opposing party in negotiation, the supervisor as well as the subordinate has a duty to correct the resulting misapprehension." Rule 5.1, Comment 5.

One should keep in mind the distinction between Rule 5.1 and tort liability, as well as the distinction, within Rule 5.1, between the failure to supervise and the ordering or ratifying of unethical conduct. For example, assume that Lawyer *A* is the supervisor of Lawyer *B*. Neither the firm nor Lawyer *A* exercises any care to assure that Lawyer *B* will protect client confidences. Even though there is no supervision, it turns out that Lawyer *B* in fact does not violate any confidences. Nonetheless, Lawyer *A* still has violated Rule 5.1(b), because of Lawyer *A*'s failure to supervise. But there is no violation of Rule 5.1(c), which governs a supervising lawyer's liability for ratifying or failure to take reasonable remedial action. A client would not have a cause of action in tort against Lawyer *A* for failure to supervise because there are no damages.

Now, let us change the facts. Assume, in the above example, that Lawyer *A* does exercise reasonable supervisory care over Lawyer *B*, but Lawyer *B* nonetheless violates a client's confidences, causing the client monetary damage. Lawyer *A* has neither violated Rule 5.1(b) because there has been adequate supervision, nor 5.1(c), because the supervising lawyer does not ratify the action and does not know about it in time to avoid or mitigate it. But the supervisory lawyer is still liable in tort under a theory *respondeat superior*.

RULE 5.2:
RESPONSIBILITIES OF
A SUBORDINATE LAWYER

A lawyer cannot escape responsibility for ethical misconduct merely by claiming that she followed orders. There is no "good soldier" defense in the law governing lawyers when a clear breach of an ethical obligation has occurred.

However, one can escape responsibility by following reasonable orders. If the ethical violation is not clear, the subordinate lawyer may defer to the judgment of the supervisory attorney. The subordinate does not violate her ethical duties if she follows the supervisor's "reasonable resolution of an arguable question of professional duty." Rule 5.2(b).

In recent years, attorneys who have been fired by their clients or their law firms, allegedly for their refusal to engage in unethical activity, have brought wrongful discharge suits. These lawyers sue even though they are employees at will. Typically, the plaintiff-lawyer asserts that he or she was discharged for not following the direction of a supervisory lawyer when that direction violated the ethics rules. Consequently, the discharged lawyers complain that the termination was wrongful. When the firing party is the law firm, normal labor rules apply. The leading case is *Wieder v. Skala* (N.Y. 1992) where the lawyer alleged that his law firm discharged him because he insisted that his firm comply with its ethical obligation to report a fellow associate to the state bar disciplinary authorities. The court held that the discharged lawyer has a cause of action for breach of contract; the duty to comply with the state bar's ethical rules is an implied-in-law condition of the employment contract. Later, New York refused to expand *Wieder* to medical doctors. *Horn v. New York Times* (N.Y. 2003).

A situation that may be different is where the firing party is the client, including cases where the lawyer is an in-house counsel. The courts have split on this issue, with several states allowing wrongful discharge suits against clients.

General Dynamics Corp. v. Superior Court of San Bernardino County (Cal.1994) held that an in-house attorney may sue in tort for retaliatory termination. In-house counsel is dependent on one employer to provide his livelihood and career success. Therefore, in-house lawyers "have, if anything, an even more powerful claim to judicial protection than their non-professional colleagues."

Some courts disagree, arguing that a lawyer is a professional and that the client should be able to terminate the lawyer for any reason (even a bad one) and not be liable for damages. *Balla v. Gambro, Inc.* (Ill.1991), holding that attorney Balla had no cause of action when he was fired for threatening to reveal (as was his duty as an Illinois attorney) that his employer's kidney dialysis devices did not comply with FDA regulations and presented a danger to patients' lives.

The Restatement of the Law Governing Lawyers, Third (ALI 2000), § 32, comment *b*, rejects *Balla*. "Giving an employed lawyer a remedy for wrongful discharge does not significantly impair the client's choice of counsel." Granted, a "client may always discharge a lawyer, regardless of cause and regardless of any agreement between them." But, the client's discharge may have adverse consequences.

Wrongful termination cases should be distinguished from cases where the lawyer sues the law firm or client for discrimination or other similar actions. These cases are typically based on state or federal statutes. For example, a tribunal may decline "to appoint new counsel for an indigent criminal defendant" or may deny "a continuance for the client to seek new counsel." Damages for wrongful discharge may be simply another adverse consequence. The lawyer-employee " has the same rights as other employees under applicable law to recover for bad-faith discharge, for example if the client dishcarged the lawyer for refusing to perform an unlawful act."

RULE 5.3: RESPONSIBILITIES REGARDING NONLAWYER ASSISTANTS

A lawyer's responsibility over nonlawyer employees parallels that over subordinate lawyers. The Comment to Model Rule 5.3 emphasizes a lawyer's duty to instruct nonlawyer employees about the ethical aspects of their employment. It is reasonable for lawyers to disclose client confidences to nonlawyer employees, such as secretaries. While the rules of ethics have no jurisdiction over these nonlawyer employees, they do require that the lawyer exercise reasonable care to prevent his employees or associates from violating the obligation regarding client confidences or secrets.

A lawyer who fails in her duty of supervision violates these disciplinary rules even though no secrets are in fact disclosed, because the disciplinary violation is the failure to supervise. Conversely, a lawyer who adequately supervises her employees has fulfilled her ethical obligation, even if the employee nonetheless violates his instructions and improperly discloses a client secret or confidence.

The lawyer may employ outside contractors for accounting, photocopying, storage, data processing, or other legitimate purposes but the lawyer must exercise due care in selecting the contractor, because these outside agencies employ nonlawyers who have some access to client files.

Lawyers must make reasonable efforts to satisfy themselves that the outside service provider does not make unauthorized disclosures of client confidences or secrets. For example, the lawyer who contracts with a recycling firm to dispose of trash should take care to instruct the recycling firm on the importance of protecting client confidences and secrets. Similarly, the law firm that hires a computer maintenance company that will have access to client files must take reasonable efforts to make sure that this outside contractor will establish reasonable procedures to protect client confidences and secrets. If there has been a "significant breach of confidentiality," then Rule 1.4(b) may obligate the lawyer to make the appropriate disclosures to the affected clients.

RULE 5.4: PROFESSIONAL INDEPENDENCE OF A LAWYER

1. Sharing Fees With Laypeople

In general, a lawyer or law firm may not share legal fees with a nonlawyer. However, there are several important exceptions to this rule.

First, lawyers may agree to pay money over a reasonable length of time after the lawyer's death to his estate or to his beneficiaries.

Second, if a lawyer buys the practice of a lawyer who is dead or who cannot be found, the lawyer may pay the money to the estate or the representative of the lawyer.

Third, a lawyer may include nonlawyer employees in the firm's compensation or retirement plan, even if the plan is based in whole or in part on a profit-sharing agreement. For example, at the end of the year a law firm may give each of its secretaries a bonus because the firm has just settled a significant case on very favorable terms. The firm's actions do not constitute a prohibited sharing of fees. However, as discussed in the next section, the law firm may not give these people any managerial control. Also, at least one court has ruled that the lawyer may not pay per-event bonuses to his non-attorney staff. *In re Holmes* (Bkrcty.N.D.Miss.2004) (lawyer's practice of paying $5.00 to his non-attorney staff each time that clients paid at least $300.00 and executed a retainer agreement constituted unethical "fee splitting" or "fee sharing" arrangement).

And, fourth, it is now clear that the lawyer may share legal fees with (or donate the legal fees to) a non-profit client, such as the ACLU or the NAACP, who recommended the lawyer or employer for the matter in question. Rule 5.4(a)(4).

Sometimes a law firm has a temporary need to hire lawyers for a specific project or staffing problem or to offer special expertise on a particular issue. In such cases, the law firm typically hires a "temporary lawyer," or "law-temp." If the law firm uses a placement agency, the agency that charges the law firm for its services (locating, recruiting, screening, and supplying temporary lawyer with particular credentials) may base its fee on a percentage of the temporary lawyer's compensation. This fee arrangement raises the question of whether it constitutes an improper sharing of legal fees with nonlawyers. ABA Formal Opinion 88–356 (Dec. 16, 1988) concluded that this payment is ethical, for the simple reason that paying it does not compromise the rationale behind Rule 5.4(a), which is to maintain the lawyer's professional independence.

Consider another factual variant involving fee sharing. Assume that an in-house lawyer who wins a case on behalf of the corporation is entitled to attorney's fees under a fee-shifting statute. ABA Formal Opinion 95–392 (April 24, 1995) concluded that it would be a violation of Rule 5.4(c) for the lawyer to "share with her corporate employer a 'reasonable attorney's fee' based on an hourly rate that exceeds the cost the corporation incurred in employing" that lawyer.

Normally, in these fee-shifting cases, the client (not the lawyer) collects the fee award and then pays his or her lawyer the agreed-upon fee. That arrangement is assumed to violate no ethics rule. Given that this arrangement is proper, why not the other way around, where the lawyer passes on the fee award to the client? Note that if the fee award is given to the client, the lawyer can always waive the fee. The ethics rules do not require lawyers to charge for their services. If lawyers can pass on the entire fee award (by declining to charge for their services) should they not be able to pass on part of the fee award? The current rule 5.4(a)(4) seems to disallow this alternative unless the corporation is a non-profit.

2.   Sharing Managerial Responsibility With Nonlawyers

Although lawyers may include lay employees in a profit-sharing arrangement, lawyers may not give these people any managerial control. Thus, lay people cannot be partners in law firms. However, they can be profit-sharing employees. "Partners" own the firm; they are the managers in control. In contrast, "employees" work for the firm; they have no managerial control even if they enjoy profit-sharing.

Because the ethics rules allow lawyers to give nonlawyer-employees a share of the profits but not a share in the management, it is unethical for a law firm to sell shares to an investing public. This ethics rule tends to limit the size of law firms because it limits their sources of capital. Large brokerage firms are publicly traded precisely because these firms needed to increase their ability to raise capital for expansion purposes.

The rule prohibiting nonlawyers from sharing managerial responsibility with lawyers applies whether or not the lawyers are practicing in the form of a partnership. If the lawyer is practicing law in the form of a professional legal corporation, no lay person may be a director or officer, or control the lawyer's legal judgment, or own any financial interest (except that a deceased lawyer's fiduciary representative may hold the lawyer's interest for a reasonable period of time during the administration of the estate).

An early draft of the Model Rules recommended that nonlawyers be permitted to form partnerships with lawyers if there would be no interference with the lawyers' independent professional judgment or with the client-lawyer relationship, client confidentiality would be maintained, and any advising and fee arrangements did not otherwise violate the Rules governing lawyers. During the ABA floor debates an ABA delegate asked: "Does this rule mean

Sears Roebuck will be able to open a law office?'' Professor Geoffrey C. Hazard, Jr., the Reporter for the Model Rules, answered ''Yes.'' The ABA promptly defeated the proposal.

The District of Columbia became the first jurisdiction to amend its Rule 5.4(b) in order to allow nonlawyers to become partners in law firms, subject to various conditions. However, even the Washington, D.C. Rules do not allow Sears, Roebuck & Co. to hold or control a law firm subsidiary: D.C. Rule 5.4(b)(1) requires that the law firm have, as its ''sole purpose'' the provision of legal services to its clients.

RULE 5.5: UNAUTHORIZED PRACTICE OF LAW; MULTIJURISDICTIONAL PRACTICE OF LAW

1. Defining the "Practice of Law"

In the United States, it is commonly understood that one needs to be licensed by a state to practice law within that state. However, in many places around the world, the concept of "unauthorized practice of law" is alien. In the United States, one does not need an M.B.A. (Master of Business Administration) to "practice business." The M.B.A. may be useful, and some employers may prefer to hire those who have it, but one may engage in business without the degree. Some foreign countries treat the practice of law the way the United States treats the practice of business.

But in this country, only licensed professionals can legally practice law. What constitutes the unauthorized practice of law is generally a matter of state law. The Model Rules mainly incorporate by reference these local rules, case law, and statutes. These state law definitions are varied and confusing. In 2003, the ABA and its Task Force on the Model Definition of the Practice of Law recommended "every state and territory adopt a definition of the practice of law." As of 2007, only 19 states defined the "practice of law" by statute or court rule. See http://www.abanet.org/cpr/model-def/ home.html. Even then, some of these definitions are, shall we say, vague. The New Hampshire S.Ct. Rules stated: "There is no satisfactory, all-inclusive definition of what constitutes the practice of law." http://www.abanet.org/cpr/model-def/model_def_stat utes.pdf. Most often one finds the definition only by trolling the case law.

If a person appears in court on behalf of another person, that appearance has historically been treated as constituting the practice of law. But the practice of law is not limited to litigation. The cases hold that lawyers who give transactional advice and engage in similar non-court representation of clients are practicing law. Beyond such general statements, the devil is in the details. Even the case law within a single jurisdiction has sometimes appeared to throw its hands into the air and given up trying to define what constitutes the "practice of law" and what Rule 5.5 therefore actually prohibits. The Connecticut Supreme Court, for example, defined the "practice of law" circularly, as the "performance of any acts by persons not admitted as attorneys, in or out of court, commonly understood to be the practice of law." *Grievance Committee v. Payne* (Conn.1941).

In general it may be said that a person practices law when he or she *applies the law to the facts of a particular case.* The practice of law relates to rendering service for others that calls for the professional legal judgment of a lawyer.

If a police officer tells you the speed limit is 55 m.p.h., or the court clerk instructs you that reply briefs should be printed on blue-backed paper, these people *use* law, but they are not *practicing* law. If a lawyer instructs these people about the law, the lawyer is not assisting unauthorized practice of law because these people, the recipients of the lawyers' aid, do not practice law.

The lawyer may delegate various tasks to secretaries, law clerks, or paralegals. So long as the lawyer supervises the work and is ultimately responsible for it, there is no unauthorized practice. While the lay investigator asks questions, or the paralegal conducts legal research, or the secretary prepares letters for the lawyer to sign, the lawyer is the person who applies the law to the facts; the lawyer decides when the cause of action lies in tort or in contract, or whether the research is useful, or whether to send a letter and what that letter should contain.

Accountants obviously can engage in accounting without practicing law. Yet, when they prepare complex income tax returns and give tax advice regarding complex transactions, there can come a time when the accountant may be said to be applying the law to the specific facts and, in effect, practicing law. If the accountant is found to be practicing law, it does not matter that he performs his service as well as, or even better than, a tax lawyer in the particular matter, because competence is not a defense to a charge of unauthorized practice of law.

If the accountant is also a lawyer admitted to the bar, the lawyer-accountant still may not practice law *if* an accounting firm employs him, because accounting firms (like corporations) may not practice law. On the other hand, if a law firm hired an accountant, there would be no problem with the accountant practicing accountancy because the Model Rules forbid the unauthorized practice of law, not of accountancy.

As one should see by now, some of the unauthorized practice rules seem designed more to protect lawyers from competition from accounting firms or other rivals than to make sure that clients receive competent advice.

In its report to the ABA House of Delegates in 2000, the Association's Commission on Multidisciplinary practice recommended that the Model Rules be amended to permit lawyers "to share fees and join with nonlawyer professionals in a practice that delivers both legal and nonlegal professional services," provided that the lawyers retain sufficient professional independence. Thus far the organized bar has largely resisted changes in the ethics rules to allow such multidisciplinary practice.

What of the paper and electronic publishing markets? Publishers market law books to lawyers and to lay people. Legal casebooks, for example, are marketed to lay people called law students. Sometimes, Unauthorized Practice Committees and others raise eyebrows when legal "how to" books are marketed to lay audiences who are not law students but simply average citizens. But the lay person can represent himself (even if it is foolish to do so), and a lawyer may counsel nonlawyers who wish to proceed pro se. Rule 5.5, Comment 3.

Yet some courts are very antagonistic to the notion that lay publishers should be able to compete with practicing lawyers. See *Unauthorized Practice of Law Committee v. Parsons Technology, Inc.* (N.D.Tex.1999) (per curiam). Parsons Technology sold computer software, including a program called *Quicken Family Lawyer*. This computer program contained various forms and asked users various questions. The initial screen displayed by the computer program stated that the program could decide which of the program's leases was appropriate for the user. "[Y]ou must use your own judgment and, to the extent you believe appropriate, the assistance of a lawyer." The trial court *enjoined* selling this computer program, even though there is no personal contact or other relationship between the publisher and the alleged client!

After the decision, the Texas legislature enacted a law providing that "the 'practice of law' does not include the design, creation, publication, distribution, display, or sale . . . [of] computer software, or similar products if the products clearly and conspicuously state that the products are not a substitute for the advice of an attorney." That law was effective immediately. The Fifth Circuit then vacated the injunction and judgment and remanded in light of the new statute.

2. Rationale and Sanctions for Unauthorized Practice

Proponents often defend unauthorized practice rules as designed to protect lay people from being injured by incompetents or by those who lack the integrity to practice law compared to those who have been licensed to practice law. But scholars have criticized these justifications as a pretext, arguing that lawyers have often used unauthorized practice rules to suppress competition by lay persons who perform services at less cost than those charged by members of the Bar. Unauthorized practice rules also make it more difficult for out-of-state lawyers to compete with those licensed within the state.

Much of the litigation involving unauthorized practice deals with subjects where nonlawyers provide services at low cost: debt collection, divorce kits or forms, kits to avoid or deal with probate, real estate closings, tax preparation and planning, and appearances before specialized administrative agencies.

Typically state laws or state common law provides that it is a defense to a lawsuit for the payment of fees that the party seeking fees engaged in the unauthorized practice of law. The client can thus avoid paying a fee even though he has no complaint as to the quality of work that the nonlawyer performed. Courts reason that a contract to provide services in violation of the prohibition against unauthorized practice of law is unenforceable as against public policy.

The unauthorized practice of law is often a criminal violation as well. Those who hold themselves out as lawyers in a jurisdiction where they are not properly admitted have been jailed and fined. Courts may also grant declaratory or injunctive relief.

Courts do not normally enforce the unauthorized practice rules by denying the client the benefit of the attorney client privilege. The Restatement of the Law Governing Lawyers, Third (ALI 2000), § 72(1) only requires that the client (including the prospective client) consult, for the purposes of obtaining legal advice, someone who is a lawyer or someone whom the client "reasonably believes to be a lawyer." If a lawyer is admitted elsewhere but not in the right jurisdiction, or the client deals with an imposter, it is "an inappropriate sanction" to deny the client the privilege as a way to punish the unauthorized practice of law. Comment *e*. The law should protect clients who deal with "legal advisers in good faith" and the law should not expose them "to the uncertainties of choice-of-law questions."

3. Aiding in the Unauthorized Practice of Law

A lawyer may engage in the unauthorized practice of law either: (1) by practicing in a jurisdiction in which she is not admitted, or (2) by assisting someone in the unauthorized practice of law.

A. *Pro Se* Litigants

A lawyer who aids a layperson to represent himself pro se cannot be aiding the unauthorized practice of law because the lay person is authorized to practice law when he only represents himself. Thus, Rule 5.5, Comment 3 makes clear: "a lawyer may counsel nonlawyers who wish to proceed pro se."

B. Aiding Disbarred or Suspended Lawyers in the Practice of Law

A lawyer may not assist a disbarred lawyer or a suspended lawyer in the practice of law. The disbarred or suspended lawyer is not authorized to practice law, and a licensed lawyer should not aid him or her in representing third parties. Some courts allow suspended or disbarred lawyers to work as paralegals, if a properly-admitted lawyer supervises the disbarred lawyer. Many other jurisdictions do not allow a suspended or disbarred lawyer to engage in such work related to the practice of law, even though a paralegal (who also is not licensed to practice law) may lawfully engage in the same tasks. Thus, for example, Louisiana prevents suspended attorneys from working during their suspensions as paralegals or legal assistants in law firms or with attorneys. *In re Comish* (La.2004).

Lawyers can use paralegals, law clerks, and other employees to engage in various tasks, as long as the lawyers adequately supervise their employees. Even then, these lay people cannot do certain things, like appear in court on behalf of a client, unless a special court rule allows it.

C. Practice of Law by Corporations, Associations, and Partnerships

While an individual may represent himself, the typical rule is that corporations, partnerships and other associations (other than law firms), may not appear *pro se*. Because a corporation is an incorporeal entity it can only appear through lawyers because the corporation cannot practice law. Courts, on their own motion, have ruled that partnerships and other organizations must be represented by counsel and no non-lawyer member of the organization can appear on the organization's behalf.

D. Jurisdictional Limitations and Crossing State Lines

The fact that a person is a graduate of a law school does not make him authorized to practice law unless he is first admitted to the bar of the relevant jurisdiction. Interstate limitations are often confusing, leading to litigation and frequent criticism.

There are an increasing number of questions involving the practice of law in multiple jurisdictions, as our society has become more mobile, with asphalt and electronic highways causing people to measure distance in minutes instead of miles. Lawyers routinely communicate in one jurisdiction to a client in a different jurisdiction about advice involving the effects or application of federal or state law in yet another jurisdiction.

El Gemayel v. Seaman (N.Y.1988) allowed a foreign attorney to collect his fees because, the court said, he did not "practice" in New York when he telephoned his client there and discussed with the client the progress of legal proceedings in Lebanon. The lawyer in *El Gemayel* was not physically present in New York and did not have an office there. He had an office at Georgetown University, in Washington, DC.

El Gemayel, in fact, specifically distinguished another New York decision, *Spivak v. Sachs* (N.Y. 1965), which held that a California attorney engaged in the unlawful practice of law by assisting an acquaintance in New York with her divorce. The California attorney became substantially involved in the client's New York affairs, spending 14 days physically in New York attending meetings, reviewing drafts of a separation agreement, discussing the client's financial and custody problems, recommending a change in New York counsel and, based on his knowledge of New York and California law, rendering his opinion as to the proper jurisdiction for the divorce action and related marital and custody issues. The court concluded that these activities plainly constituted the "practice of law."

A controversial decision that adopts a view of unauthorized practice of law that makes life difficult for multistate law firms is *Birbrower, Montal-*

bano, Condon & Frank, P.C. v. Superior Court (ESQ Business Services, Inc.) (Cal.1998). A New York firm represented ESQ, a California corporation, in claims it had against Tandem Computers, Inc., relating to a software marketing contract. California law governed the contract, and the New York firm partners traveled to California for a few brief trips on several occasions. The parties settled the dispute, and the firm asked for the million dollar fee due under its agreement with ESQ. The client refused to pay, and the California Supreme Court agreed, over a vigorous dissent, because it said that the New York law firm was engaged in the unauthorized practice of law in California. Commentators have also vigorously attacked the decision.

Model Rule 5.5, after the 2002 revisions, allows such *temporary* presence in the "foreign" jurisdiction in these circumstances. See Rule 5.5(c)(2), (3).

The 2002 revisions substantially modified Rule 5.5 in several important respects:

- If the lawyer is admitted in State #1, she may practice law anywhere within State #1. Rule 5.5(a).

- The lawyer admitted in State #1 may practice in State #2 on a temporary basis if she associates with a lawyer admitted in State #2 who "actively participates" in the matter. Rule 5.5(c)(1).

- The lawyer admitted in State #1 may provide temporary services reasonably related to a proceeding before a tribunal or potentially before a tribunal if the lawyer reasonably expects to be admitted *pro hac vice*. Rule 5.5(c)(2). Such services would include meeting with clients, interviewing witnesses, and reviewing documents. Comments 9 & 10.

- She may practice before any tribunal or administrative agency of any other state or the federal government if she complies with the temporary or regular admission rules of that tribunal or agency. For example, she may be admitted *pro hac vice*. Lawyers who are litigating in court but who are not admitted in a particular state typically ask the tribunal for admission for the purposes of the particular case. Lawyers who give advice in putting together various transactions have no procedure to become admitted for purposes of a particular transaction. A lawyer litigating in federal court has to be admitted to the bar of that court, either permanently or *pro hac vice*. If a lawyer is admitted in State #1 (but not State #2) and she is also admitted in the federal court that sits in State #2, she can practice law before the federal court in state #2 as long as she complies with the federal court's admission rules and her practice is limited to cases filed in the federal court for State #2. Rule 5.5(c)(2), Rule 5.5(d)(2).

- She may practice on a temporary basis within a jurisdiction in which she is not admitted to the extent that her activities in the matter arise out of or are otherwise reasonably related to the lawyer's practice under parts (1) or (2), above. Rule 5.5(c)(2),(3).

- She may provide legal services to her employer (i.e., as in-house counsel or government lawyer) in a jurisdiction in which she is not admitted, as long as she is not before a tribunal. Rule 5.5(d) and Comment 16. If she is before a tribunal, she must secure *pro hac vice* admission. In-house lawyers often render legal services to the client in various out-of-state offices and facilities of the client. The employer is unlikely to be deceived about the training and expertise of these lawyers, so the Model Rules also offer a safe harbor for this multijurisdictional practice of law.

Note that even the revised Model Rules are concerned with lawyers who open up offices. Rule 5.5(d) gives only two circumstances where a lawyer may open an office or have a continuous presence and practice law in State #2 while only being admitted in State #1. The first example, mentioned above, deals with in-house lawyers and similar types. The second example is for cases where federal law or other relevant law authorized this practice of Law. See Comments 15–18.

For example, assume that Lawyer is admitted in State A and has an office there. Some of her clients are residents of State B, where Lawyer is not admitted. She may represent these residents of State B and research the law of State B, but she may not open a law office in State B for the general practice of law in that state unless she is first admitted there.

Similarly, assume that Lawyer represents a regulated utility ("Utility") in State A near the border with State B. Sometimes, to service her client, Lawyer must research the law of State B as well as the law of State A and federal law. Lawyer may do that as well as travel to State B to deal with governmental officials with respect to environmental issues arising out of Utility's activities. In fact, she may represent Utility in rate applications in other states, even though that will involve her in extensive presence and activities in each of the other states until the necessary rates have been established, as long as she reasonably believes she will obtain *pro hac vice* admission at the appropriate time, or if she has retained local counsel.

Finally, assume that Lawyer is admitted in Illinois and drafts a will and estate plan for Client A, in Illinois. Later, Client A moves to Florida, and requests Lawyer to draft a codicil to A's will. Lawyer does so and visits Client A in Florida to obtain the necessary signatures. Then Client A introduces Lawyer to Client B, also in Florida. Client B also asks Lawyer to draft an estate plan for him, and she does so, conducting legal research in Illinois and conferring with Client B by telephone and letter. Lawyer then travels back to Florida so that Client B and the necessary witnesses can sign the documents. The Restatement of the Law Governing Lawyer, Third, § 3, Illustration 5 (Official Draft 2000) concludes that this activity is permissible. It should also be permissible under Rule 5.5(c)(4), which uses language taken from Restatement, § 3(3).

Model Rule 5.5 should be influential in persuading courts not to interpret vague criminal statutes drafted in an earlier era to create complex entry barriers to multistate legal practice that are not necessary to protect clients from incompetent representation.

RULE 5.6: RESTRICTIONS ON RIGHT TO PRACTICE

The ABA Model Rules prohibit a lawyer from either requiring or agreeing to accept an employment contract restricting his or her right to practice law after termination of the relationship created by the agreement. Such restrictive covenants violate the discipline rules even if they are limited to a stated period and geographic area.

For example, a lawyer may not accept or propose a restriction in an employment agreement prohibiting counsel for a corporation from representing anyone in any future action against the corporation. The former lawyer for the corporation could not ethically engage in subsequent adverse representation that is *substantially related* to the prior representation. To go beyond that and prohibit *all* future adverse representation, including matters that are *unrelated,* violates Rule 5.6(a). ABA Formal Opinion 94–381 (May 9, 1994).

Most courts will not enforce a restrictive agreement that violates this rule. *Stevens v. Rooks Pitts and Poust* (Ill.App.1997) (a law firm cannot create a financial penalty that goes into effect if the lawyer leaves the law firm and then competes with it because that penalty is a form of restriction).

California is a notable exception to this rule. *Howard v. Babcock* (Cal.1993), concluded, over a vigorous dissent, that law firms should be treated no differently from other business partnerships, such as accountants' and doctors' practices, which California permits to enter into agreements restricting competition: "A revolution in the practice of law has occurred requiring economic interests of the law firm to be protected as they are in other business enterprises."

Kennard, J., dissenting, objected. The majority was implementing the restrictive covenant although the California ethics rules, like the ABA Model Rules, prohibit lawyers "from entering into agreements that 'restrict' their right to practice law after leaving a firm." The "majority, contrary to the unambiguous language of the rule, holds that this rule does not bar law firms from entering into noncompetition agreements with their attorneys if such agreements are 'reasonable.' "

A law firm may impose a restrictive covenant as a condition to the law firm's payment of retirement benefits to one of its lawyers. Rule 5.6(a). If the lawyer is really retiring from the practice of law, then a restriction on her right to practice would not interfere with the right of her former clients to choose her as their lawyer because she is retiring from the practice of law. If there really is not an authentic and genuine retirement, the restrictive covenant is invalid.

For the retirement agreement to comply with Rule 5.6(a), it must affect benefits that are available only to a lawyer who is in fact retiring from the practice of law. It cannot impose a forfeiture of income that the lawyer had already earned. For example, a law firm could not place a "retirement benefit" label on income that the partner already earned and seek to deprive the lawyer of those funds if she competed with the law firm. "Beyond that, law firms and employers have significant latitude in shaping the nature and scope of the restrictions on practice and the penalties for noncompliance." ABA Formal Opinion 06–444 (Sept. 13, 2006).

Rule 5.6 does not apply to restrictions that may be included in the terms of the sale of a law practice. Rule 1.17, discussed above, deals with such provisions.

Rule 5.6(b) also makes clear that lawyers may not restrict their right to practice as part of the settlement of a client's controversy. Clients always have a right to discharge their lawyers at any time and hire new counsel. And a lawyer can turn down a prospective client. But if lawyers were forced to (or were allowed to force others to) agree to restrictive covenants, then these covenants would impose restraints, not only on the lawyer's professional autonomy, but also on the new client's freedom to choose a lawyer. Rule 5.6(b) is based on two rationales—lawyer freedom and client freedom. Therefore, Rule 5.6 limits Rule 1.2(a), which provides, in general, that the lawyer must abide by the client's decisions concerning settlement: a lawyer may not accept or be part of a settlement agreement that would limit the ability of the lawyer to accept representation of future clients.

A disciplinary authority or government agency, as part of a settlement of its controversy with a lawyer, may impose restrictions on that lawyer's right to practice. In this case, the lawyer is the party (the defendant or respondent). The lawyer is not settling a claim on behalf of a client; he is settling a disciplinary proceeding or other claims against him. ABA Formal Opinion 95–394 (July 24, 1995).

RULE 5.7: RESPONSIBILI-TIES REGARDING LAW–RELATED SERVICES

Someday, Sears may be able to own a law firm. In the meantime, may a law firm (or partners of a law firm) invest in, or own and operate a department store? Absolutely. The department store is not a "law-related" business. It is not ancillary to the business of a law firm, so the Model Rules do not concern themselves with this issue.

May a law firm also own a business that is "law-related" or ancillary to the practice of law, such as a title insurance firm?

"Law-related services" are services that are reasonably performed in conjunction with, and are related to, legal services, but these services would not constitute the unauthorized practice of law if a nonlawyer performed them. Examples include title insurance, financial planning, accounting, trust services, real estate advice, legislative lobbying, economic analysis, social work, psychological counseling, tax return preparation, patent, medical or environmental consulting, and so forth. Rule 5.7, Comment 8.

Customers of these law-related businesses may include clients and nonclients. One-stop shopping makes the law firm more convenient for the client when the client has a problem that requires the services of several professionals. In addition, in these non-law subsidiaries, the law firm can ethically give nonlawyer professionals—the former ambassador, a former economist for the federal reserve, or a former chief trade negotiator—the status and titles that they believe they deserve. Having affiliates may help the firm retain existing clients and bring in new clients, thus offering new sources of revenue. Accordingly, various law firms, particularly in the Washington, D.C. area (where there is a disproportionate number of former ambassadors, former agency heads, and so forth), have created subsidiaries to perform law-related services.

Clients may become confused when dealing with these law-related services because they may think that they are still dealing with lawyers and have the protection of the attorney-client privilege and the rules governing conflicts of interest. Hence the existence of Rule 5.7.

Whether or not a jurisdiction adopts Rule 5.7, the lawyer is still governed by Rule 1.8(a), which already regulates business transactions with a client. In fact, one can think of Rule 5.7 as an elaboration of the general principles found in Rule 1.8(a). Thus, *Florida Bar v. Slater* (Fla.1987) suspended a lawyer for two years and four months for referring law clients who sustained personal injuries to a physical therapy clinic of which he was a principal. He *concealed* from his clients his involvement in the clinic.

Rule 5.7(a) provides that a lawyer is subject to *all* of the Model Rules when providing these services *if*: (1) she provides them in circumstances that are indistinct from her provision of legal services to clients, *or* (2) the lawyer (individually or with others) controls a separate, distinct entity that provides these law-related services *but* she does not take reasonable measures to make sure that the recipient of the law-related services knows that these services are not legal services and that therefore the typical protections of the lawyer-client relationship (*e.g.*, attorney-client privilege, conflict of interest rules) are inapplicable.

Rule 5.7(a) significantly motivates the lawyer to make sure these law-related services are distinct from her legal business in order to avoid the more demanding and stringent requirements of several of the sections in the Model Rules. If the law-related services are distinct from her provision of legal services to clients, and the lawyer makes clear that the protections of the lawyer-client relationship do not apply, then with respect to those law-related services she is not subject to those provisions of the Rules that apply to lawyers only when acting as lawyers (*e.g.*, advertising, conflicts of interest, disclosure of confidential information). She still would be subject to those other portions of the Model Rules that apply to lawyers whether or not they are acting in their capacity as lawyers (*e.g.*, prohibition of deceit).

If the ancillary business (the real estate firm, or the consulting firm) bills the customer separately and does not engage in the practice of law, then the fact that both the law firm and the ancillary business are involved in the same matter does not constitute illegal fee-splitting with non-lawyers, even if non-lawyers have ownership interests or exercise management powers in the ancillary enterprise.

Still, a lawyer involved with ancillary businesses must take care to avoid typical pitfalls. First, a lawyer who advises a client in dealing with the business entity that is really the lawyer's affiliate may not have the independent judgment needed to give sound advice, such as the advice to fire the affiliate. The lawyer must be sure that her self-interest in promoting the ancillary business does not distort her judgment in recommending the lawyer's own ancillary services to the client. While all the conflict of interest rules may not apply to these ancillary businesses, there remains the ethical risk that the affiliate will expand the number of situations disqualifying the law firm. For example, the affiliate may work on behalf of one of its customers, who has an interest conflicting with that of a different client of the law firm.

RULE 6.1: VOLUNTARY *PRO BONO PUBLICO* SERVICE

Pro Bono Publico means, "for the public good," or for the welfare of the whole. As applied to the work of lawyers, it usually refers to work that lawyers do with no expectation of a fee, or for a reduced fee, for persons of limited means. Lawyers may also represent charitable organizations, such as the Y.M.C.A., the Boy Scouts, the A.C.L.U., and the N.A.A.C.P. on a no-fee or reduced-fee basis. The Model Rules encourage, but do not require, lawyers to engage in fifty hours of pro bono activities each year.

Law reform activities (when a lawyer, without fee, represents a cause rather than a client) are also considered part of pro bono work. Such activities may include: (1) testifying before legislative or administrative hearings urging law reform; (2) lobbying for law reform in the selection and retention of judges; and (3) participating in bar association activities.

Rule 6.1 is the only Rule that never uses the word "shall," and instead uses the word "should." Rule 6.1 is not intended to be enforced through the disciplinary process. Rule 6.1, Comment 12.

When the ABA initially adopted the Model Rules in 1983, Rule 6.1 was a vague call urging lawyers to engage in pro bono work for people of limited means, or for public service or charitable groups. In February 1993, the ABA House of Delegates approved a much more specific Rule, although it remains aspirational. The Ethics 2000 reforms specified even more clearly that "*every* lawyer has a professional responsibility to provide legal services to those unable to pay." Rule 6.1 urges lawyers to aspire "to render at least (50) hours of *pro bono publico* legal services per year." The hours are in parentheses because the ABA recognized that states might well choose a different figure. States may choose a higher or lower number, or express the number as a percentage of a lawyer's professional time.

The ABA Commission that drafted the Model Rules wrestled with the question of whether the Model Rules should *require* lawyers to engage in pro bono work for clients of limited means. For years, commentators have proposed or criticized compulsory *pro bono*. In 1976 in California, for example, the state legislature considered, and defeated, a bill requiring active members of the bar to engage in a minimum of 40 hours per year of mandatory pro bono work for no fee or a "substantially reduced" fee.

In *Schwarz v. Kogan* (11th Cir.1998), plaintiff challenged the constitutionality of a Florida rule that merely required Florida lawyers to report the number of pro bono hours they worked each year.

The rule also encouraged them to pay $350 to a legal aid organization if they did not want to do pro bono work themselves. The court held that the Florida program was a rational way to highlight the need for pro bono service before Florida lawyers, and that a lawyer may be professionally disciplined for a failure to report. The Eleventh Circuit said Florida "undoubtedly has a legitimate interest" in encouraging pro bono service and "the free provision of legal services to the poor has long been recognized as an essential component of the practice of law." Indeed, the court said, a "traditions of the legal profession is that a lawyer, as an officer of the Court, is 'obligated to represent indigents for little or no compensation upon court order.' "

Judges have the power to compel attorneys to accept appointment to cases before the court. In *Powell v. Alabama* (S.Ct.1932), a case that helped inspire Harper Lee to write *To Kill a Mockingbird*, the Supreme Court declared that, "Attorneys are officers of the court, and are bound to render service when required by such an appointment." Less certain is the extent to which the law may require counsel to assume this burden with little or no compensation. A related question is the extent to which a state bar association or the state disciplinary machinery can or should require mandatory pro bono representation in civil, rather than criminal cases, and mandatory pro bono counseling and advice in non-litigious situations.

These issues are occasionally litigated. While courts have held that there is no constitutional right to compensation for compelled jury service, the difference between compelled jury service and compelled legal representation is not only in the amount of time and effort typically required, but also in the nature of the limited and discrete class burdened. The burden of uncompensated criminal defense representation is borne only by lawyers while the burden of jury service does not single out any discrete class of individuals. Thus the Alaska Supreme Court held that, under that state's Constitution, the court could not compel a private attorney to represent an indigent criminal defendant unless the state paid just compensation, defined as, "the compensation received by the average competent attorney operating on the open market." *DeLisio v. Alaska Superior Court* (Alaska 1987).

Because pro bono activities are professionally voluntary, albeit morally expected, it is a fact of life that some lawyers are more forthcoming than others in offering free (or reduced fee) legal services to those unable to pay the normal fee. The legal needs of the poor are not entirely met by lawyers who donate their time by engaging in personal pro bono activities. Hence, state and federal governments and some foundations fund various legal service organizations that hire lawyers to represent the poor.

The bar often uses "Interest on Lawyer Trust Account," or "IOLTA," to fund these organizations.

These accounts grew out of a series of trust law and tax law provisions. See the discussion of Rule 1.15, above, which notes that the constitutionality of these plans is the subject of litigation. Opponents argue that they take away the clients' property (the earned interest) without compensation because typical rules do not require the lawyer to secure the knowing consent of his or her client. The Supreme Court has not yet accepted that argument. *Brown v. Legal Foundation of Washington* (S.Ct.2003).

RULE 6.2: ACCEPTING APPOINTMENTS

A lawyer is not like the cab driver waiting at a taxi stand. The lawyer need not accept any client who walks through the door. However, it is improper for a lawyer to refuse an *appointed* case for the wrong reason. To achieve the goal of making legal services fully available, a lawyer should not lightly decline proffered employment; even employment that may be unattractive both to him and to the bar generally.

A lawyer *must* refuse a case if he is too busy to give it his competent attention. A lawyer also must refuse a case if the client seeks to maintain a frivolous action or one brought only to harass another. And a lawyer must refuse a case if he cannot deal with it competently.

On the other hand, a lawyer should not decline an appointment by a tribunal merely because the client, or the client's cause, is unpopular, or because influential members of the community oppose the lawyer's involvement. In addition, a lawyer need not refuse a case merely because he or she does not believe in the merits of a client's case, or believes, in a criminal case, that the client is guilty. However, if the lawyer's personal feelings are so intense that his effective representation is impaired, he must not take the case. Indeed, it would be unethical for the lawyer to accept such a case, because the first rule of legal ethics is competence.

RULE 6.3: MEMBERSHIP IN LEGAL SERVICES ORGANIZATIONS

An attorney in a private law firm may also be a member, officer, or director of a legal services organization engaged in pro bono activities. After Congress established the federal Legal Services Corporation in 1974, to offer noncriminal legal services to indigents, relevant regulations required that at least 60% of the local governing bodies should be attorneys admitted in that state and supportive of the delivery of quality legal services to the poor. The pro bono activities of the legal services organization may include lawsuits against private parties represented by the attorney's private firm. Such a situation may raise a conflict of interest question. Rule 6.3 deals with this issue.

If an attorney in private practice is on a legal services board, it may come to pass that the staff members of the legal services organization, on behalf of an indigent client, will file suit against one of the private attorney's private clients, or defend the indigent against suit brought by the private client. This situation may raise a practical problem: the private client may not approve of the fact that its private lawyer is serving on the legal services board. However, there is no formal conflict of interest because the private attorney who is a member of the Board does not have an attorney-client relationship with the Legal Service Organization's clients. The individual legal service clients do not confer with the Board members; nor do they place any confidences or secrets with these Board members. The Board's role is restricted solely to establishment of broad policy for the Program, and not the management of or the direct participation in Program client representation.

Rule 6.3 tries to solve the problem of any perceived conflicts by selectively screening the private lawyer from the decision-making process of the legal services organization. If the private lawyer is also a member, director, or officer of the legal services organization, then the private lawyer should not "knowingly" participate in any decision or action of the legal services organization if such participation would be inconsistent with the lawyer's obligation, under Rule 1.7, to his or her private clients. Similarly, the private lawyer should not knowingly participate in a decision on behalf of the legal services organization if the decision could have a "material adverse effect" on a legal services' client whose interests are adverse to the lawyer's private client. The private lawyer, then, is not disqualified from serving on the Board, but is sometimes disqualified from participating in certain Board decisions.

RULE 6.4: LAW REFORM ACTIVITIES AFFECTING CLIENT INTERESTS

It is not generally considered a conflict of interest for a lawyer to engage in law reform activities even though such activities are adverse to the financial interests of the lawyer's private clients. A lawyer only represents a client in the lawyer's professional capacity. It is not necessary that the lawyer personally agree with, adopt, or support his or her client's views. Lawyers who abhor cigarettes may represent tobacco companies and still participate in a bar association group that advocates bans on smoking. Their clients may object, and of course they may fire their lawyer, but they have no complaint that their lawyer (or former lawyer) acted unethically.

Thus, Rule 6.4 states that a lawyer may be a director, officer, or member of a group involved in law reform activities "notwithstanding that the reform may affect the interests of a client of the lawyer." If there is no breach of loyalty when the lawyer is a member of an organization advocating law reform contrary to a client's interest, there should be little legal argument that there is a breach of loyalty when the lawyer speaks out on his own behalf. The client could not validly charge that the lawyer acted unethically in taking the contrary position, unless the lawyer is violating client secrets.

The client's interest and the personal law reform interests of the lawyer may of course coincide. If the lawyer is representing a private client while, for example, appearing before a legislative committee and asking for law reform, the lawyer may not mislead the committee as to the true identity of the client. Thus Rule 6.4 provides that when the lawyer knows that the interests of a client may be materially *benefited* by a decision in which the lawyer participates, he "shall disclose that fact but need not identify the client." The disclosure of the fact of representation helps to preclude the suspicion that the lawyer exercised improper influence on behalf of a client. If the identity of the client is privileged or secret, the lawyer should at least alert the legislative committee or similar entity that she is representing a private client whose identity cannot be revealed. See also Rule 3.9.

RULE 6.5: NON–PROFIT AND COURT–ANNEXED LIMITED LEGAL– SERVICES PROGRAMS

Bar associations and other groups often set up programs such as hotlines, etc. to assist people with short-term limited legal advice. Even though there may be no expectation of life-long or other long-term service from hotlines, the lawyer may sometimes establish a true lawyer-client relationship. Often such programs are not operated under conditions that allow for systematic conflict checks. In 2002, the ABA added Rule 6.5, to protect a lawyer who inadvertently creates a conflict through such representation.

The "short-term" lawyer must inform the client that the scope of his representation is limited. Rule 6.5, Comment 2. If this is done, the lawyer is held to the basic conflicts Rules 1.7 and 1.9(a) only if he *knows* of a conflict. He is also subject to the imputation restrictions of Rule 1.10 only if he *knows* that another lawyer in his firm is disqualified by 1.7 or 1.9(a). This means that the firm will not be disqualified from representing the adversary to the hotline client. Otherwise the conflicts rules would impose a considerable burden on the lawyer, thus discouraging participation in these programs.

If the representation becomes ongoing, however, the basic conflicts rules assume their full force at that time. Rule 6.5, Comment 5.

RULE 7.1: COMMUNICATIONS CONCERNING A LAWYER'S SERVICES

1. The Origins of the Restrictions on Legal Advertising

The Canons of Ethics of 1908 originally allowed lawyers to advertise, and advertise they did. Lawyers published their but some advertisements were and also advertized their specialities, unseemly or misleading. For example, one 1911 lawyer's advertisement in the *Los Angeles Daily Times* included the following (in all capital letters): "WE GET THE COIN."

By 1937 a complete redraft of Canon 27 severely restricted lawyer advertising. The organized bar maintained this virtual prohibition until the 1970s when consumer groups, some attorneys, and others began actively opposing the bar's position, leading to court decisions that forced the bar to change the rules.

Consequently, before considering Rule 7.1 and the other Rules in Part 7—all dealing with regulations governing the way that lawyers communicate to the lay public information about legal services— we shall first very briefly consider and analyze the major U.S. Supreme Court cases that focus on the special issue of the commercial speech of lawyers. These decisions are important because they slowly forced the organized bar to remove its restrictions on free speech. Rule 7.1, after the 2002 revisions, now only prevents false or misleading speech and no longer provides that certain statements are, by *ipse dixit*, considered misleading.

2.   The *Bates* Case and Its Progeny

All commercial speech constitutional law cases dealing with lawyer advertising are the progeny of *Bates v. State Bar* (S.Ct.1977). *Bates* struck down state limitations on attorney advertising and held that the right of free speech protects truthful newspaper advertising of availability and fees for routine legal services. However, the Court allowed the states to subject legal advertising to reasonable restrictions on time, place and manner, and to prohibit false or misleading advertising.

The Court in *Bates* was tentative in expanding the right of free speech as applied to advertising by lawyers. The majority noted that the case involved neither person-to-person solicitation nor advertising as to the quality of legal services, but only the question of whether lawyers may constitutionally advertise truthful information about the prices of routine services, such as uncontested divorces, simple personal bankruptcies, and changes of name. This advertising, the Court ruled, is constitutionally protected under the First Amendment.

The Court left open the extent to which certain types of advertising may be misleading, though it

found appellants' particular advertisement not misleading. The Court also raised the questions of: (1)
whether advertising claims as to the *quality* of
services "may be so likely to be misleading as to
warrant restriction," and (2) whether "the special
problems of advertising on the electronic broadcast
media will warrant special consideration."

Following *Bates*, the Supreme Court developed a
four-part test for commercial speech cases, in *Central Hudson Gas & Electric Corporation v. Public
Service Commission* (S.Ct.1980). The Court declared:

> "At the outset we must determine whether the
> expression is protected by the First Amend-
> ment. For commercial speech to come within
> that provision, it at least [1] must concern
> lawful activity and not be misleading. [2] Next
> we ask whether the asserted governmental in-
> terest is substantial. If both inquiries yield pos-
> itive answers, we must determine [3] whether
> the regulation directly advances the govern-
> mental interest asserted, and [4] whether it is
> not more extensive than is necessary to serve
> that interest."

Now, keeping the *Central Hudson* four-part test
in mind, let us consider some specific fact scenarios
involving lawyer advertising.

A.   Allegedly Misleading Advertising

Some states responded to *Bates* by, in effect,
declaring that certain types of legal advertising

were inherently misleading. In a significant opinion, which identified the lawyer only by initials, *In re R.M.J.* (S.Ct.1982), a unanimous Supreme Court rejected this approach. The Missouri supreme court had reprimanded R.M.J. because he had deviated from the precise listing of areas of practice included in the state's Rule governing lawyer advertising; his advertisement listed "real estate" instead of "property," and he listed "contracts" and "securities," although the state's Rule did not list that term. Because the state did not show that R.M.J.'s listing was deceptive, and because the state could show no substantial interest that its restriction on advertising promoted, the Court invalidated it.

The Court also invalidated a Rule prohibiting a lawyer from identifying the jurisdictions in which he is licensed to practice law. R.M.J. had emphasized in large boldface type that he was a member of the U.S. Supreme Court bar, a "relatively uninformative fact" but not (according to the evidence submitted) misleading.

Finally, the *R.M.J.* Court invalidated a prohibition against the lawyer mailing announcement cards to persons other than lawyers, former clients, personal friends, and relatives. These cards announced the opening of his law office to a wide range of people. The state produced no evidence justifying such a restrictive prohibition.

The facts of *Peel v. Attorney Registration and Disciplinary Commission of Illinois* (S.Ct.1990) were unusual. Illinois rules did not permit an attorney to hold himself out as "certified" or a "specialist" except for patent, trademark, and admiralty lawyers. The Illinois Supreme Court publicly censured Peel, an Illinois attorney, because his letterhead *truthfully* stated that he is a civil trial specialist certified by the National Board of Trial Advocacy (NBTA), a bona fide private group that developed a set of objective and demanding standards and procedures for periodic certification of lawyers with experience and competence in trial work. In *Peel*, a splintered U.S. Supreme Court reversed and found that Peel's claims were constitutionally protected. Illinois argued that Peel's letterhead implied a higher quality or ability than for uncertified lawyers. Justice Stevens' plurality opinion explained that Illinois had confused "the distinction between statements of opinion or quality and statements of objective facts that may support an inference of quality."

Ibanez v. Florida Department of Business and Professional Regulation, Board of Accountancy (S.Ct.1994) held that the Florida Board of Accountancy violated the First Amendment when it reprimanded Silvia Ibanez, an attorney, because she had *truthfully* stated in her advertising that she is a Certified Public Accountant (CPA) and a Certified Financial Planner (CFP). The state Board of Accountancy had licensed her as a CPA, and a bona fide private organization had licensed her as a CFP. Justice Ginsburg wrote, for a unanimous Court: "[W]e cannot imagine how consumers can be misled by her truthful representation" that she is a CPA. *Ibanez* also held (7 to 2 this time) that Ms. Ibanez could not be sanctioned for truthfully stating that she was a CFP.

Zauderer v. Office of Disciplinary Counsel (S.Ct. 1985) limited the power of the state to mandate detailed disclosures. The Court explained, "unjustified or unduly burdensome disclosure requirements might offend the First Amendment by chilling protected commercial speech." However, the Court held that the state could discipline an attorney if he failed to include in his advertisements some information reasonably necessary to make his advertisement not misleading. The lawyer advertised that he was available to represent clients on a contingent fee basis and that "if there is no recovery, no legal fees are owed by our clients." The advertisement failed to disclose that the clients might be liable for significant litigation costs even though their lawsuits were unsuccessful. *Zauderer,* also held that the state may not discipline an attorney who solicits business by running newspaper advertisements containing nondeceptive illustrations and legal advice.

B. Solicitation of Legal Business

In the year following the *Bates* decision, the Court began to define the limits of state regulation of attorney solicitation of clients. Two leading cases were decided the same day, *Ohralik v. Ohio State Bar* (S.Ct.1978) and *In re Primus* (S.Ct.1978). Justice Powell, for the Court, said in *Ohralik* that the distinction between other types of speech and commercial speech is a "commonsense" one, though later he stated in *Primus* that the line between commercial and noncommercial speech "will not always be easy to draw." The decisions in the two cases, taken together, indicate that the state may regulate a lawyer's face-to-face or in-person solicitation of clients in order to protect the public from false or deceptive commercial practices, so long as the regulations are reasonable and are not applied to speech that does not clearly present such dangers to the public.

Ohralik recognized that the state has an interest in protecting the "unsophisticated, injured, or distressed lay person" from "those aspects of solicitation that involve fraud, undue influence, intimidation, overreaching, and other forms of 'vexatious conduct.' " This rule is justified in part because of the special nature of "in-person" solicitation. In general advertising, the recipient may simply turn away, but in-person solicitation may exert pressure and seek an immediate response from the prospective client, who then has less opportunity for reflection.

Justice Marshall's thoughtful concurring opinion specifically would allow "benign" commercial solicitation, that is "solicitation by advice and information that is truthful and that is presented in a noncoercive, nondeceitful, and dignified manner to a potential client who is emotionally and physically capable of making a rational decision either to accept or reject the representation with respect to a legal claim or matter that is not frivolous."

In the companion case, *In re Primus,* a lawyer whose firm was cooperating with the American Civil Liberties Union (ACLU) wrote to a woman who had been sterilized as a condition of receiving public medical assistance. The lawyer offered the ACLU's services to represent her. The state disciplined the attorney for this action, but the Supreme Court reversed that decision and distinguished *Ohralik* because of the nature of the interests involved. Solicitation for private gain under the circumstances of *Ohralik* could be proscribed without showing harm in a given case because the circumstances were likely to result in misleading, deceptive, and overbearing conduct, but solicitation on behalf of nonprofit organizations that litigate as a form of political expression may be regulated only when actual harm is shown in the particular case. The Court reviewed the record in *Primus* and found nothing indicating fraud, overreaching or other behavior that the state could regulate. Under*Ohralik,* states are free to proscribe in-person solicitation for gain in circumstances where it is likely to be fraudulent, misleading, or overreaching, but under *Primus* they may only proscribe solicitation on behalf of nonprofit political organizations if it is in fact misleading.

In re R.M.J. (S.Ct.1982) invalidated a state rule that prohibited lawyers from mailing cards (which announced the opening of his office) to persons other than "lawyers, former clients, personal friends and relatives." Later, *Shapero v. Kentucky Bar Association* (S.Ct.1988) protected targeted, direct mail advertising. Thus, letters and other non-face-to-face solicitation are not illegal "in-person" solicitation for the purposes of *Ohralik,* even if the lawyer seeks pecuniary gain. Of course, the state can always prohibit actual misrepresentation and overreaching.

The Supreme Court back-tracked from *Shapero* when it considered targeted mail sent to prospective clients soon after an accident. A Florida ethics rule prohibited personal injury lawyers from sending targeted direct mail soliciting employment to victims and their relatives until 30 days following an accident or disaster. This rule prevented the personal injury *plaintiff's* attorney from contacting the accident victim or a relative, but it imposed no restrictions on the *defense* attorney from contacting either the victim or the relative. *Florida Bar v. Went For It, Inc.* (S.Ct.1995) held (5 to 4) that, even though targeted mailing is constitutionally protected under *Shapero*, Florida may ban targeted mailing by plaintiffs' attorneys for 30 days after the cause of action has occurred. Justice O'Connor, who dissented in *Shapero*, wrote the majority opinion in *Went for It*.

In a significant passage, the Court announced an important limitation on any broad reading of this case:

> "Florida permits lawyers to advertise on prime-time television and radio as well as in newspapers and other media. They may rent space on billboards. They may send *untargeted letters* to

the general population, *or to discrete segments thereof*.'' (emphasis added).

The majority justified the Florida prohibition as a means to protect the public perception of lawyers. Justice Kennedy ominously complained in his dissent that, ''for the first time since *Bates v. State Bar of Arizona*, the Court now orders a major retreat from the constitutional guarantees for commercial speech in order to shield its own profession from public criticism.''

3. The Overarching Principle: No Misleading Speech

Rule 7.1 broadly prohibits ''false or misleading communication about the lawyer or the lawyer's services.'' Subject to the requirements of this Rule, Rule 7.2 permits a lawyer to advertise through a broad spectrum of media. Rule 7.1 states that communication regarding a lawyer's services is false or misleading if it contains material misrepresentations of law or fact, or (even if, for instance, the communication is literally truthful) if it has *omissions* that are ''necessary to make the statement considered as a whole not materially misleading.'' This phrase is derived from federal securities laws.

Prior to the 2002 revisions, Rule 7.1 not only forbade ''misleading'' speech but also contained a provision, Rule 7.1(c), that the 2002 revisions deleted. This subsection simply announced that an advertisement that compares one lawyer's services with another is misleading unless the comparison

can be "factually substantiated." The drafters of
the revised Rule 7.1 concluded that "a prohibition
of all comparisons that cannot be factually substantiated is unduly broad. Whether such comparisons
are misleading should be assessed on a case-by-case
basis in terms of whether the particular comparison
is substantially likely to mislead a reasonable person to believe that the comparison can be substantiated."

So, an unsubstantiated comparison of the lawyer's fees with the fees of other lawyers would be
misleading if presented in a way that would lead a
consumer to believe apples are apples when they
are in fact being compared to oranges. Rule 7.1,
Comment 3.

RULE 7.2: ADVERTISING

The Model Rules now permit truthful advertising through any medium except it imposes extra restrictions on "in-person solicitation," which is narrowly defined and governed by its own rule, Rule 7.3.

While some jurisdictions have tried to prohibit advertising going beyond specified facts about a lawyer or "undignified" advertising, these efforts are often unconstitutional. Lawyers have the right to free speech. The ABA no longer attempts to forbid or even regulate "undignified" advertising. If the advertising is "undignified," the free market can take care of the problem, because consumers need not hire a lawyer whose advertisements they find distasteful or inappropriate. "Questions of effectiveness and taste in advertising are matters of speculation and subjective judgment." Rule 7.2, Comment 3.

One thing that the Supreme Court has left untouched is restrictions on paid referrals. Rule 7.2(b) forbids a lawyer from giving anything of value in exchange for a recommendation, except that she may pay for media advertising and the "usual charges" of not-for-profit lawyer referral services or legal service plan. Because the Model Rules allow a lawyer to purchase a law practice, Rule 7.3 makes clear that it does not forbid such a purchase pursuant to Rule 1.17.

The old Model Code, in precise and elaborate detail, defined the types of legal service organizations from which a lawyer may accept a recommendation or client referral. In contrast, the present Model Rule 7.2, Comment 8 simply requires a lawyer to guarantee his or her professional independence, as Rule 5.4(c) already requires. In addition, there are a few general restrictions regarding solicitation in Rule 7.3.

Rule 7.2(b) does not, in general, allow a lawyer to pay money to a person to recommend his services. There are, however, several important exceptions. First, the lawyer may pay the reasonable costs of advertisements. Rule 7.2(b)(1).

Rule 1.5(e). Second, the lawyer may pay the "usual charges" of a legal service plan, or non-for-profit or qualified legal service plan. Rule 7.2(b)(2). A "legal service plan" is "a prepaid or group legal service plan or a similar delivery system that assists prospective clients to secure legal representation." A "lawyer referral service" is "any organization that holds itself out to the public as a lawyer referral service." A "qualified lawyer referral service" is one that the appropriate regulatory authority has approved "as affording adequate protections for prospective clients." Rule 7.2, Comment 6. The lawyer is not supposed to distort the judgment of these plans by paying more than their "usual charges."

Third, the lawyer can buy a law practice if he follows the requirements of Rule 1.17.

Fourth, the lawyer may refer clients to other lawyers or other nonlawyer professionals pursuant to agreement if the reciprocal agreement is not exclusive and if he tells the client about the existence and nature of the agreement.

Rule 7.2 does not refer to Rule 1.5(e) but it should. Rule 1.5(e) allows a lawyer to pay a referral fee from a lawyer in another firm (1) if the client agrees, (2) the total fee is reasonable, and (3) the division is in proportion to services performed *or* each lawyer assumes joint responsibility for the representation.

For ease of enforcing Rule 7.2, the Rule also requires that any communication a lawyer makes under this Rule include the name and address of at least one lawyer responsible for it.

RULE 7.3: DIRECT CONTACT WITH PROSPECTIVE CLIENTS

1. Introduction

Solicitation may be considered a form of advertising, but on a retail, rather than a wholesale, level. The Model Rules, as they have been amended in response to various Supreme Court decisions, now make a distinction that forbids "in-person" [*i.e.,* face to face] or "live [*i.e.,* non-prerecorded] telephone contact," and "real-time electronic contact" of a prospective client if the lawyer engages in such actions where his "pecuniary gain" is a "significant motive."

Rule 7.3(a) does not apply if the lawyer contacts another lawyer, or a family or close personal friend, or someone with whom he has had a prior professional relationship.

In all cases, even those within the exceptions of Rule 7.3(a)(1) and (a)(2), the lawyer may not solicit if the prospective client has told the lawyer that he does not wish to be solicited, or if the solicitation involves coercion, duress, or harassment.

The 1983 version of the Rules used to distinguish between mass mailings (allowed as advertising) and targeted mail (not allowed). In February of 1987 two ABA entities initially proposed that Rule 7.3 should allow targeted mailing, but they withdrew this proposal after the ABA Board of Governors opposed it. Then the Supreme Court gave the bar no choice but to allow targeted mail. In *Shapero v. Kentucky Bar Association* (S.Ct.1988) the Court ruled that, under the First Amendment, states may not categorically prohibit lawyers from seeking business by sending truthful, nondeceptive letters to potential clients known to face particular legal problems. In February 1989, the ABA responded to *Shapero* by amending Rule 7.3, which no longer prohibits targeted mail. Targeted mail is simply a more efficient form of mailing than mass mailing. The First Amendment does not require advertisers to be inefficient when mailing advertising blurbs, so the Supreme Court invalidated the restriction.

Any written solicitation must include the words "Advertising Material" on the "outside envelope" and at the beginning and ending of any recorded or electronic message. Rule 7.3(c). The touchstone of the new Rule is to protect the prospective client from direct, personal encounters or live telephone persuasion from a lawyer because those situations are fraught with the possibility of undue influence, intimidation, and over-reaching.

2. Departing Lawyers Soliciting Clients of the Former Law Firm

One does not normally think of soliciting *present* clients. These clients have already hired the law firm, and when the firm sends them unsolicited information about their possible legal needs, it is only being pro-active, taking the initiative. However, there are situations where lawyers within a firm have a falling out, and some lawyers depart without buying the entire law practice from the other lawyers. The partnership agreement may provide how the law firm should handle these break-ups, but any agreement must comply with the ethical rule that provides that a partnership or employment agreement may not restrict the right of a lawyer to practice after leaving the firm except an agreement concerning benefits upon retirement. Rule 5.6. Thus, when lawyers leave the firm, they retain the right to practice law in competition with the firm from which they departed.

To what extent may the departing lawyers seek to take with them the clients of that firm (or, in the view of the departing lawyers, "their clients")? Many years ago, joining a law firm was a little like marriage: it was expected to be a lifetime commitment. Now, joining a law firm is a lot like modern marriage: it often is not a lifetime commitment. The fact that some lawyers prosper from grabbing business from the law firm and then leaving reflects this new reality.

The clients may wish to follow the individual lawyers with whom they have dealt in the past. Clients are not merchandise; they have the right to follow the lawyer when she changes law firms. There are also some free speech interests at stake. A lawyer should be able to tell the truth, *e.g.,* that she is leaving one firm and starting a new firm or joining a different firm and the clients are free to follow her. However, the right of free speech is not the right to lie. The departing lawyer may not lie or mislead others. Thus, *In re Smith* (Ore.1992) suspended a lawyer for four months because he misled his clients: when he opened his new firm, he sent letters to clients that implied that nothing material had changed.

Restatement of the Law Governing Lawyers, Third, § 9(3) (Official Draft 2000) advises that, prior to the time a lawyer leaves a law firm, she may solicit clients on whose matters she had previously worked actively and substantially, *but* only *after* she has adequately and timely informed the firm of her intent to contact clients for that purpose. After she has left the firm, she may contact the old firm's clients to the same extent as any other nonfirm lawyer.

When a lawyer decides to leave a law firm, she might not leave alone. She ethically may consult with other partners and associates and employees who decide to leave together. The lawyers leaving Firm #1 should not use the resources of Firm #1 to solicit clients for Firm #2. The lawyers may agree to depart as a group, or to serial departures, so long as, first, "the lawyers and personnel do nothing prohibited to either of them (including impermissibly soliciting clients);" second, they must not "misuse firm resources (*such as copying files or client lists without permission or unlawfully removing firm property from its premises*);" or third, they must take no other action "detrimental to the interests of the firm or of clients, aside from whatever detriment may befall the firm due to their departure." Restatement of the Law Governing Lawyers, Third, § 9 (Official Draft 2000), at Comment *i* (emphasis added).

Courts, in general, do not favor departing lawyers making statements disparaging of their former law firm. However, one should distinguish disparaging remarks that are factually verifiable and true from other types of disparaging remarks. Lawyers should have the right to tell the truth. For example, if a lawyer left the firm because it had discriminated against him on account of race, the free speech interests dictate that he should be able to tell that to his clients at Law Firm #1.

3. Solicitation and Legal Service Plans

The Rules make clear that an attorney may contact the representatives of a group, such as a union, companies, etc., and urge these representatives to set up a prepaid legal services plan for their members. These third parties (the union, a company, etc.) can then contact (*i.e.*, solicit) their members. Rule 7.3, Comments 6, 8.

The rationale is that when a lawyer is soliciting the representatives of a proposed plan, she is not engaging in solicitation but in advertising because this "form of communication is not directed to a prospective client," but to the representatives of the plan who are "acting in a fiduciary capacity seeking a supplier of legal services for others who may, if they choose, become prospective clients of the lawyer.'' Rule 7.3, Comment 6.

This Rule allows the lawyer to contact directly a prepaid or group legal services plan, and allows that plan to solicit its members. To make sure that the lawyer cannot use the plan to evade the restrictions that the Rule places on the lawyer's own solicitation, the Rule prohibits the lawyer from owning or directing the plan. Comment 8.

The legal services plan, when it solicits members, may not target particular persons who are known to need legal services in a particular matter. In-person, face-to-face solicitation, or telephone solicitation, comes under this Rule. Rule 7.3, Comment 8. After *Shapero,* which gave constitutional protection to targeted, direct mail advertising, the Rule 7.3 prohibition, to the extent is applies to targeted mail, is questionable.

RULE 7.4:
COMMUNICATION OF
FIELDS OF PRACTICE
AND SPECIALIZATION

The Rules place some regulations on a lawyer's communication of fields of practice. A lawyer may communicate through advertising that the lawyer's practice does or does not include particular fields of law. Prior to February 1989, the Comment to Rule 7.4 had provided that the lawyer may not state that his practice "is limited to" or is "concentrated in" a particular area. Now, there is no such restriction. In light of modern lawyer-advertising cases, the pre–1989 version would be unconstitutional, unless the state could meet the difficult burden of demonstrating that the use of language such as "is limited to" is misleading (while "is not limited to" is not misleading).

The current Rule 7.4, after the 2002 revisions, recognizes that many of the battles of the past have ended with the ABA's long-standing position as the loser. Thus, in light of free speech interests, Rule 7.4 imposes only three basic rules governing communication of a field of practice and specialization. First, the lawyer may communicate that she does or does not practice in particular fields of law. Second, if she is admitted to practice before the U.S. Patent and Trademark Office, she may use the designation of "Patent Attorney" or similar designation. And, third, she may use the designation of "Admiralty" or "Proctor in Admiralty" if she engages in Admiralty practice.

The lawyer may not state or imply that she is "certified as a specialist" in a particular field of law unless the appropriate state authority or the ABA has approved the organization. The lawyer must also clearly identify the name of the certifying organization in her communication.

RULE 7.5: FIRM NAMES AND LETTERHEADS

One cannot appreciate the simplicity of the Model Rules regarding the lawyer's professional cards, signs, and letterheads unless one first acknowledges the extensive regulations found in the former Model Code. The old Model Code had specific, intricate, and detailed regulations governing professional cards, signs, and letterheads, and so forth. That is all in the past.

Rule 7.5(a) simply prohibits the use of a "firm name, letterhead or other professional designation that violates Rule 7.1," which is the general rule that bans misleading or false statements.

For example, it is increasingly common for a law firm to be located in more than one jurisdiction, although all the lawyers within that firm are not admitted to practice in all the jurisdictions. The Model Rules allow the law firm to use the same name in each jurisdiction, but as to lawyers licensed in different jurisdictions, each lawyer's jurisdictional limitations should be indicated on the letterhead and on other permissible publicity. Rule 7.5(b).

Sometimes, holding a public office is a full time job, and a statute or the pressure of the office precludes the office holder from engaging in another occupation. But, in many other instances statutes may allow a lawyer to hold a public position and to practice law or another occupation. For example, a part-time mayor, state legislator, or city council member typically may continue the practice of law. The law firm should not use the name of a public official unless that official is actively and regularly practicing with the law firm. Rule 7.5(c). If the lawyer is not so engaged, it is considered misleading to allow the firm to continue to use his name in firm communications because it may imply a connection that no longer exists.

What about trade names? The old Model Code prohibited lawyers in private practice from practicing under a trade name whether or not it was misleading. In other words, a law firm could not call itself, ''The 47th Street Law Office,'' even though it really was located on 47th Street. However, the old Model Code did allow a law firm to use the name of one or more deceased partners or retired members of the firm, even thought that really is a trade name.

The Model Rules are more logical and avoid thorny constitutional issues by prohibiting the use of a trade name in private practice only if the name is misleading or implies a connection with a government agency or charity or public legal services organization that does not exist. For example, ''State of Alabama Legal Clinic'' may be misleading if it is not connected with the state and is not a public legal aid agency. In that case, an express disclaimer may be necessary. Otherwise, the ''47th

Street Law Office'' or the ''ABC Legal Clinic'' is a perfectly valid name for a law office. Rule 7.5, Comment 1.

The Model Rules also allow the use of the name of a deceased or retired member, but only if there has been a continuing line of succession. In other words, a law firm cannot call itself ''Law Offices of William O. Douglas & Hugo Black'' if Douglas and Black were never members of that firm.

RULE 7.6: POLITICAL CONTRIBUTIONS TO OBTAIN GOVERNMENT LEGAL ENGAGEMENTS OR APPOINTMENTS BY JUDGES

Lawyers have the right to participate in the political process. But Rule 7.6 distinguishes what is often called "pay to play" as unprofessional and unethical. Pay to play occurs when a lawyer accepts a government legal engagement or an appointment by judge (for example, as a "special master") if the lawyer makes or solicits a political contribution "*for the purpose of* obtaining or being considered for that type of legal engagement."

Note that Rule 7.6 applies to a lawyer "or law firm." This is the first time that the ABA House of Delegates approved a rule that can be used to discipline a "law firm."

There is a roughly parallel provision in the ABA Model Code of Judicial Conduct (2007)—Judicial Rule 2.13(B)—that provides (subject to a few common sense exceptions) that the judge should not appoint someone to a position (such as special master) if the person has contributed more than a certain amount of money (each state is supposed to insert a figure) within a certain number of years prior to the judge's election campaign (each state is supposed to insert a figure here too).

Rule 7.6 is not limited to bribery, which requires proof of a *quid pro quo*. Indeed, if there were a bribe or other crime involved, Rule 8.4(b) already takes care of that matter. Instead, Rule 7.6 deals with the non-criminal situations.

It will often be difficult to clearly prove the subjective intention behind the donation. That is because the Rule requires that the lawyer or law firm would not have made the political contribution "but for the desire to be considered for the legal engagement or appointment." Comment 5.

The rule does not apply to those government officials in the legislative or executive branch who accept the donation; by it own term it applies to lawyers or law firms who "make" the contribution.

Rule 7.6 only applies to "political contributions," which are defined as any "gift, subscription, loan, advance, or deposit of anything of value made directly or indirectly to" a candidate, judicial incumbent, etc. Comment 2. Endorsements may not be included in this definition because they do not fit under the examples given, which all seem to refer to money. Indeed, Comment 2 specifically announces (without any effort to explain) that "political contribution" does not include "uncompensated services." So, if a lawyer endorses the political campaign of a judge for the specific intention of securing a judicial appointment as a special master, or if the lawyer devotes many hours of her time to secure the election of a judge, for the same specific intention, she does not violate Rule 7.6. But, if she gives $1 to the judge's campaign with that same specific intention, she violates Rule 7.6.

RULE 8.1: BAR ADMISSION AND DISCIPLINARY MATTERS

The Model Rules, in general, do not govern non-lawyers. However, an important exception concerns the case of a nonlawyer who seeks to become a lawyer and who intentionally makes a materially false statement in her bar application. That misstatement constitutes "dishonesty" or a "fraud," and thus is disciplinable, even if the person was not a lawyer at the time because the duty of Rule 8.1 extends to persons seeking admission to the bar as well as to lawyers. Though the applicant is not, at the time of the application, governed by the Rules of that jurisdiction, a violation of Rule 8.1(a) may form the basis of discipline if the applicant is already a member of the bar in one jurisdiction and is seeking admission elsewhere. Even if the applicant has not yet been admitted to any bar, she would become subject to discipline if she is subsequently admitted.

A statement is *material* if it has "the effect of inhibiting efforts of the bar to determine an applicant's fitness to practice law." *Grievance Commission v. Howe* (N.D.1977). The misstatement also must be *knowingly* false when made. Rule 8.1(a).

This Rule has a *scienter* requirement. Because of this *scienter* requirement, there arises the question of what the lawyer or applicant should do if she *un*knowingly makes a material false statement, but later comes to know of its falsity. Can she now take advantage of the misinformation because she did not act with *scienter*? The Rule 8.1(b) is clear on this point. The lawyer or applicant may *not* "*fail to disclose* a fact necessary to correct a misapprehension known by the person to have arisen in the matter...." Consequently, she must disclose her earlier false statement even though she did not know it was false when she originally made it. The Rules impose on the applicant an affirmative duty to clarify "any misunderstanding on the part of the admissions or disciplinary authority of which the person involved becomes aware." Comment 1.

In the case of either an application for admission or a bar disciplinary matter, if the bar authorities request information, Rule 8.1(b) and Comment 2 make clear that the lawyer or applicant may assert a *bona fide* evidentiary or constitutional privilege.

Thus, if the bar application asks if the applicant has ever been arrested, even if that arrest has been expunged from the record, the applicant should either answer the question truthfully (*e.g.*, she was arrested 15 years earlier, but that juvenile arrest was expunged from her record), or challenge the legal authority of the bar authorities to ask about expunged records.

There are constitutional limits on the ability of the bar authorities to investigate applicants and deny them admission. For example, the bar may lawfully discipline a lawyer or refuse to admit an applicant who unlawfully obstructs the investigation. But the bar authorities, because of free speech concerns, may not punish persons simply because they are or have been members of the Communist Party. *Schware v. Board of Bar Examiners of State of N.M.* (S.Ct.1957). However, the state may refuse a person admission if that person, with *scienter*, was a member in an organization advocating the unlawful overthrow of the Government, and had the *specific intent* to further these unlawful goals of the organization. *Law Students Civil Rights Research Council, Inc. v. Wadmond* (S.Ct.1971).

Lawyers are often asked to supply character references for bar applicants. If the lawyer is asked, the lawyer obviously must reply truthfully, unless the lawyer claims a privilege such as a constitutional privilege. If the lawyer is representing the applicant, then she must claim the attorney-client privilege. No provisions of the Rules require (or even urge) a lawyer to *volunteer* unfavorable information about an applicant. The Model Rules impose no requirement that the lawyer become a self-appointed investigator.

RULE 8.2: JUDICIAL AND LEGAL OFFICIALS

Rule 8.2 makes a lawyer subject to discipline if he or she knowingly makes any false charges against a judge, judicial candidate, or public legal officer. The lawyer also must not knowingly speak with "reckless disregard" as to the truth or falsity of his or her statements.

The Rules prohibit a lawyer from making any knowingly false statements (or false statements made with reckless disregard as to their truth), when the statements relate to the judge's, or judicial candidate's, or public legal officer's qualifications or integrity. However, this Rule seems to allow even inflamed opinions. Thus, Rule 8.2 would *not* approve of *In re Raggio* (Nev.1971) (per curiam), which reprimanded an attorney for calling a judicial opinion "shocking."

It is not unusual for judges to believe that lawyers should defend judges from unjust criticism. Hence, the final version of Rule 8.2, as approved by the House of Delegates, added Comment 3, which encourages lawyers "to continue traditional efforts to defend judges and courts unjustly criticized."

Judges running for retention or reelection are governed in their campaign activities by the ABA

Model Code of Judicial Conduct (2007), as enacted by the individual states. This prevents lawyers campaigning for judicial office from having an unfair competitive advantage over sitting judges. Needless to say, no code of judicial conduct or lawyer conduct can limit essential First Amendment rights.

RULE 8.3: REPORTING PROFESSIONAL MISCONDUCT

1. The Lawyer's Role Regarding Reporting Disciplinable Violations of Lawyers

In general, lawyers have an obligation to volunteer information of another lawyer's serious disciplinable violations that raise a substantial question about that lawyer's honesty or fitness as a lawyer in other respects unless the information is privileged.

The Illinois Supreme Court, in 1988, became the first court to discipline a lawyer solely for failing to report another lawyer's misconduct, under circumstances where the disciplined lawyer's client specifically told him not to report the other lawyer's conduct. *In re Himmel* (Ill.1988). In October 1978, Tammy Forsberg, who had been injured in a motorcycle accident, retained an attorney named John R. Casey to represent her. Casey worked out a settlement of $35,000, one-third to go to him and two-thirds to Ms. Forsberg. However, when Casey received the $35,000 settlement check, he converted the funds. After several unsuccessful attempts to collect her share, Ms. Forsberg hired James H. Himmel to represent her. Himmel offered not to collect any fees until Forsberg had recovered her full $23,233.34; he would then collect one-third of any funds recovered in excess of that amount. After Himmel entered the case, Casey agreed to pay Forsberg $75,000 in settlement of all claims she might have against him including any claims for punitive damages. Under the settlement agreement, Ms. Forsberg also agreed not to initiate any criminal, civil, or disciplinary action against Casey. Casey did not honor this agreement to pay $75,000, and so Himmel, on behalf of his client, sued Casey and won a judgment of $100,000. Himmel was never able to collect this entire award, but, because of Himmel's efforts, Ms. Forsberg eventually collected a total of $15,400 from Casey. Himmel therefore received no fee for his efforts because, pursuant to his agreement with Ms. Forsberg, the amount was less than the full amount owed her.

Neither before nor after the $100,000 judgment against Casey did Himmel report Casey to the disciplinary authorities, because Forsberg had specifically instructed him not to do so. She said she simply wanted her money back. Ms. Forsberg may have been concerned that having her attorney report Casey would make it that much more difficult to collect any money from Casey. The Hearing Board recommended a private reprimand against Mr. Himmel; on appeal, the Review Board recommended dismissal of the disciplinary complaint. The Illinois Supreme Court disagreed with the two prior rulings and suspended Mr. Himmel for one year. The court's opinion noted that Himmel would have possibly profited from his decision not to report Casey to the bar.

In contrast to *Himmel*, Model Rule 8.3 "does not require disclosure of information otherwise protected by Rule 1.6 . . . ." And Rule 1.6 protects all "client information," a term that is broad enough to cover both evidentiary "confidences" and ethical "secrets." Once Ms. Forsberg filed her case in a court, her complaint against her former lawyer, Mr. Casey was "public" in the sense that someone could uncover it and read about it. Yet, after the complaint was filed, information about it might still be "secret" in the sense that the information had not become "generally known." And, if it were "generally known," then the Illinois Supreme Court should have at least suggested disciplinary proceedings against the trial judge, who apparently reported nothing, and Casey's lawyer, who knew at least as much public information about the case as did Mr. Himmel.

The *Himmel* decision is significant because it disciplines a lawyer solely for the failure to report. Other jurisdictions have not followed *Himmel*, and Model Rule 8.3(c) now makes clear that the reporting obligation does not require disclosure of information that Rule 1.6 protects.

2. The Different Reporting Obligation of the Model Rules

Substantial Questions. The whistle-blowing duty only covers conduct that raises a "substantial question'' regarding the other lawyer's "honesty, trustworthiness or fitness as a lawyer." The drafters of the Rules hoped that, by limiting the obligation to report only the more serious violations, the duty would be more realistic and therefore might be more enforceable.

The Rules define "substantial" to mean "a material matter of clear and weighty importance." Model Rules, Terminology, Rule 1.0(*l*). Thus, "substantial" refers not to the amount of evidence of which the lawyer is aware, but to the "seriousness of the possible offense." Rule 8.3, Comment 3.

No Self–Reporting. There is no obligation to "self-report" under Rule 8.3, which explicitly refers to knowledge regarding "another lawyer."

Knowledge. Rule 8.3(a) requires a lawyer to report if he "knows" that another lawyer committed a reportable violation. "Knows" does not mean absolute certainty. It does mean "actual knowledge of the fact in question." Rule 1.0(f). The standard is objective. "[M]ere suspicion does not impose a duty of inquiry." But there is "knowledge" if "a *reasonable* lawyer in the circumstances would have a *firm opinion* that the conduct in question *more likely than not occurred*." Restatement of the Law Governing Lawyers, Third, § 5, comment *i* (Official Draft 2000) (emphasis added).

Thus, *In re Riehlmann* (La.2005) disciplined attorney Riehlmann for failing to report that Deegan, a former prosecutor, had once suppressed exculpatory blood evidence in a case. Riehlmann met Deegan for a drink after work one day in 1994, when Deegan revealed he was dying of cancer, and confessed to the misconduct. Riehlmann urged Deegan to remedy the matter, but Deegan died three months later. In 1999, Riehlmann learned that the case in question involved a death row inmate. Riehlmann contacted the defense attorneys, and signed an affidavit regarding Deegan's statement. At that time, Riehlmann also reported the violation.

The initial hearing committee found that Riehlmann did not violate the reporting requirement, because Deegan's statement was "equivocal," since Deegan had said only that the evidence "might" have been exculpatory. The disciplinary board and the Louisiana Supreme Court disagreed, relying on the "more likely than not" test, quoted above. The court imposed a public reprimand on the lawyer.

Reporting of Non–Practicing Lawyer. Rule 8.3(a) requires a lawyer to report relevant professional misconduct by "committed at any time by a licensed but non-practicing lawyer." The lawyer must report professional misconduct "must be reported even if it involves activity completely removed from the practice of law." ABA Formal Opinion 04–433 (Aug. 25, 2004).

Reporting of Lawyers Who Suffer from Disability or Impairment. Rule 1.16(a)(2) requires that a lawyer withdraw from representing a client if her "physical or mental condition materially impairs the lawyer's ability to represent the client." A lawyer who believes that another lawyer's mental condition materially impairs her ability to represent clients, and who knows that that lawyer continues to do so in violation of Rule 1.16(a)(2), must report that other lawyer's violation. ABA Formal Opinion 03–431 (Aug. 8, 2003).

3.   Applicability of Privileges

The Rules explicitly provide that whistle-blowing is not required if information is protected by Rule 1.6. Rule 1.6, of course, protects all client information, a category that is much broader than the attorney-client evidentiary privilege.

A Lawyer Assistance Program (often called by the acronym LAP) is designed to help lawyers and judges who suffer from alcoholism or drug abuse. Lawyers and judges help other lawyers and judges afflicted with these problems. LAPs promise confidentiality to their participants in order to encourage their involvement in the program. It would severely undercut LAP if the Rules required lawyers who are active in a LAP to reveal the confidential information that they learn from their colleagues who suffer from alcohol or substance abuse. Consequently, Rule 8.3(c) makes it clear that the reporting requirements that it imposes do not apply in this situation. The Rule treats the relationship between the volunteer lawyers and judges in a LAP and the impaired lawyers or judges as if it were a client-lawyer relationship for purposes of this Rule.

The drafters of Rule 8.3 made sure that the reporting obligation did not override the client's right to keep client information confidential under

Rule 1.6. But, what of the other privileges, such as the Fifth Amendment right against self-incrimination? Moreover, the drafters specifically refer to the self-incrimination privilege in Rule 8.1, further suggesting that Rule 8.3 does not incorporate that privilege or any privilege other than the attorney-client privilege. However, it would be incorrect to read this reference to the attorney-client privilege as a negative pregnant, excluding all other privileges not specifically mentioned. The Rule cannot apply to knowledge protected by a constitutional privilege, such as the privilege against self-incrimination because then the rule would be unconstitutional. To preserve the constitutionality of these Rules, the self-incrimination protection must be read into them.

As a constitutional matter, bar authorities cannot discipline or otherwise sanction a lawyer simply because he or she has asserted the privilege against self-incrimination. However, the attorney may be disciplined for refusing to testify if that testimony would not expose him to criminal prosecution.

If the attorney's testimony would incriminate him, the state can grant the lawyer ''use immunity''—*i.e.*, a guarantee that the compelled testimony will not be used against the person in a *criminal* prosecution—and then use the lawyer's compelled testimony to disbar or otherwise discipline him. The justification for allowing the use of this compelled testimony for bar discipline is that bar discipline is not a criminal matter. Bar prosecutors can use the compelled testimony (given pursuant to use immunity) in the disciplinary proceeding but the criminal prosecutors cannot use that immunized testimony in the lawyer's criminal prosecution.

4. Reporting Misconduct of Judges

The Model Rules clearly require a lawyer to volunteer to the appropriate authorities any nonconfidential information showing that a judge (whether or not a lawyer) violated the judicial rules if the conduct raises "a substantial question as to the judge's fitness for office...." Rule 8.3(b).

RULE 8.4: MISCONDUCT

1. Defining Professional Misconduct

Rule 8.4 defines when a lawyer engages in "misconduct." In general it provides that a lawyer may be disciplined for violating a mandatory requirement of the Rules, or for engaging in conduct forbidden by other laws if that conduct demonstrates that the lawyer should not be entrusted with the confidence that clients normally place in a lawyer.

A lawyer may be disciplined for wrongful conduct even though she was not acting in her capacity as a lawyer while she was engaging in the wrong, *if* the conduct functionally relates to her capacity to practice law. Any "illegal conduct" or any conduct "involving dishonesty, fraud, deceit, or misrepresentation" adversely affects the lawyer's capacity to practice law.

For example, if a news reporter interviews several people near the courthouse about judicial candidates, and if one of those interviewed is a lawyer who knowingly makes a false statement of fact about a judicial candidate, he has evidenced lack of trustworthiness and is subject to discipline. If the lawyer, not acting in his capacity as a lawyer, misappropriates money from a bank, or defrauds a homeowner, the lawyer is subject to discipline because those crimes have a functional relationship to the qualities required to practice law. Lawyers routinely handle client funds and make representations to the court. Crimes that reflect adversely on a lawyer's honesty and trustworthiness relate to his ability to practice law.

In contrast, other Rules, such as Rule 3.6, governing trial publicity, or Rule 7.2, governing advertising, relate to a lawyer only in her professional capacity. So, if a lawyer/accountant, acting in her capacity as an accountant, solicits accounting clients in a way that is non-misleading but would be improper for a lawyer—*e.g.*, she engages in face-to-face solicitation—she would not be subject to discipline under Rule 7.2.

2.   Categories of Misconduct

A.   Violating or Attempting to Violate a Disciplinary Rule: Rule 8.4(a)

It is, of course, misconduct to violate a Disciplinary Rule. The Model Rules add that it is misconduct to "attempt to violate the Rules."

The ABA Model Rules of Professional Conduct distinguish between what *must* be done, what *should* be done, and what *may* be done. When the Rules use imperatives such as "shall" or "shall not," violations are misconduct. Some provisions of the Model Rules also use the term "may" in order to define areas of permissible lawyer discretion.

Many of the Comments and some of the Rules also use the term "should" or "preferably." When

Comments use the term "should," they do "not add obligations to the Rules but provide guidance for practicing in compliance with the Rules." Model Rules Preamble/Scope, ¶ 14. Similarly, there should be no discipline for violating Rule 6.1, which uses the word "should," or Rule 1.5(b), which advises that non-contingency fee agreements are "preferably" in writing.

B. Violating a Disciplinary Rule Through Another: Rule 8.4(a)

It is misconduct to assist or induce another to violate a Disciplinary Rule. For example, if a lawyer cannot engage a prospective client in a hospital room in a face-to-face encounter in an effort to solicit legal business, Rule 8.4(a) makes it clear that the lawyer may not avoid his responsibilities by hiring a hospital orderly to speak on his behalf.

Consider another, more complicated, example. Rule 4.2 provides that a lawyer may not communicate about the subject of the representation with a person the lawyer knows is represented by his own lawyer. The lawyer must communicate through the opponent's lawyer. However, because this Rule governs lawyers and not their lay clients, parties to a matter may communicate directly with each other. This Rule does not prohibit lawyers from advising their clients to speak directly with their counterparts. Rule 8.4, Comment 1, Rule 42, Comment 4.

However, Rule 4.2, in connection with Rule 8.4(a) *does* preclude a lawyer from using one of their agents, e.g., a paralegal, to carry a message from the lawyer to the opposing party. If lawyer *A* (on behalf of Party *A*) makes a settlement offer to the opposing party's lawyer (lawyer *B*), but lawyer *A* believes that lawyer *B* will not communicate that offer to Party *B*, lawyer *A* may not communicate directly with Party *B* to determine whether the offer has been communicated. Nor may lawyer *A* hire a detective or paralegal to communicate directly with Party *B* because lawyer *A* may not violate the Rules of Professional Conduct "through the acts of another." Lawyer *A* may advise Party *A* that Party *A* may communicate directly with Party *B* about the offer.

C. Criminal Acts: Rule 8.4(b)

Not all criminal conduct is professional misconduct. The Rule specifies that "a lawyer should be professionally answerable only for offenses that indicate lack of those characteristics relevant to law practice." Rule 8.4, Comment 2. Rule 8.4(b) limits criminal acts to those that reflect "adversely on the lawyer's honesty, trustworthiness or fitness as a lawyer in other respects."

Examples of criminal acts that are also professional misconduct include crimes of fraud or breach of trust; willful (rather than negligent) failure to file an income tax return, or "serious interference with the administration of justice." Comment 2.

Comment 2 includes crimes of "violence" in the category of professional misconduct even though violence does not necessarily indicate lack of trustworthiness or dishonesty: a drunken barroom brawl may only indicate an isolated case of poor judgment and bad temper in a situation far removed from the things that relate what lawyers do.

Comment 2 also advises that even a pattern of repeated minor offenses could be disciplinable if it indicates "indifference to legal obligation." The drafters give no examples, but repeated violations involving minor offenses may just as likely indicate an indifference only to a *particular* violation. For example, a lawyer may own a grocery store that repeatedly is open on Sunday, in violation of a local "blue law." This would not necessarily show any general indifference to other legal obligations.

D. Conduct Involving Dishonesty: Rule 8.4(c)

Conduct that involves dishonesty, fraud, deceit, or misrepresentation, is misconduct, even if it is not a crime. The tort of non-criminal fraud would fall under this rubric. Similarly, violations of fiduciary obligations (whether or not undertaken in one's capacity as a lawyer) would be misconduct if they indicate dishonesty.

E. Conduct Prejudicial to the Administration of Justice: Rule 8.4(d)

It is misconduct for a lawyer to "engage in conduct that is prejudicial to the administration of justice." This is a vague, catch-all provision. Disciplinary authorities occasionally discipline a lawyer under this rather loose standard, typically in factual situations that are atypical.

If a lawyer makes racist and sexist remarks, that speech may be deplorable and even heinous. But is it misconduct under the Model Rules? Such prosecutions raise important free speech concerns. Speech, even hateful speech, is not action, and the First Amendment gives the Ku Klux Klan and other racists the right to march on the public streets and spread their hate.

Comment 3 to 8.4 provides:

"A lawyer who, in the course of representing a client, knowingly manifests by *words* or conduct, bias or prejudice based on race, sex, religion, national origin, disability, age, sexual orientation or socioeconomic status, violates paragraph (d) [Rule 8.4(d)] when such actions are prejudicial to the administration of justice. *Legitimate* advocacy respecting the foregoing factors does not violate paragraph (d). A trial judge's finding that peremptory challenges were exercised on a discriminatory basis does not alone establish a violation of this rule." (emphasis added).

This Comment allows racist speech and other hateful speech when it is part of "legitimate advocacy." However, the Comment does not define when advocacy is "illegitimate." Nor does it explain why a lawyer's decision to exercise a peremptory challenge in a racially discriminatory way that violates the U.S. Constitution is "not a violation of this rule." This Comment may give less protection to a lawyer who exercises pure speech to complain about the idle rich ("socioeconomic status") than it gives to a lawyer who engages in unconstitutional and racist conduct when choosing a jury.

F. Implying an Ability to Influence Improperly a Government Official: Rule 8.4(e)

Rules 8.4(e) forbids a lawyer from stating or implying an ability to influence improperly a government agency or official, or to achieve results unethically or illegally.

A lawyer, whether or not a public official, may not state or even "imply" to anyone that she has the power to influence a public official or agency on improper or irrelevant grounds. This prohibition applies whether or not the lawyer actually exercises the influence and whether or not the lawyer could, in fact, exercise such influence. Such suggestions by lawyers serve no valid purpose and undermine public confidence in the legal system, even if the implication is false.

Consider *Matter of Sears* (N.J.1976), where the attorney wrote an official of his company/client implying that the attorney would or could improperly influence a federal judge in connection with an S.E.C. investigation of that company. Though there was no evidence that the attorney communicated *ex parte* with the judge, the state supreme court found an ethics violation because it fostered an impression that the lawyer could influence the SEC.

G. Assisting a Judicial Official to Violate the Judicial Code: Rule 8.4(f)

A lawyer may not improperly influence a government agency or official, or knowingly assist a judge to violate the Code of Judicial Conduct. Rule 8.4(f) dovetails with the Model Judicial Code, so that lawyers are prohibited from giving judges that which the judges are not allowed to accept under the Model Code of Judicial Conduct.

RULE 8.5: DISCIPLINARY AUTHORITY: CHOICE OF LAW

A state disciplinary authority has, in general, the power to discipline a person admitted to the bar in that jurisdiction even though the acts complained of occurred outside the jurisdiction. That simple statement leads to many complex and intriguing legal questions.

To understand the intricate legal issues, let us begin by considering three cases: (1) Lawyer 1 is admitted in State *A,* yet commits misconduct in State *Y* in several cases after being admitted there *pro hac vice* (*i.e.,* for purposes of one case only). (2) Lawyer 2 is admitted in State *A* and State *Y,* but practices only in State *Y,* where he commits misconduct. (3) Lawyer 3 is admitted in State *A,* does not practice law at all, but he engages in misconduct in State *Y* (he lies to secure a real estate license), and this misconduct reflects on his ability to practice law.

In all of these cases, State *A* has jurisdiction to discipline the lawyer, even though the improper conduct occurs outside of State *A*'s jurisdiction. In addition, State *Y* also has jurisdiction to discipline Lawyer 1 for misconduct growing out of Lawyer 1's special appearance in State *Y*. Of course, because Lawyer 1 is not generally admitted in State *Y*, State *Y* cannot disbar him. However, State *Y* can revoke its permission for him to appear *pro hac vice* for that case and for future cases.

The rationale for the extraterritorial application of ethics rules is easy to understand. The purpose of lawyer discipline is not to punish (although the lawyer may be deprived of her livelihood) but rather to seek to determine the fitness of the lawyer to continue in that capacity. Given this rationale, if the lawyer engages in improper conduct—even if she engages in the conduct while not acting as a lawyer (*e.g.,* lying to secure a real estate license), and even if the improper conduct occurs outside of the jurisdiction of State *A,* that conduct still reflects on the ability of that lawyer to practice law. It is the lawyer's admission to practice in State *A* (even though State *A* is not the site of her improper act) that gives State *A* the jurisdiction to discipline.

Now consider the case where State *A* seeks to punish conduct that occurred in State *B*, but the conduct *did not violate the rules of State B*. Choice of law problems are inevitable because there is no uniform rules governing ethics. Each jurisdiction adopts its own rules. The ABA Rules are only a model. If a lawyer practices in two jurisdictions, it is conceivable that conduct *forbidden* in one jurisdiction is permissible or perhaps even ethically *compelled* in another. For example, State *A* may demand disclosure of client confidences in a situation where State *B* may forbid it.

The Model Rules tackle this issue in Rule 8.5(b). The goal of this Rule is to ensure that any particular conduct of a lawyer should be subject to only one set of rules. Both jurisdictions may impose discipline, but they should both be using the same substantive rules against which they measure the conduct. Disciplinary authorities should avoid proceeding against a lawyer on the basis of two inconsistent rules. The choice of law issue is: which jurisdiction's ethics rules should apply to a lawyer admitted in more than one jurisdiction?

In general, if the conduct at issue takes place before a tribunal, the disciplinary authority should apply only the rules of the jurisdiction where that tribunal sits (unless the rules of that tribunal provide otherwise). Thus, let us assume that a lawyer is admitted generally in State *A*, and is admitted *pro hac vice* in a case heard in State *B*. If that lawyer then violates the rules of the court in State *B*, State *A* should apply the ethics rules of State *B*, which are the rules applicable to that case. Rule 8.5(b)(1).

For all other conduct, the ethics law applied should be the law of the jurisdiction in which the lawyer's conduct occurred, unless the "predominant effect of the conduct" is in a different jurisdiction, in which case that jurisdiction's rules should apply. Rule 8.5(b)(2).

The Model Rules, after the 2002 revisions, create a safe harbor. A lawyer is not subject to discipline if he reasonably believes that his conduct is predominantly related to a particular jurisdiction and his conduct conforms to the rules of that jurisdiction. Rule 8.5(b)(2).

The Rules do not create any statute of limitations for disciplinary actions. Because the purpose of discipline is to protect the public rather than punish the attorney, the time when the misconduct occurred is relevant only to the extent that it bears on the lawyer's present fitness to practice law. Hence, if the disciplinary authorities accuse a lawyer of conduct that also is a tort or criminal wrong, the mere fact that the statute of limitations has run in either the civil or criminal case does not preclude disciplinary action.

INDEX

References are to Pages

485

†